First World War

and Army of Occupation

War Diary

France, Belgium and Germany

62 DIVISION
1 Highland Brigade Headquarters,
Princess Louise's (Argyll & Sutherland Highlanders)
10th Battalion,
Queen's Own Cameron Highlanders 5th Battalion,
Gordon Highlanders 52nd, 4th, 1/5th and 51st Battalion,
Black Watch (Royal Highlanders)
6th (Perthshire) Battalion (Territorial) and 8th (Service)
and Seaforth Highlanders
(Ross-shire Buffs, the Dukc of Albany's) 4th Battalion
1 March 1919 - 30 August 1919

WO95/3092

The Naval & Military Press Ltd
www.nmarchive.com
Published in association with The National Archives

Contents

Document type	Place/Title	Date From	Date To
Heading	BEF Highland Div Formerly 62 Div 1 Highland Bde 52 Bn Gordons 1919 Apr To 1919 Aug		
Heading	War Diary of 52nd Battalion Gordon Highlands From 6/4/19 To 31/5/19 Volume I		
War Diary	Dunkirk	06/04/1919	08/04/1919
War Diary	En Route	09/04/1919	09/04/1919
War Diary	Zulpich	10/04/1919	10/04/1919
War Diary	Embken	11/04/1919	08/05/1919
War Diary	Fussenich	09/05/1919	31/05/1919
Heading	52nd Gordon Hldrs War Diary for July 1919		
War Diary	Duren	01/07/1919	01/07/1919
War Diary	Blens	02/07/1919	31/07/1919
Heading	War Diary For 52nd. Battalion Gordon Highlanders Period 1/8/19 To 17/8/19		
War Diary	Blens Germany	01/08/1919	17/08/1919
Heading	BEF Highland Div Formerly 62 Div 3 Highland Bde H.Q 1919 May To 1919 Aug		
Heading	War Diary of 3rd Highland Brigade From 1st May 1919 To 31st May 1919 Volume 2		
Miscellaneous	Cover For Documents. Nature Of Enclosures.		
War Diary		01/05/1919	31/05/1919
Miscellaneous	3rd Highland Brigade Warning Order No.1	23/05/1919	23/05/1919
Miscellaneous	3rd Highland Brigade Warning Order No.2	26/05/1919	26/05/1919
Miscellaneous	Table "A" Issued With 3rd Highland Brigade Warning Order No.2 dated 26th May 1919		
Miscellaneous	Table "B" Issued With 3rd Highland Brigade Warning Order No. 2 dated 26th May 1919		
Miscellaneous	3rd Highland Brigade Administrative Instructions in The Event of Advance issued in Conjunction with 3rd Highland Brigade Warning Orders Nos.1 and 2	29/05/1919	29/05/1919
Miscellaneous	3rd Highland Brigade		
Miscellaneous	Appendix I		
Heading	War Diary of 3rd Highland Brigade From 1st June 1919 To 30th June 1919 Volume III		
War Diary		01/06/1919	30/06/1919
Miscellaneous	Addenda And Corrigenda To 3rd Highland Brigade Warning Order No.2 dated May 26th 1919	05/06/1919	05/06/1919
Miscellaneous	Table 'A' Issued With 3rd Highland Brigade Warning Order No.2 dated May 26th 1919		
Miscellaneous	Table 'B' Issued With 3rd Highland Brigade Warning Order No.2 dated May 26th 1919		
Miscellaneous	3rd Highland Bde No. BM/35	16/06/1919	16/06/1919
Miscellaneous	3rd Highland Bde No. BM/35	21/06/1919	21/06/1919
Miscellaneous	3rd Highland Brigade Warning Order No.3	22/06/1919	22/06/1919
Operation(al) Order(s)	3rd Highland Brigade Order No.1	23/06/1919	23/06/1919
Miscellaneous	Addenda No. 1 To 3rd Highland Brigade Warning Order No.3	24/06/1919	24/06/1919

Miscellaneous	3rd Highland Brigade Administrative Instructions Issued in Conjunction with 3rd Highland Brigade Warning Order No.3 Dated 22nd June 1919 and Addenda No.1 Dated 24th June 1919	25/06/1919	25/06/1919
Miscellaneous	3rd Highland Brigade		
Operation(al) Order(s)	3rd Highland Brigade Order No.2	25/06/1919	25/06/1919
Miscellaneous	Table Issued With 3rd Highland Brigade Order No.3 dated 25th June 1919		
Heading	War Diary of 3rd Highland Brigade From 1st July 1919 To 31st July 1919 Volume No.IV		
Miscellaneous	Cover For Documents. Nature Of Enclosures.		
War Diary		01/07/1919	31/07/1919
Miscellaneous	3rd Highland Brigade Transport Competition	13/07/1919	13/07/1919
Heading	War Diary of 3rd Highland Brigade From 1st August 1919 To 31st August 1919 Volume No.V		
Miscellaneous	Cover For Documents. Nature Of Enclosures.		
Miscellaneous	3rd Highland Brigade B.M./57.A	12/09/1919	12/09/1919
War Diary	Maubach Germany	01/08/1919	11/08/1919
War Diary	England Folkestone	12/08/1919	12/08/1919
War Diary	Brocton	13/08/1919	13/08/1919
War Diary	Brocton England	14/08/1919	31/08/1919
Miscellaneous	3rd Highland Brigade Administrative Instructions Concerning Departure of Equipment Trains	07/08/1919	07/08/1919
Miscellaneous	Equipment Trains	08/08/1919	08/08/1919
Operation(al) Order(s)	3rd Highland Brigade Order No.3	07/08/1919	07/08/1919
Miscellaneous	3rd Highland Brigade Administrative Instructions Issued in Conjunction with 3rd Highland Brigade Order No.3 dated 7th August 1919	08/08/1919	08/08/1919
Operation(al) Order(s)	3rd Highland Brigade Order No.4	14/08/1919	14/08/1919
Heading	BEF Highland Div Formerly 62 Div 2 Highland Bde 1/4 Bn Gordons 1919 May To 1919 Aug From 51 154 Bde		
Heading	War Diary of 1/4 Batt The Gordon Highlanders From 1st May 1919 To 31st May 1919		
Miscellaneous	Cover For Documents. Nature Of Enclosures.		
War Diary	Duren	01/05/1919	31/05/1919
Miscellaneous	Nominal Roll of Officers As At 31/5/19		
Heading	War Diary of 1/4th Battalion The Gordon Highlanders From 1st June To 30th June 1919 Volume LIII		
War Diary	Duren	02/06/1919	17/06/1919
War Diary	Solingen	18/06/1919	30/06/1919
Miscellaneous	1/4th Battalion The Gordon Highlanders		
Heading	War Diary of 1/4th Battalion The Gordon Highlanders From 1st To 31st July 1919 Volume 54		
War Diary	Solingen	01/07/1919	02/07/1919
War Diary	Duren	03/07/1919	31/07/1919
Miscellaneous	1/4th Battalion The Gordon Highlanders Nominal Roll of Officers as at 30/7/19		
Heading	War Diary of 1/4th Bn, The Gordon Highlanders August 1st 31st 1919 Vol 55		
War Diary	Duren	01/08/1919	09/08/1919
War Diary	Calais	10/08/1919	10/08/1919
War Diary	Clipstone Camp	11/08/1919	30/08/1919
Miscellaneous	1/4th Battalion The Gordon Highlanders Strength On 31/8/19		

Heading	Highland (62nd) Division 3rd Highland Bde 8th Royal HDRS (Black Watch) 1919 Mar-1919 Aug From 9div 26 Bde)		
Heading	War Diary of 8th Bn The Black Watch (R 26) 1st March To 31st March 1919 Volume		
Miscellaneous	Cover For Documents. Nature Of Enclosures.		
War Diary	Solingen	01/03/1919	01/03/1919
War Diary	Burvenich	02/03/1919	06/03/1919
War Diary	Merzenich	07/03/1919	14/03/1919
War Diary	Germany Malmedy & Duren	15/03/1919	17/03/1919
War Diary	Vettweiss & Malmedy	18/03/1919	31/03/1919
War Diary	Germany	31/03/1919	31/03/1919
War Diary	Vettweiss Germany	31/03/1919	31/03/1919
Miscellaneous	8th Bn The Black Watch (R.H.)	08/03/1919	08/03/1919
Miscellaneous	To Units Of Brigade Group Warning Order	01/03/1919	01/03/1919
Miscellaneous	187th. (Highland) Infantry Brigade Warning Order No.1	02/03/1919	02/03/1919
Miscellaneous	187th Inf. Bde. No. BM/57 (b)	10/03/1919	10/03/1919
Miscellaneous	8th. Bn. The Black Watch (R.H.)	08/03/1919	08/03/1919
Miscellaneous	8th Black Watch	16/03/1919	16/03/1919
Miscellaneous	To All Units 9th (Scottish) Division	17/03/1919	17/03/1919
Heading	War Diary of 8th Bn. The Black Watch From 1st May 1919 To 31st May 1919		
Miscellaneous	Cover For Documents. Nature Of Enclosures.		
War Diary	Buir	01/05/1919	09/05/1919
War Diary	Maubach	09/05/1919	31/05/1919
War Diary	Buir-Maubach	31/05/1919	31/05/1919
Heading	War Diary of 8th Bn, The Black Watch (R.N.) From 1st June 1919 To 30th June 1919 (Volume III)		
War Diary	Maubach	01/06/1919	17/06/1919
War Diary	Birks-Dorf-Benrath	18/06/1919	18/06/1919
War Diary	Benrath	19/06/1919	30/06/1919
War Diary	Maubach	30/06/1919	30/06/1919
Heading	War Diary of 8th Bn. Black Watch (R.H) From 1st July 1919 To 31st July 1919 Volume IV		
Miscellaneous	Cover For Documents. Nature Of Enclosures.		
War Diary	Benrath	01/07/1919	01/07/1919
War Diary	Birkesdorf-Maubach	01/07/1919	02/07/1919
War Diary	Maubach	02/07/1919	28/07/1919
Heading	War Diary of 8th Bn. The Black Watch From 1st August 1919 To 31st August 1919		
War Diary	Maubach Germany	01/08/1919	10/08/1919
War Diary	Duren	11/08/1919	13/08/1919
War Diary	Brocton Camp	14/08/1919	31/08/1919
War Diary	Brocton Camp England	31/08/1919	31/08/1919
Heading	BEF Highland Div Formerly 62 Div 2 Highland Bde H.Q. 1919 May To 1919 Sept		
Heading	War Diary of 2nd Highland Brigade H.Qrs May 1st 1919 To May 31st 1919.		
War Diary	Duren	01/05/1919	31/05/1919
Miscellaneous	Reference Duren Defence Scheme	04/05/1919	04/05/1919
Miscellaneous	Reference Duren Defence Scheme	09/05/1919	09/05/1919
Miscellaneous	2nd Highland Brigade Warning Order No.215	22/05/1919	22/05/1919
Miscellaneous	Amendments to Highland Brigade Warning Order No.215 dated 22.5.19	23/05/1919	23/05/1919
Miscellaneous	Amendments No. 2 To Highland Bde Warning Order No.215 of 22.5.19	25/05/1919	25/05/1919

Heading	War Diary of Headquarters 2nd Highland Brigade From 1st June 1919 To 30th June 1919 (Volume XXX)		
War Diary	Duren	01/06/1919	17/06/1919
War Diary	Solingen	18/06/1919	30/06/1919
Miscellaneous	2nd Highland Brigade B.M.J 353	04/06/1919	04/06/1919
Miscellaneous	Reference Duren Defence Scheme	07/06/1919	07/06/1919
Miscellaneous	Reference Duren Defence Scheme	09/06/1919	09/06/1919
Miscellaneous	Reference Duren Defence Scheme	15/06/1919	15/06/1919
Miscellaneous	Reference Duren Defence Scheme	14/06/1919	14/06/1919
Miscellaneous	2nd Highland Brigade Instructions	21/06/1919	21/06/1919
Miscellaneous	Provisional Instructions Regarding The Maintainance of Law and Order Within The 2nd Highland Brigade Sub-Area	20/06/1919	20/06/1919
Miscellaneous	2nd Highland Brigade B.M.J.534/1	21/06/1919	21/06/1919
Miscellaneous	2nd Highland Brigade B.M.J.566/1	23/06/1919	23/06/1919
Miscellaneous	2nd Highland Brigade B.M.J.580/1	26/06/1919	26/06/1919
Heading	War Diary of Headquarters 2nd Highland Brigade From 1st July 1919 To 31st July 1919 Vol 31		
War Diary	Solingen	01/07/1919	02/07/1919
War Diary	Duren	03/07/1919	31/07/1919
Miscellaneous	Reference Duren Defence Scheme	06/06/1919	06/06/1919
Miscellaneous	Reference Duren Defence Scheme	14/07/1919	14/07/1919
Miscellaneous	Reference Duren Defence Scheme	29/07/1919	29/07/1919
Heading	War Diary of Headquarters 2nd Highland Brigade From 1st August 1919 To 31st August 1919 Volume No.32		
War Diary	Duren	01/08/1919	08/08/1919
War Diary	Calais	09/08/1919	09/08/1919
War Diary	Duren	09/08/1919	09/08/1919
War Diary	Calais	10/08/1919	11/08/1919
War Diary	Clipstone	11/08/1919	31/08/1919
Heading	War Diary of Headquarters 2nd Highland Brigade From 1st September 1919 To 31st September 1919 Volume No.33		
War Diary	Clipstone	01/09/1919	30/09/1919
Heading	Highland Div 1 Highland Bde 10 A & S H 1919 Mar-1919 Aug From 32 Div 97 Bde		
Heading	War Diary of 10th Argyll & Sutherland Highrs 1st March 1919 To 31st March 1919 (Volume)		
Miscellaneous	Cover For Documents. Nature Of Enclosures.		
War Diary	Menden	01/03/1919	11/03/1919
War Diary	Embken	12/03/1919	31/03/1919
Heading	War Diary of 10th Battalion Argyll And Sutherland Highlanders From 21st May 1919 To 31st May 1919		
War Diary	Gladbach	21/05/1919	31/05/1919
Heading	War Diary of 10th Bn Argyll & Sutherland Highlanders From 1 July 1919 To 31 July 1919 (Volume 7)		
War Diary	Hausen	07/07/1919	30/07/1919
Heading	10th (S) Bn, Argyll & Sutherland Hdrs War Diary For August 1919		
War Diary	Hausen	05/08/1919	13/08/1919
War Diary	Calais	14/08/1919	14/08/1919
War Diary	Catterick Camp Yorkshire	15/08/1919	15/08/1919
Heading	BEF Highland Div Formerly 62 Div 3 Highland Bde 1/4 Seaforths 1919 Mar 1919 Aug		
Heading	War Diary of 1/4th Bn Seaforth Highlanders Vol 54 From March 1st 1919 To March 31st 1919		

Miscellaneous	Cover For Documents. Nature Of Enclosures.		
War Diary	In Germany Embken	01/03/1919	06/03/1919
War Diary	Golzheim	07/03/1919	07/03/1919
War Diary	In Germany Golzheim	08/03/1919	31/03/1919
Heading	War Diary of 1/4th Bn. Seaforth Highlanders From 1st May 1919 To 31st May 1919		
Miscellaneous	Cover For Documents. Nature Of Enclosures.		
War Diary	Golzheim	01/05/1919	11/05/1919
War Diary	Nideggen	12/05/1919	31/05/1919
Heading	War Diary of 1/4th Bn, Seaforth Highlanders From 1st June 1919 To 30th June 1919 (Volume III)		
War Diary	Nideggen	01/06/1919	16/06/1919
War Diary	Duren	17/06/1919	17/06/1919
War Diary	Ohligs	18/06/1919	30/06/1919
Heading	War Diary of 1/4th Bn Seaforth Highlanders From 1st July 1919 To 31st July 1919 Volume IV		
Miscellaneous	Cover For Documents. Nature Of Enclosures.		
War Diary	Ohligs	01/07/1919	02/07/1919
War Diary	Nideggen	03/07/1919	19/07/1919
War Diary	Lendersdorf	20/07/1919	31/07/1919
Heading	War Diary of 4th Bn. Seaforth Highlanders From 1st August 1919 To 31st August 1919		
Miscellaneous	Cover For Documents. Nature Of Enclosures.		
War Diary	Lendersdorf	01/08/1919	11/08/1919
War Diary	Brocton Camp	13/08/1919	31/08/1919
Heading	Highland Div Formerly 62 3 High Bde 1/6 Bn R. Highlanders (Black Watch) 1919 Mar To 1919 Aug		
Heading	War Diary of 6th Bn Black Watch Vol 56 From March 1st 1919 To March 31st 1919		
Miscellaneous	Cover For Documents. Nature Of Enclosures.		
War Diary	Mechernich	01/03/1919	11/03/1919
War Diary	Merzenich	12/03/1919	31/03/1919
Miscellaneous	6th Battalion The Black Watch Operation Orders	20/03/1919	20/03/1919
Miscellaneous	6th Battalion The Black Watch Operation Orders		
Miscellaneous	6th Battalion The Black Watch (R.H) Addendum To Operation Orders	08/03/1919	08/03/1919
Miscellaneous	6th Battalion The Black Watch		
Miscellaneous	6th Battalion The Black Watch (R.H)		
Miscellaneous	6th Battalion The Black Watch Officers And Other Ranks Awarded Decoration During Month		
Miscellaneous	6th Battalion The Black Watch List Of Officers		
Miscellaneous	6th Battalion The Black Watch List Of Appendices		
Heading	War Diary of 6th Bn.The Black Watch From 1st May 1919 To 31st May 1919		
Miscellaneous	Cover For Documents. Nature Of Enclosures.		
Heading	War Diary of 6th (Perthshire) Battalion The Black Watch (R.H) From 1st May To 31st May 1919 Volume 58		
War Diary	Merzenich	01/05/1919	31/05/1919
Miscellaneous	6th Battalion The Black Watch Operation Orders	12/05/1919	12/05/1919
Miscellaneous	6th Battalion The Black Watch Operation Orders	18/05/1919	18/05/1919
Miscellaneous	1/6th Black Watch Warning Order No.2	27/05/1919	27/05/1919
Miscellaneous	6th Battalion The Black Watch Operation Orders	29/05/1919	29/05/1919
Miscellaneous	6th Battalion The Black Watch Warning Order No.3	29/05/1919	29/05/1919
Miscellaneous	6th Battalion The Black Watch		

Miscellaneous	6th Battalion The Black Watch Officers And Other Ranks Joined During Month Of May 1919		
Miscellaneous	6th Battalion The Black Watch List Of Officers		
Miscellaneous	6th Battalion The Black Watch List Of Appendices		
Heading	War Diary of 6th Bn The Black Watch (R.N.) From 1st June 1919 To 30th June 1919 (Volume 59)		
Heading	War Diary of 6th (Perthshire) Battalion The Black Watch (R.H) From 1st June To 30th June 1919 Volume 59		
War Diary	Lendersdorf	01/06/1919	18/06/1919
War Diary	Hilden	19/06/1919	30/06/1919
Miscellaneous	6th Battalion The Black Watch Warning Order	10/06/1919	10/06/1919
Miscellaneous	6th Battalion The Black Watch Warning Order No.1		
Miscellaneous	6th Battalion The Black Watch Addendum To Warning Order No.1		
Miscellaneous	Addendum To Warning Order No.1	16/06/1919	16/06/1919
Miscellaneous	6th Bn. The Black Watch Addendum To Warning Order No.1	17/06/1919	17/06/1919
Miscellaneous	6th Battalion The Black Watch Operation Orders	04/06/1919	04/06/1919
Miscellaneous	Addendum To Warning Orders No.1	16/06/1919	16/06/1919
Miscellaneous	6th Battalion The Black Watch Addendum To Warning Order No.1		
Miscellaneous	6th Battalion The Black Watch Warning Order No.1	23/06/1919	23/06/1919
Miscellaneous	6th Battalion The Black Watch Warning Order No.2	26/06/1919	26/06/1919
Miscellaneous	6th Battalion The Black Watch Amendment To Warning Order No.2	29/06/1919	29/06/1919
Miscellaneous	6th Battalion The Black Watch		
Miscellaneous	6th Battalion The Black Watch Officers & Other Ranks Joined During Month Of June 1919		
Miscellaneous	6th Battalion The Black Watch Officers & Other Ranks Awarded Decoration During Month		
Miscellaneous	6th Battalion The Black Watch List Of Officers		
Miscellaneous	List Of Appendices		
Heading	War Diary of 6th Bn Black Watch (R.H) From 1st July 1919 To 31st July 1919 Volume IV		
Miscellaneous	Cover For Documents. Nature Of Enclosures.		
Heading	War Diary of 6th (Perthshire) Battalion The Black Watch (R.H) From 1st July 1919 To 31st July 1919 Volume 60		
War Diary	Hilden	01/07/1919	01/07/1919
War Diary	Lendersdorf	02/07/1919	19/07/1919
War Diary	Bruck	20/07/1919	31/07/1919
Miscellaneous	6th Battalion The Black Watch Warning Order	17/07/1919	17/07/1919
Miscellaneous	6th. Battalion The Black Watch Addendum To Warning Order Of 17/7/19	18/07/1919	18/07/1919
Miscellaneous	6th. Battalion The Black Watch Further Addendum of Warning Order Of 17/7/19	18/07/1919	18/07/1919
Operation(al) Order(s)	6th. Battalion The Black Watch Operation Orders No.1	02/07/1919	02/07/1919
Operation(al) Order(s)	6th. Battalion The Black Watch Operation Orders No.2	02/07/1919	02/07/1919
Miscellaneous	6th. Battalion The Black Watch		
Miscellaneous	6th. Battalion The Black Watch Officers And Other Ranks Joined During Month Of July 1919		
Miscellaneous	6th. Battalion The Black Watch List Of Officers		
Miscellaneous	List Of Appendices		
Heading	War Diary of 6th Bn. The Black Watch From 1st August 1919 To 31st August 1919		

Miscellaneous	Cover For Documents. Nature Of Enclosures.		
Heading	War Diary of 6th (Perthshire) Battalion The Black Watch (R.H) From 1st August 1919 To 31st August 1919 Volume 61		
War Diary	Nideggan	01/08/1919	08/08/1919
War Diary	Duren	09/08/1919	10/08/1919
War Diary	Calais	11/08/1919	12/08/1919
War Diary	Brocton	13/08/1919	31/08/1919
Miscellaneous	6th Battalion The Black Watch (R.H) Warning Order No.1		
Operation(al) Order(s)	6th Battalion The Black Watch Operation Orders No.3		
Operation(al) Order(s)	6th Battalion The Black Watch Operation Orders No.4	09/08/1919	09/08/1919
Miscellaneous	6th Battalion The Black Watch		
Miscellaneous	6th Battalion The Black Watch Officers And Other Ranks Joined During Month Of August 1919		
Miscellaneous	6th Battalion The Black Watch Other Ranks Awarded Decorations during Month		
Miscellaneous	6th Battalion The Black Watch List Of Officers		
Miscellaneous	List Of Appendices		
Heading	B.E.F. Highland Div Formerly 62 Div 1 Highland Bde H.Q 1919 May To 1919 Aug		
Heading	War Diary of 1st Highland Brigade Headquarters From 1st May 1919 To 31st May 1919 British Army Of The Rhine Germany		
War Diary		01/05/1919	30/05/1919
War Diary	Blens	31/05/1919	31/05/1919
Heading	War Diary of 1st Highland Brigade Headqrs From 1st June 1919 To 30th June 1919 Volume 6		
War Diary	Germany Blens	01/06/1919	18/06/1919
War Diary	Opladen Germany	19/06/1919	30/06/1919
Operation(al) Order(s)	1st Highland Brigade Movement Order No.1	17/06/1919	17/06/1919
Miscellaneous	Ammendment to Warning Order No.1	15/06/1919	15/06/1919
Miscellaneous	1st Highland Brigade Amendment to Warning Order No.1 dated 27/5/1919	05/06/1919	05/06/1919
Miscellaneous	1st Highland Brigade B.M.H. /1361	19/06/1919	19/06/1919
Miscellaneous	Addendum To 1st Highland Brigade Warning Order No. 1 of 27-5-19	17/06/1919	17/06/1919
Miscellaneous	Demo To Units Of Brigade Group	18/06/1919	18/06/1919
Operation(al) Order(s)	1st Highland Brigade Order No.2	19/06/1919	19/06/1919
Miscellaneous	Addendum To Amendment To 1st Highland Brigade Warning Order No.1 dated 5/5/19 para 3	17/06/1919	17/06/1919
Miscellaneous	1st Highland Brigade	21/06/1919	21/06/1919
Miscellaneous	1st Highland Brigade B.M.H /1370	21/06/1919	21/06/1919
Miscellaneous	1st Highland Brigade B.M.H./ 1361	19/06/1919	19/06/1919
Miscellaneous	1st Highland Brigade Warning Order No.2	24/06/1919	24/06/1919
Heading	Headquarters 1st Highland Brigade War Diary For July 1919		
War Diary	Blens	01/07/1919	13/07/1919
War Diary	Hauson	14/07/1919	18/07/1919
War Diary	Blens	19/07/1919	31/07/1919
Heading	War Diary of 1st Highland Brigade 1st August 31st August 1919		
War Diary	Blens	01/08/1919	11/08/1919
War Diary	Duren	11/08/1919	15/08/1919
War Diary	Blens	01/08/1919	11/08/1919
War Diary	Duren	11/08/1919	15/08/1919

War Diary	Catterick	16/08/1919	31/08/1919
Miscellaneous	Orders By Camp Commandant 1st Highland Brigade	07/08/1919	07/08/1919
Miscellaneous	Train Circular H/ S.G /1 Equipment Trains		
Miscellaneous	Schedule 1		
Miscellaneous	Administrative Instructions M/ S.C. /2.2	09/08/1919	09/08/1919
Heading	Highland (62) Division 1st Highland Bde 5th Cameron Hdrs 1919 Mar-1919 Aug		
Heading	War Diary of 5th Cameron Highlanders 1st March 1919 To 31st March 1919 (Volume)		
Miscellaneous	Cover For Documents. Nature Of Enclosures.		
War Diary	Solingen Germany	01/03/1919	20/03/1919
War Diary	Geich	21/03/1919	31/03/1919
Heading	War Diary of 5th Battalion Cameron Highlanders From 1st May 1919 To 31st May 1919 And From 1st April 1919 To 30th April 1919 British Army Of The Rhine Germany		
War Diary	Fussenich Geich Tuntersdorf Germany	01/04/1919	21/05/1919
War Diary	Hausen	22/05/1919	31/05/1919
Heading	War Diary of Appendix For July 1919 Vol II		
War Diary	(Drove-Thumboich) H.Q. Drove	01/07/1919	01/07/1919
War Diary	Hausen	02/07/1919	31/07/1919
Operation(al) Order(s)	Operation Order No.1 By Lieut Colonel R. Campbell D.S.O. Commanding 5th Bn Cameron Highlanders	29/06/1919	29/06/1919
Miscellaneous	Appendix to O.O. No.1	29/06/1919	29/06/1919
Miscellaneous	Appendix "B" to Operation Order No.1	30/06/1919	30/06/1919
Heading	6th Battalion The Queens Own Cameron Highlanders War Diary Vol III and Appendices August 1919		
War Diary	Hausen	01/08/1919	10/08/1919
War Diary	Duren Barracks	11/08/1919	13/08/1919
War Diary	Calais	14/08/1919	14/08/1919
War Diary	Catterick	15/08/1919	26/08/1919
War Diary	Yorks	27/08/1919	31/08/1919
Miscellaneous	General Fayolle's Review		
Operation(al) Order(s)	5th Bn Cameron Highlanders Operation Order No.2 By Lieut Colonel R. Campbell D.S.O. Commanding 5th Bn Cameron Highlanders	09/08/1919	09/08/1919
Miscellaneous	Appendix No.1 to O.O. No.2		
Miscellaneous	Appendix No.2 to O.O. No.2	11/08/1919	11/08/1919
Miscellaneous	5th Bn Cameron Highlanders Operation Order No.2	09/08/1919	09/08/1919
Miscellaneous	Appendix No.1 to O.O No.2		
Heading	BEF Highland Div Formerly 62 Div 2 Highland Bde 1/5 Gordons 1919 Mar To 1919 Aug		
Heading	War Diary of 5th Battalion The Gordon Highlanders From 1st March 1919 To 31st March 1919 Volume No.47		
War Diary	Roggandorf	01/03/1919	09/03/1919
War Diary	Kerpen	10/03/1919	31/03/1919
Miscellaneous	Appendix I		
Heading	War Diary of 5th Battn. The Gordon Highlanders May 1st 1919 To May 31st 1919		
War Diary	Birkesdorf	01/05/1919	31/05/1919
Miscellaneous	Effective Strength		
Heading	War Diary of 5th Battalion Gordon Highlanders From 1st June 1919 To 30th June 1919 (Volume IV)		
War Diary	Birkesdorf	01/06/1919	17/06/1919
War Diary	Solingen	17/06/1919	17/06/1919

War Diary	Wald	17/06/1919	30/06/1919
Miscellaneous	Effective Strength	31/05/1919	31/05/1919
Heading	War Diary of 5th Battn. The Gordon Highlanders From 1st July 1919 To 31st July 1919 Volume No.51		
War Diary	Wald	01/07/1919	02/07/1919
War Diary	Birkesdorf	03/07/1919	31/07/1919
Miscellaneous	Effective Strength	28/06/1919	28/06/1919
Heading	War Diary of 5th Battn. The Gordon Highlanders From 1st August 1919 To 31st August 1919 Volume No.52		
War Diary	Birkesdorf	01/08/1919	03/08/1919
War Diary	Merzenich	04/08/1919	09/08/1919
War Diary	Calais	10/08/1919	10/08/1919
War Diary	Folkestone	10/08/1919	10/08/1919
War Diary	Clipstone Camp	11/08/1919	31/08/1919
Miscellaneous	Effective Strength	26/07/1919	26/07/1919
Operation(al) Order(s)	Operation Order No.11	07/08/1919	07/08/1919
Operation(al) Order(s)	5th Battn. The Gordon Highlanders Operation Order No. 9 2nd August 1919	02/08/1919	02/08/1919
Heading	B.E.F. Highland Div Formerly 62 Div 2 Highland Bde 51 Gordons 1919 Mar To 1919 Aug		
Heading	War Diary of 51st Bn. Gordon Highlanders 1st March 1919 To 31st March 1919 Volume 1		
Miscellaneous	To Headquarters 186 Infantry Brigade	03/04/1919	03/04/1919
War Diary	Dunkerque	21/03/1919	22/03/1919
War Diary	Horrem	24/03/1919	24/03/1919
War Diary	Turnich	25/03/1919	31/03/1919
Heading	War Diary of 51st Bn. Gordon Highlanders From 1st May 1919 To 31st May 1919		
War Diary	Duren	01/05/1919	31/05/1919
Heading	War Diary of 51st Battn, Gordon Highlanders From 1st June 1919 To 30th June 1919 Volume IV		
War Diary	Duren	02/06/1919	30/06/1919
Heading	War Diary of 51st Battn. Gordon Highlanders From 1st July 1919 31st July 1919		
War Diary	Solingen	01/07/1919	02/07/1919
War Diary	Duren	05/07/1919	29/07/1919
Heading	War Diary of 51st Gordon Highlanders R 1st August 1919 To 31st August 1919		
War Diary	Duren	01/08/1919	09/08/1919
War Diary	Clipstone	19/08/1919	30/08/1919

BEF

HIGHLAND DIV formerly
62 DIV

1 HIGHLAND Bde

52 BN GORDONS

1919 APR TO 1919 AUG

NO BOX

1st Highland Inf Bde

Highland Div [illegible] 62

CONFIDENTIAL

CONFIDENTIAL

WAR DIARY

OF

52nd. Battalion Gordon Highlanders

from:- 6/4/19. To 17-8-19 to 31/5/19.

VOLUME I.

J. W. Browning-Allinson Capt. Adjt.

Instructions regarding War Diaries and Intelligence Summaries are contained in F. S. Regs., Part II, and the Staff Manual respectively. Title pages will be prepared in manuscript.

WAR DIARY
or
INTELLIGENCE SUMMARY.

(Erase heading not required.)

Army Form C. 2118.

Place	Date	Hour	Summary of Events and Information	Remarks and references to Appendices
Dunkirk	6/4/19		The Battalion arrived at Dunkirk at 1600 hours and proceeded to the Rest Camp. On reaching the Camp the men received a hot meal. Tent accommodation proved to be insufficient and over-crowding was unavoidable.	F.W.B-A. Capt. Adjt.
Dunkirk	7/4/19		As no instructions were received for proceeding further leave was granted to the extent of 50% to Officers and Other Ranks. Instructions to entrain the following day were received from the O.C. Detail Camp at 2200 hours.	F.W.B-A. Capt. Adjt.
Dunkirk	8/4/19		Battalion paraded at 1000 hours in readiness to move off on receipt of instructions for time of entraining. Instructions were received at 1100 hours, to entrain 1230 hours.	F.W.B-A. Capt. Adjt.
en Route	9/4/19		Arrangements for Hot meals during the night of the 8th. and during the day of the 9th. were extremely satisfactory. Case of influenza left at CHALEROI.	F.W.B-A. Capt. Adjt.
ZULPICH	10/4/19		Train arrived at ZULPICH at 0500 hours and instructions received to march to EMBKEN where arrangements were made for the billeting of the Battalion. Battalion detrained at 0700 hours and marched to its destination arriving there at 1000 hours. On arrival it was found in view ofthe strength of the Battalion it would be necessary to billet in the two adjacent villages of GINNICK and PISSENHEIM. Companies were allotted as follows:- Headquarters Personnel, "B" and "D" Coys. to EMBKEN. "A" Company to GINNICK. "C" Company to PISSENHEIM. Companies were reported to have completed arrangements by 1230 hours.	F.W.B-A. Capt. Adjt.
EMBKEN.	11/4/19		Nothing to report.	F.W.B-A. Capt. Adjt.
EMBKEN	12/4/19		Wire from Brigade to the effect that the Divisional Commander will inspect the Battalion at 1200 hours on Monday 14th. instant at JUNTERSDORF.	

D. D. & L., London, E.C.
(A8004) Wt. W1771/M2931 750,000 5/17 Sch. 52 Forms/C2118/14

Army Form C. 2118.

Instructions regarding War Diaries and Intelligence Summaries are contained in F. S. Regs., Part II. and the Staff Manual respectively. Title pages will be prepared in manuscript.

WAR DIARY
or
INTELLIGENCE SUMMARY.

(*Erase heading not required.*)

Place	Date	Hour	Summary of Events and Information	Remarks and references to Appendices
EMBKEN	13/4/19		Nothing to report.	F.W.B-A. Capt. Adjt.
EMBKEN	14/4/19		The Battalion inspected by Major-General Sir David Campbell, K.C.B., Divisional Commander, who expressed his appreciation of the fine appearance of the Battn. and its steadiness on parade.	F.W.B-A. Capt: Adjt.
EMBKEN	15/4/19		The Battalion marched to NIDDEGAN where the men cooked their own dinners. The afternoon was devoted to Sports and General Recreational Training. Nothing further to report.	F.W.B-A. Capt. Adjt.
EMBKEN.	16/4/19		Nothing to report.	F.W.B-A. Capt. Adjt.
EMBKEN	17/4/19		Nothing to report.	F.W.B-A. Capt. Adjt.
EMBKEN	18/4/19		Nothing to report.	F.W.B-A. Capt. Adjt.
EMBKEN	19/4/19		~~Nothing to report~~ Lt.G.B.Godson,Lt. F.H. Davison, and 2nd.Lt.C.H.Roberts and 100 O.R. proceeded on attachment to 15th. Husars, Kerpen.	F.W.B-A. Capt. Adjt.
EMBKEN	20/4/19		Nothing to report.	F.W.B-A. Capt. Adjt.
EMBKEN	21/4/19		Nothing to report.	F.W.B-A. Capt. Adjt.
EMBKEN	22/4/19		Nothing to report.	F.W.B-A. Capt. Adjt.
EMBKEN	23/4/19		~~Nothing to report~~ Capt.J.L.Riddel,M.C.2nd.Lts. W.J.Hadden, P.J. Bett and D. Langlands and 151 O.R. are attached to 3rd. Hussars, GROTTENHERTEN.Capt.R.K.Gordon Lieut. A.E.Ashman,2nd.Lts.R.L.Tanner and C.Beattie and 150 O.R.to 10th.Hussars,Turnich.	F.W.B-A. Capt. Adjt.
EMBKEN	24/4/19		Nothing to report.	
EMBKEN	25/4/19		2/Lieut. W.E. Winsall reported to A.D.R.T. Cologne for one month's probation.	F.W.B-A. Capt. Adjt.
EMBKEN	26/4/19		Nothing to report.	
EMBKEN	27/4/19		In accordance with Brigade instructions other ranks will not proceed outside t	F.W.B-A.

D. D. & L., London, E.C. (A8004) Wt. W1771/M2 31 750,000 5/17 Sch. 52 Forms/C2118/14

Instructions regarding War Diaries and Intelligence Summaries are contained in F. S. Regs., Part II. and the Staff Manual respectively. Title pages will be prepared in manuscript.

WAR DIARY
or
INTELLIGENCE SUMMARY.
(Erase heading not required.)

Army Form C. 2118.

Place	Date	Hour	Summary of Events and Information	Remarks and references to Appendices
EMBKEN	27/4/19		(Cont'd.) the village in which they are billeted without sidearms.	J.W.B-A. Capt. Adjt.
EMBKEN	28/4/19		Nothing to report.	J.W.B-A. Capt. Adjt.
EMBKEN	29/4/19		In accordance with Corps orders Thursdays will be observed as a whole holiday.	J.W.B-A. Capt. Adjt.
EMBKEN	30/4/19		Brigade Order 402 sanctioned the holding of Labour Demonstrations by the Civil population on May 1st. Lieut. R.McD. Smellie took over the duties of Battalion Spor s Officer vice Lieut. J.A. Tinning. The undernoted Officers proceeded on Detachment duty with 3rd. Hussars, GROTTENHERTEN with effect from 23/4/19. Captain J.L. Riddel, M.C. 2/Lieuts. W.J. Hadden, F.J. Bett and D. Langlands. The undernoted Officers proceeded on detachment with 10th. Hussars, TURNICH with effect from 23/4/19:- Captain R.K. Gordon, M.C. 2/Lieuts. R.L. Tanner and C. Beattie.	J.W.B-A. Capt. Adjt.
EMBKEN	1/5/19		Information received from 1st. Highland Brigade that the Battalion would form part of the Brigade and will remain as a complete Bn. in this formation.	J.W.B-A. Capt. Adjt.
	2/5/19		Nothing to report.	J.W.B-A. Capt. Adjt.
	3/5/19		Captain J.F. Mackintosh, M.C. proceeds to the Army Reconnaissance School, MONTJOIE. Nothing further to report.	J.W.B-A. Capt. Adjt.
	4/5/19		Nothing to report.	
	5/5/19		Captain W.A. Fraser, M.C., R.A.M.C. reported for duty vice Lieut. E.B. Verney, proceeding to England.	J.W.B-A. Capt. Adjt.
	6/5/19		Nothing to report.	J.W.B-A. Capt. Adjt.

D. D. & L., London, E.C.
(A8004) Wt. W1771/M2231 750,000 5/17 Sch. 52 Forms/C2118/14

Army Form C. 2118.

Instructions regarding War Diaries and Intelligence Summaries are contained in F. S. Regs., Part II. and the Staff Manual respectively. Title pages will be prepared in manuscript.

WAR DIARY
or
INTELLIGENCE SUMMARY.

(Erase heading not required.)

Place	Date	Hour	Summary of Events and Information	Remarks and references to Appendices
MBKEN.	7/5/19		Nothing to report.	F.W.B-A. Capt. Adjt.
MBKEN	8/5/19		Major P.B. Anderson, D.C.M. assumed Temporary Command of the Battalion from this date vice Temp. Lieut.-Colonel G.R.V. Hume-Gore, M.C. appointed 2nd. in Command of the 53rd. Bn. Gordon Highlanders. Headquarters and Details of "C" Company moved into Fussenich. "A" Company moves to PISSENHEIM. Transport to GINNICK. Nothing further to report.	F.W.B-A. Capt. Adjt. F.W.B-A. Capt. Adjt.
USSENICH	9/5/19		Nothing to report.	F.W.B-A. Capt. Adjt.
USSENICH	10/5/19		Nothing to report.	
USSENICH	11/5/19		Nothing to report.	
USSENICH	12/5/19		2/Lieut. C.H. Roberts proceeded on 3 months' leave to England prior to joining Regimental Depot and is struck off strength from this date. Nothing further to report.	F.W.B-A. Capt. Adjt.
SSENICH	13/5/19		Nothing to report.	F.W.B-A. Capt. Adjt.
USSENICH	14/5/19		Nothing to report.	
SSENICH	15/5/19		3 men attached 2/1st. Field Ambulance with effect from 16th. 16 men attached Divisional Train with effect from 16th. 1 attached to Brigade Headquarters. Nothing further to report.	F.W.B-A. Capt. Adjt.
USSENICH	16/5/19		Nothing to report.	F.W.B-A. Capt. Adjt.
USSENICH	17/5/19		Nothing to report.	
USSENICH	18/5/19		Nothing to report.	F.W.B-A. Capt. Adjt.

D. D. & L., London, E.C.
(A8004) Wt. W1771/M2231 750,000 5/17 Sch. 52 Forms/C2118/14

Instructions regarding War Diaries and Intelligence Summaries are contained in F. S. Regs., Part II. and the Staff Manual respectively. Title pages will be prepared in manuscript.

WAR DIARY
or
INTELLIGENCE SUMMARY.

(*Erase heading not required.*)

Army Form C. 2118.

Place	Date	Hour	Summary of Events and Information	Remarks and references to Appendices
FUSSENICH	19/5/19		"A" and "D" Companies move to JUNTERSDORF from PISSENHEIM and GINNICK respectively. Nothing further to report.	F.W.B-A. Capt Adjt
FUSSENICH	20/5/19		Transport moved to FUSSENICH from GINNICK. Nothing further to report.	F.W.B-A. Capt Adjt
FUSSENICH	21/5/19		Transport inspection by Divisional Commander, Sir David Campbell, K.C.B., postponed.	F.W.B-A. Capt Adjt
FUSSENICH	22/5/19		Instructions received from 1st. Highland Brigade that move to Training Area on 23rd instant. (Operation Order No. 2). Further wire received regarding this instruction from 1st. Highland Brigade B.M.111 reads as follows:- Operation Order No. 2 aaa Move to training area is postponed. Received at 2215 hours. Secret instructions received from 1st. Highland Brigade Warning Order BMH/1195:- The Brigade will prepare to move to OPLADEN by train on or after the 25th. instant. 52nd. Gordon Highlanders less detachment to the Cavalry will be prepared to move to the DROVE Area on the night previous to entraining. Entraining stations will be either NIDDEGAN or KRESAU. With reference to BMH/1195 the following wire was received at 1805 hours:- paras 1 and 2 cancelled. Duren will be entraining station f r the Brigade aaa If forward movement begins to-morrow Brigade will await orders to concen rate DUREN BARRACKS aaa If no forward move orders to move to training area holds good.aaa Units will be informed by 0600 hours to-morrow. Acknowledge. Receipt of this wire was acknowledged.	F.W.B-A. Capt Adjt
FUSSENICH	23/5/19		Nothing to report.	F.W.B-A. Capt Adjt
FUSSENICH	24/5/19		The G.O.C. Brigade, Brigadier-General J. Campbell, C.B., C.M.G., D.S.O. inspected Battalion Guard Mounting at 1030 hours.	
FUSSENICH	25/5/19		Lieut.-Colonel A.B. Robertson, C.M.G., D.S.O. assumed Command of the Battalion from Major P.B. Anderson, D.C.M.	F.W.B-A. Capt Adjt

D. D. & L., London, E.C.
(A8004) Wt. W1771/M2131 750,000 5/17 Sch. 52 Forms/C2118/14

Army Form C. 2118.

Instructions regarding War Diaries and Intelligence Summaries are contained in F. S. Regs., Part II. and the Staff Manual respectively. Title pages will be prepared in manuscript.

WAR DIARY
or
INTELLIGENCE SUMMARY.

(*Erase heading not required.*)

Place	Date	Hour	Summary of Events and Information	Remarks and references to Appendices
FUSSENICH	26/5/19		Nothing to report.	F.W.B-A. Capt. Adjt.
FUSSENICH	27/5/19		Secret instructions received from Brigade with reference to the advance of the Army of the Rhine. (Adjutant's reference A.16)	F.W.B-A. Capt. Adjt.
FUSSENICH	28/5/19		The Commanding Officer held a conference of all Company Commanders and Specialist Officers at which detailed instructions were given in connection with Warning Order A.16. Further instructions received from Brigade copy 4 Adjutant's reference A.17. Captain J.S. Brander proceeded for demobilisation.	F.W.B-A. Capt. Adjt. F.W.B-A. Capt. Adjt.
FUSSENICH	29/5/19		Transport ibstructions received from 1st. Highland Brigade in continuation of copy 4.	F.W.B-A. Capt. Adjt.
FUSSENICH	30/5/19		2/Lieut. W. Barclay, Gordon Highlanders reported for duty with this Battn. as from 27/5/19. Cross-posted from 5th. Bn. Cameron Highlanders. Further instructions in connection with copy 4 Adjutant's reference A.19 received from 1st. Highland Brigade. Brigade moves to Training Area at BLENS reference copy 5 Adjutant's reference A.20.	
FUSSENICH	31/5/19		Nothing to report.	F.W.B-A. Capt. Adjt.

APPENDIX.

The Battalion left England with a strength of 43 Officers and 981 Other Ranks. During the period from 10th. April to 31st. May 8 Officers and 12 Other Ranks were demobilised or struck off strength for other reasons.
3 Officers have been taken on strength.
The Battn. strength on 31/5/19 is as follows:- 38 Officers
969 O.R's.

F.W. Bagnall-Allinson Capt. Adjt.

D. D. & L., London, E.C. (A8004) Wt. W1771/M2-31 750,000 5/17 Sch. 52 Forms/C2118/14

Confidential

52ND Gordon Hldrs

Original

War Diary

Nov. – July 1919.

Army Form C. 2118.

Instructions regarding War Diaries and Intelligence Summaries are contained in F. S. Regs., Part II. and the Staff Manual respectively. Title pages will be prepared in manuscript.

WAR DIARY
or
INTELLIGENCE SUMMARY.

(Erase heading not required.)

Place	Date	Hour	Summary of Events and Information	Remarks and references to Appendices
DUREN.	1/7/19.		Battalion entrained at DUREN Station for BLENS arriving there at 1400 hours. J.B.M. a/adjt.	
BLENS.	2/7/19.		Nothing to report. J.B.M. a/adjt.	
do.	3/7/19.		Nothing to report. J.B.M. a/adjt.	
do.	4/7/19.		Reconnaissance of HEIMBACH, ABENDEN, and ~~HAUSEN~~ HASENFELD to provide accommodation for Companies returning from Cavalry. J.B.M. a/adjt.	
do.	5/7/19.		~~Nothing to report.~~ D COY. MOVED TO BILLETS IN ABENDEN J.B.M. a/adjt.	
do.	6/7/19.		R.S.M. and 3 O.R. proceeded to PARIS to take part in Allied Victory March. J.B.M. a/adjt.	
do.	7/7/19.		Nothing to report. J.B.M. a/adjt.	
do.	8/7/19.		1 Officer and 60 O.R. proceeded on Rhine Trip. J.B.M. a/adjt.	
do.	9/7/19.		Capt. J.L.Riddel, M.C. Lieut. MacKay, Lieut. Davidson, 2/Lieuts. D. Langlands, P.J. Bett, and 330 Other Ranks rejoined the Battalion from 10th. and 15th. Hussars. J.B.M. a/adjt. Lieut. A.E. Ashman proceeded on attachment to Demobilization Camp, DUREN BARRACKS, as Company Commander. J.B.M. a/adjt.	
do.	10/7/19.		Nothing to report. J.B.M. a/adjt.	
do.	11/7/19.		Nothing to report. J.B.M. a/adjt.	
do.	12/7/19.		Nothing to report. J.B.M. a/adjt.	
do.	13/7/19.		Nothing to report. J.B.M. a/adjt.	
do.	14/7/19.		Nothing to report. J.B.M. a/adjt.	
do.	15/7/19.		Nothing to report. J.B.M. a/adjt.	
do.	16/7/19.		Nothing to report. J.B.M. a/adjt.	

(A8004) Wt. W177/M2431 750,000 5/17 D. D. & L. Ltd. F.C. Sch. 52 Forms/C2118/14

Instructions regarding War Diaries and Intelligence Summaries are contained in F. S. Regs., Part II. and the Staff Manual respectively. Title pages will be prepared in manuscript.

WAR DIARY
or
INTELLIGENCE SUMMARY.
(Erase heading not required.)

Army Form C. 2118.

Place	Date	Hour	Summary of Events and Information	Remarks and references to Appendices
BLENS.	17/7/19.		Nothing to report. J.B.M. a/adjt.	
do.	18/7/19.		Battalion Sports. J.B.M. a/adjt.	
do.	19/7/19.		Peace Day Holiday and Celebrations. J.B.M. a/adjt.	
do.	20/7/19.		Nothing to report. J.B.M. a/adjt.	
do.	21/7/19.		Nothing to report. J.B.M. a/adjt.	
do.	22/7/19.		Nothing to report. J.B.M. a/adjt.	
do.	23/7/19.		Nothing to report. J.B.M. a/adjt.	
do.	24/7/19.		Nothing to report. J.B.M. a/adjt.	
do.	25/7/19.		Nothing to report. J.B.M. a/adjt.	
do.	26/7/19.		Nothing to report. J.B.M. a/adjt.	
do.	27/7/19.		Nothing to report. J.B.M. a/adjt.	
do.	28/7/19.		Nothing to report. J.B.M. a/adjt.	
do.	29/7/19.		Nothing to report. J.B.M. a/adjt.	
do.	30/7/19.		Nothing to report. J.B.M. a/adjt.	
do.	31/7/19.		2/Lieut. J.G. McLeod proceeded for duty to Chinese Labour Corps, NOYELLES, and struck off strength of this Battalion from this date. J.B.M. a/adjt.	

**** ***** *****

D. D. & L., London, E.C.
(A8004) Wt. W1771/M2731 750,000 5/17 Sch. 52 Forms/C2118/14

W A R   D I A R Y

for

52nd. Battalion Gordon Highlanders.

Period:- 1/8/19.   To 17/8/19.

Army Form C. 2118.

Instructions regarding War Diaries and Intelligence Summaries are contained in F. S. Regs., Part II. and the Staff Manual respectively. Title pages will be prepared in manuscript.

WAR DIARY
or
INTELLIGENCE SUMMARY.
(Erase heading not required.)

Place	Date	Hour	Summary of Events and Information	Remarks and references to Appendices
Blens.Germany	1/8/19.		Nothing to report.	
	2/8/19.		Brigade Sports.	
	4/8/19.		Nothing to report.	
	5/8/19.		Rhine Trip. One Officer and 59 Other Ranks to attend from each Company.	
	6/8/19.		Nothing to report.	
	7/8/19.		Brigade Ceremonial Parade cancelled.	
	8/8/19.		Lieut.L.L.R.F. Preau and Captain G.H.Gordon struck off strength from 6/8/19. Orders to move to U.K. received.	
	9/8/19.		Advance party 1 Officer and 5 Other Ranks proceed to Duren in view of move to U.K. 2/Lt.G.Foster proceeds to Duren Bcks. to make arrangements to take over billets for Battalion.	
	10/8/19.		Battalion commences Move to U.K. 1 Platoon of "B" Company to act as rearvparty under Command of Lieut. R.McD. Smellie.	
	11/8/19.		Battalion stays night in Duren Barracks and entrains at 1800 hours at Duren Station.	
	12/8/19.		En route for Calais.	
	13/8/19.		Arrive at Calais at 0600. Embarked Calais at 1000 hours. Disembarked Dover 1145 hours.	
	14/8/19.		Arrived Catterick Camp at 0700 hours. Occupy "Y" Lines.	
	15/8/19.		Nothing to report.,	
	16/8/19.		Nothing to report.	
	17/8/19.		do.	

BEF

HIGHLAND DIV formerly
62 DIV

3 HIGHLAND BDE H.Q.

1919 MAY to 1919 AUG

Original.

Confidential

War Diary

of

3rd Highland Brigade

from 1st May 1919 to 31st May 1919

Volume 2

(6392) Wt. 1 5192/P875 1,500,000 4/18 McA & W Ltd (E 2815) Forms W3091/4. Army Form W.3091.

Cover for Documents.

Nature of Enclosures.

Notes, or Letters written.

Instructions regarding War Diaries and Intelligence Summaries are contained in F. S. Regs., Part II. and the Staff Manual respectively. Title pages will be prepared in manuscript.

Army Form C. 2118.

WAR DIARY
or
INTELLIGENCE SUMMARY.

3rd Highland Brigade.

(Erase heading not required.)

Place	Date	Hour	Summary of Events and Information	Remarks and references to Appendices
	1919 May 1		B.G.C. attended a Sports Conference at IV Corps Headquarters. Advanced detachment of 4th Seaforths moved by train to NIDEGGEN Station. Draft from 9th Seaforths joined 4th Seaforths. Lecture by Commander Viscount Broome, R.N. to 4th Seaforths at GOLZHEIM at 1800 hours.	
	2.		Headquarters 53rd Gordons moved to SCHLISH to billets vacated by 9th Seaforths.	
	3.		Units Training.	
	4.		Church Parades.	
	5.		Capt. D.McCALLUM M.C., East Yorkshire Regt. arrived to take over duties of Brigade Major.	
	6.		Brigadier-General Commanding proceeded on leave to United Kingdom. Lt.Col. W.GREEN, 6th Bn. The Black Watch assumed command of the Brigade. Capt. D.McCALLUM took over duties of Brigade Major from Major G.de C.GLOVER, D.S.O.,M.C.	
	7.		Major G.de C.GLOVER proceeded to join IV Corps H.Q. as G.S.O.2 (operations). Brigade Major and Staff Captain visited the new Brigade area.	
	8.		Units training.	
	9.		8th Bn. The Black Watch moved by train from BUIR to MAUBACH. Staff Captain present at entraining.	
	10.		Units Training. Brigade Major visited HERBESTHAL and MALMEDY detachments. Cadre of 9th Seaforth Highrs. moved to VETTWEISS.	
	11.		Church Parades.	
	12.		1/4th Seaforth Highrs. moved from GOLZHEIM to BRUCK (less isolated company left at ESCHWEILER)	

A7092 Wt. W128.9/M1293 750,000. 1/17. D. D & L. Ltd. Forms/C2118/14.

Army Form C. 2118.

Instructions regarding War Diaries and Intelligence Summaries are contained in F. S. Regs., Part II. and the Staff Manual respectively. Title pages will be prepared in manuscript.

WAR DIARY
or
~~INTELLIGENCE SUMMARY.~~ 3rd Highland Brigade.

(Erase heading not required.)

Place	Date	Hour	Summary of Events and Information	Remarks and references to Appendices
	1919 May 13.		6th Bn. The Black Watch took over Brigade Guards from 'A' Company 53rd Bn Gordon Highrs. Units Training.	
	14.		Units Training	
	15.		Units Training.	
	16.		Divisional Commander visited Brigade Headquarters. Brigade Major reconnoitred training areas of 8th Bn. The Black Watch and 1/4th Bn. Seaforths.	
	17.		Marshall Foch visited DUREN, Guard of Honour found by 2nd Highland Brigade. Units Training.	
	18.		Mr. BRUNTON of the Army Schoolmasters Branch reported for duty and was attached to 1/4th Bn. Seaforth Highrs. Brigade Major, Staff Captain and O.C. L.T.M.Battery visited UDDIGEN reference move of T.M.Battery.	
	19.		Units Training.	
	20.		Conference of Brigadiers at Divisional Headquarters at 1700 hours. Units training.	
	21.		Units training. Conference at Divisional Headquarters. Brigade Commander attended it. Orders received that moves to training area to be cancelled for the present. C.Os and Staff Officers to be recalled from leave. Orders issued for conference at Brigade Headquarters tomorrow 22nd at 1100 hours. All C.Os to attend. 9th Bn. Seaforth Highrs to move with 3rd Brigade if move takes place.	

Army Form C. 2118.

WAR DIARY
or
INTELLIGENCE SUMMARY.
(Erase heading not required.)

3rd Highland Brigade.

Instructions regarding War Diaries and Intelligence Summaries are contained in F. S. Regs., Part II. and the Staff Manual respectively. Title pages will be prepared in manuscript.

Place	Date	Hour	Summary of Events and Information	Remarks and references to Appendices
	1919 May 22		Conference of C.Os at Brigade Headquarters reference move forward in event of Armistice terminating. Brigadier-General A.H.MARINDIN, D.S.O. returned from leave. Units Training. Highland Division Warning Order No. 7 and amendments received.	
	23.		Brigadier visited Divisional H.Q., 8th Bn. The Black Watch and 1/4th Bn. Seaforth Highrs. Brigade Major proceeded to reconnoitre BENRATH area and visited 2nd and 3rd Lowland Brigade H.Qs. reference projected move forward. 3rd Highland Brigade Warning Order No.1 issued (See appendix "A") 2/3rd W.R.F.Ambulance moved from GIRBELSRATH to LEHRER-SEMINAR, DUREN relieving 2/2nd W.R. F.Ambulance who proceed to GIRBELSRATH prior to being disbanded.	Appendix A.
	24.		Inspection of 6th Bn. The Black Watch transport by Divisional Commander. B.G.C. was also present.	
	25.		B.G.C. attended Church Parade of 8th Bn. The Black Watch at MAUBACH. B.G.C. visited Divisional H.Q. in afternoon. Range construction party of 9th Bn Seaforth Highrs returned to Battn at VETTWEISS.	
	26.		B.G.C. inspected transport of 8th Bn. The Black Watch and 1/4th Bn. Seaforth Highrs.	
	27.		9th Bn Seaforth Highrs relieved detachment of 8th Bn. The Black Watch at MALMEDY. Detachment of 8th Bn. The Black Watch rejoined Battalion at MAUBACH. 3rd Highland Bde Warning Order No 2 issued (See Appendix B.)	Appendix B.
	28.		B.G.C. inspected training of 6th Bn. The Black Watch.	
	29.		B.G.C. visited Divisional Headquarters and 8th Bn. The Black Watch. Administrative Instructions in conjunction with Warning Orders No.1 and 2 issued	Appendix C.

(A7092). Wt. W12839/M1293. 750,000. 1/17. D. D. & L., Ltd. Forms/C.2118/14.

Army Form C. 2118.

Instructions regarding War Diaries and Intelligence Summaries are contained in F. S. Regs., Part II. and the Staff Manual respectively. Title pages will be prepared in manuscript.

WAR DIARY or ~~INTELLIGENCE SUMMARY.~~ 3rd Highland Brigade.

(*Erase heading not required.*)

Place	Date	Hour	Summary of Events and Information	Remarks and references to Appendices
	1919 May 30.		6th Bn. The Black Watch moved from MERZENICH to LENDERSDORF. 3rd Highland T.M.Battery moved from ROMMELSHEIM to UDINGEN. Brigade Signal School moved from BINSFELD to UDINGEN. Divisional Commander inspected transport of 8th Bn. The Black Watch and 1/4th Bn. Seaforth Highrs.	
	31.		Brigade Headquarters moved from DUREN to UNT MAUBACH. Brigadier and Brigade Major attended Sports Meeting of 51st Bn. Gordon Highlanders at IV Corps Sports Club ground.	

Brigadier-General.
Commanding 3rd Highland Brigade.

A7092. Wt. W128 9/M1293. 750,000. 1/17. D. D & L., Ltd. Forms/C2118/14.

Appendix A

War Diary

SECRET.

Copy No.........

3rd HIGHLAND BRIGADE WARNING ORDER NO. 1.

23rd May, 1919.

1. In the event of the Army of the Rhine being ordered to advance, three days only will be available for preparatory moves and re-distribution of troops. Thus, if J day is the day on which the advance commences, J - 3 day will be the first day on which movements take place.

2. The earliest date which J-3 day can be is midnight 22/23rd May, 1919. From this hour troops of the Highland Division will be prepared to move by tactical trains and road at short notice. The 3rd Highland Brigade may possibly receive 24 hours notice to move.

3. The Highland Division will take over the OPLADEN - SOLINGEN-BENRATH Area from units of the II Corps. The IX Corps will take over from the IV Corps the area west of the line ESCH - BACHEM - BLATZHEIM.

The 6th Bn. The Black Watch (R.H.)., will hand over the Railway Guards and the IV Corps Salvage Dump Guard to the Battalion of the Midland Division relieving them in MERZENICH. All other Guards with the exception of the HERBERTSTHAL and MALMEDY Detachments will be withdrawn upon the receipt of orders to move.

On receipt of orders to move, however, the Railway and Salvage Dump Guards of the 6th Bn. The Black Watch (R.H.)., will not wait to be relieved by troops of the Midland Division.

4. The 9th Bn. Seaforth Highlanders will move under orders of the 3rd Highland Brigade.

5. The 461st Field Company, R.E., will move by road under orders of the C.R.E.

6. The 2/3rd West Riding Field Ambulance will move by road to SOLINGEN with 2nd Highland Brigade transport, under orders of the 2nd Highland Brigade.

7. The Headquarters Staff for Civil matters will move to the new area with Brigade Headquarters.

8. Further orders will be issued regarding the action to be taken by units on receipt of the order to move.

9. ACKNOWLEDGE.

[signature] Captain.

Brigade Major. 3rd Highland Brigade.

Issued through Signals at 1030 hours to -

Copy No. 1. 6th Bn. The Black Watch.
2. 8th Bn. The Black Watch.
3. 4th Bn. Seaforth Hldrs.,
4. 9th Bn. Seaforth Hldrs.,
5. 3rd Highland L.T.M.Batty.
6. 461st Field Coy., R.E.,
No. 7. 528 Coy.,R.A.S.C.,
8. 2/3 W.R.F.Ambulance.,
9. B.G.C.,
10. Brigade Major.
11. Military Staff Captain.
12. Civil Staff Captain.
13. Brigade Signal Officer.
14. 1st Highland Bde.
15. 2nd Highland Bde.

Appendix B

SECRET Copy No.....

3rd Highland Brigade Warning Order No. 2.

26th May 1919.

In continuation of 3rd Highland Brigade Warning Order No.1 of 22nd May 1919, the following movements will be carried out by units on receipt of the orders to move -

1. The 3rd Highland Brigade will concentrate in the vicinity of DUREN on J - 3 days preparatory to moving to the BENRATH area by tactical train and road in accordance with the attached Table 'A'.

2. The move to the BENRATH area on J - 2 days will be carried out in accordance with the attached Table 'B'.

3. The 9th Seaforth Highlanders will NOT move with the 3rd Highland Brigade but will remain at MALMEDY until further orders are issued.
The Company of the 6th Bn. The Black Watch will remain at HERBESTHAL until relieved, when further orders will be issued for it to rejoin its battalion in the new area.

4. Troops will move in "Marching Order".

5. The greater part of units First Line Transport will move from DUREN to the BENRATH area by train, the remainder proceeding by road, brigaded, under orders of Capt. R.G.A.DICKSON, The Black Watch.

6. While on the line of march particular attention will be paid to march discipline and the keeping of the proper intervals laid down in G.H.Q. pamphlet dated May 22nd 1919.

7. Units will move with ammunition echelons full.

8. Each unit will send forward by train, 24 hours in advance of the troops, the necessary billetting party to report to the H.Q. of the Unit of the 3rd Lowland Brigade it is taking over from.

9. Rations to be taken on the trains will consist of the unexpended portion of the day's ration plus the following day's ration.

10. On arrival in the new area battalions will take over the following out-posts, guards etc. at present found by battalions of the 2nd and 3rd Lowland Brigades :-

6th Bn. The Black Watch at HILDEN ... 1 Coy. to take over duties at LANGENFELD until relieved by troops from OPLADEN or Machine gunners.

8th Bn. Black Watch at BENRATH

Nature of duty.	Location.	Offs.	O.Rs.
No.1 Perimeter Post.	KEMPERDICK	1	21
No.2 do	DICKHAUS	1.	19
No.3 do	REUSHOLZ	1.	32
No.4 do	FRIEDHOF	1.	16
No.5 do	HOLTHAUSEN	2	37
No.6 do	HIMMELGEIST	2.	24
Guard on RHENANIA Petroleum Works.		1 Platoon minimum.	
Guard on Electric Power Station close to above.		1 Platoon.	
* Examining Post	HILDEN Rly. Stn.	3 offs.	23 O.Rs.
* do	REISHOF Rly. Stn.	4 offs.	26 O.Rs.

* It is possible that these two latter duties will be found by the Allied Railway Commission in the near future.

	Nature of Duty	Location.	Offs.	O.Rs.
1/4th Seaforth Highrs.	Examining Post	OHLIGS Rly.Stn.	4.	40

(Particulars of other duties to be taken over by 1/4th Seaforths will be notified later).

A map showing locations of all Perimeter Posts, guards, etc., will be issued to battalions as soon as the necessary sheetsare received from the Higher Authorities.

11. Completion of arrival and taking over of their respective duties will be reported to 3rd Highland Brigade Headquarters.

12. 3rd Highland Brigade will close at SCHOELLERSTRASSE, DUREN on J + 2 days at an hour to be notified later and will re-open at the BAHNHOF HOTEL, BENRATH, on arrival.

13. Headquarters, Civil Administration Staff will report to Lowland Division H.Q. at OHLIGS on the afternoon of J - 2 days.

14. 3rd Highland Brigade area will include HAAN - OHLIGS - HILDEN - BENRATH.

15. The two R.E. detachments of the 461st Field Coy. R.E, consisting of 2 officers, 2 N.C.Os and 1 clerk each, will remain with Brigade H.Q. until fetched by the Lowland Division Engineers from whom they are to take over.

16. ACKNOWLEDGE.

Captain.
Brigade Major.
3rd Highland Brigade.

Issued through Signals at 1030 hours 27.5.1919.

Copies to -

1. 6th Black Watch
2. 8th Black Watch
3. 1/4th Seaforth Highlanders
4. 9th Seaforth Highlanders
5. 3rd Highland T.M.Battery
6. 461st Field Coy. R.E.
7. 528 Coy. R.A.S.C.
8. 1st Highland Brigade
9. 2nd Highland Brigade
10. Highland Division 'G'
11. Highland Division 'Q'
12. 62nd M.G.Battalion
13. Highland Division R.A.
14. Lowland Division.
15. 2nd Lowland Brigade
16. 3rd Lowland Brigade
17. 2/3rd W.R.F.Ambulance
18. B.G.C.
19. Brigade Major.
20. Staff Captain
21. Staff Captain for civil duties
22. Brigade Signal Officer
23. Capt. R.G.A.Dickson.

Table 'A' issued with 3rd Highland Brigade Warning Order No.2 dated May 26th May 1919.

Serial No.	Date.	Unit.	From.	To.	How moving	Remarks
1.	J - 3 day.	6th Black Watch	Remain at MERZENICH			
* 2.	do	8th Black Watch	MAUBACH	BIRKESDORF	March Route	
* 3.	do	1/4th Seaforths	BRUCK	DUREN BARRACKS	March Route	
4.	do	3rd Highland T.M.B.		Remain at ROMMELSHEIM		
5.	do	3rd Highland Bde H.Q.		Remain at DUREN		
6.	do	R.E. detachments of 461 Field Coy. R.E.	FRAUWULLERSHEIM	DUREN	March Route	To join 3rd Highland Bde H.Q.
7.	do	338 Coy. R.A.S.C.		Remain at DISTELRATH		

* Arrangements are being made for lorries to convey surplus kit, blankets etc. on J - 3 days.

Table '[illegible]' issued with 3rd Highland Brigade Warning Order No.2 dated 26th May 1919

Serial No.	Date.	Unit.	From	To.	How Moving.	Entraining Stn.	Relieving	Remarks.
1.	J - 2 day	3rd Highland Bde H.Q.	DUREN	BENRATH	Train	DUREN	3rd L[illegible] land Bde	
2.	do	3rd HighlandT.M.B.	ROMMELSHEIM	BENRATH	Train	do	---	
3.	do	6th Black Watch	MERZENICH	HILDEN	Train	do	8th Scot.Rifles & 4th Royal Scots	One coy. to be dropped at LANGENFELD to take over duties at that place until relieved by troops from OPIADEN or Machine Gunners
4.	do	5th Black Watch	BIRKESDORF	BENRATH	Train	do	9th Scot.Rifles	
5.	do	1/4th Seaforths	DUREN BARRACKS	OHLIGS	Train	do	5/6th Royal Scots	To take over also Perimeter posts found by 11th Royal Scots in HAAN.
6.	do	R.E.detachments of 461 Field Coy.R.E.	DUREN	BENRATH	Train	do	---	To remain with Brigade H.Q. until fetched by Lowland Divn. R.E.
7.	do	528 Coy. R.A.S.C.	DISTELRATH	HILDEN	Train	do	No.4 Coy. Low-Land Div. Train.	Only such personnel as are not required to proceed with transport.

Table 'B' continued

8.	J - 2 day.	Units Transport Brigaded.	DUREN area	BENRATH area	Road	---	---	Such portion as is unable to proceed by [illegible]ain. Transport of units will rendezvous at junction of MERZENICH and Main DUREN ~~Road~~ COLOGNE Road at 0300 hours and proceed to MUNGERSDORF via Main COLOGNE Road.
9.	J - 1 day	do	MUNGERSDORF	OPLADEN	do	---	---	Keep North of COLOGNE and cross RHINE by Bridge of boats at RIEHL.
10.	J day	do	OPLADEN	Units respective billetting areas.	do	---	---	By shortest routes to respective billetting areas.

(a) Brigade Transport Column will move as one column under Capt. R.G.A.Dickson, The Black Watch.

(b) Accommodation for transport staging will be obtained from H.Q. 42nd Bn. M.G.C. at FORT for MUNGERSDORF, at OPLADEN from Civil Administrator.

(c) Train arrangements will be notified later.

(d) Arrangements are being made for lorries to convey surplus kit, blankets, etc. to entraining Station on J - 2 day.

Appendix C.

SECRET. Copy No. 22......

3rd Highland Brigade.

ADMINISTRATIVE INSTRUCTIONS IN THE EVENT OF ADVANCE ISSUED IN CONJUNCTION WITH 3RD HIGHLAND BRIGADE MARCHING ORDERS NOS. 1 and 2.

29th May, 1919.

1. ENTRAINMENT.

Units will entrain in accordance with the attached train table.

(a) Captain R.G.A. DICKSON, The Black Watch (R.H.)., will generally superintend the entraining of the whole Brigade Group.

(b) Units will each detail one Entraining Officer to report to the Brigade Representative at the Entraining Station half an hour before the time specified for transport to arrive. He should be in possession of an entraining state in duplicate showing -

No. of Officers.
No. of Other Ranks.
No. of Animals.
No. of two wheeled vehicles.
No. of four - ditto -

to be entrained.

2. AMMUNITION.

S.A.A., up to 120 rounds per man will be issued before entrainment from the dump at Quartermasters' Stores kept for that purpose.

3. SUPPLIES.

(a) The unconsumed portion of the day's rations will be carried on the man.
Rations for the two following days will be taken on the Personnel train for troops travelling by rail.

(b) Transport moving by road will carry the unexpended portion of the day's ration on the man and the two following days' rations and forage on the vehicles.

(c) Details as to when and where the two additional days' rations are to be delivered will be issued as soon as received.

4. MEDICAL ARRANGEMENTS.

Medical Arrangements will be issued as soon as received from the A.D.M.S., Highland Division.

5. VETERINARY ARRANGEMENTS.

The 2/1st (West Riding) Mobile Veterinary Section will move with the Highland Divisional Artillery.

6. LORRIES.

Three lorries each will be allotted to the 8th Bn. The Black Watch (R.H.)., and 4th Bn. Seaforth Highlanders on J-3 Day to convey blankets and surplus kit to staging area.

Three lorries will be allotted to each Battalion on J-2 Day to convey stores and blankets to entraining station.

One lorry for one journey only will be allotted to the 3rd Highland Light Trench Mortar Battery.

Lowland Division have been asked to supply a similar number to move stores from Detraining Station.

On no account will these lorries be sent through to new area.

7. SURPLUS KIT, STORES, ETC.,

(a) Only war equipment will be taken forward in the first instance.

(b) All surplus kit, R.E.Stores, Palliases, Beds, Blankets, etc., will be stored in units' dumps.

The location, approximate number of lorry loads and the number of men left on guard will be wired to Brigade Headquarters.

Four days rations will be left with this party.

(c) All tents will be struck and left in this Dump, the number of tents being reported to this office.

(d) R.E.Stores, Cookhouses, Latrines, etc., that cannot be collected will be handed over to the Burgomeister of the village concerned.

List of the stores will be made out in quadruplicate, one copy will be handed to the Burgomeister, one to the incoming Civil Staff Captain and two copies to Brigade Headquarters.

The Burgomeister will be warned that he is responsible for the safety of these stores until they are taken over by the British Military Authorities.

These lists will be prepared forthwith.

Note - For full details of procedure see this office S.C.477 of 8.5.1919.

(e) If time permits surplus kit and stores of the 3rd Highland L.T.M.Battery will be moved to Brigade Headquarters, DUREN.

8. ORDNANCE.

An Advance Ordnance Store will be at OHLIGS on J. Day. This will consist of Lewis Gun Barrels and spare parts and a reserve of 500 Box Respirators and 250 Containers.

9. ANIMAL COLLECTING CAMP.

The present Staff of the Animal Collecting Camp will remain and carry on the Camp at DUREN pending further instructions.

10. CANTEEN.

The Highland Divisional Canteen has arranged to move forward as facilities permit.

11. CIVIL ADMINISTRATION.

The 3rd Highland Brigade will take over the Civil Administration of BENRATH, HILDEN, OHLIGS and HAAN at 1800 hours on J Day.

Further instructions will be issued with regard to handing over the present area to the Midland Division.

12. BATHS.

The Officer i/c Divisional Baths is taking over Lowland Divisional Clothing Store, at DUNKELNBURGHER STR, SCHOOL, OHLIGS and the Lowland Divisional Delouser, Great Hospital, SOLINGEN.

There are Baths in this area which will be taken over by units concerned.

No. 2 Army Laundry and Clothing Exchange are at HILDEN.

13. PERSONNEL FOR DEMOBILIZATION will be sent by units to report to No. 1 Concentration Camp, COLOGNE.

14. LEAVE AND RECEPTION CAMP will continue pending further instructions.

(a) After the Brigade has left the Divisional Area personnel proceeding on leave will report under Battalion arrangements to Rhine Army Reception Camp, BRUGELMAN HOUSE, COLOGNE (¼ mile East of Hohenzollern Bridge) 3 hours prior to departure of trains which leave COLN-DEUTZ 1341 daily.
The leave party Conducting Officer will report at the same time.

(b) Until a Battalion has left DUREN Area personnel will be sent from DUREN under existing arrangements.

(c) O.C., Highland Divisional Reception Camp is making arrangements for dealing with returning leave men as follows -

He will meet each incoming leave train at DUREN and ensure that only those men alight, whose Units have not left DUREN Area, or who will not have left before the men are able to reach it. All other men are to be instructed to proceed to COLOGNE and report to Rhine Army Reception Camp.

15. ACKNOWLEDGE by Units of Brigade Group only.

[signature]

Captain.
Staff Captain. 3rd Highland Brigade.

Issued through Signals at 1030 hours, 29.5.1919.

Copies to -

1. G.O.C.,
2. Brigade Major.
3. Staff Captain.
4. Staff Captain for Civil Duties.
5. Brigade Signal Officer.
6. 6th Bn. The Black Watch (R.H.).,
7. 8th Bn. The Black Watch (R.H.).,
8. 4th Bn. Seaforth Highlanders.,
9. 9th Bn. Seaforth Highlanders.,
10. 3rd Highland L.T.M.Battery.,
11. 461st Field Company, R.E.,
12. 528 Company, R.A.S.C.,
13. Highland Division 'Q'.
14. 2nd Lowland Brigade.
15. 3rd Lowland Brigade.
16. ~~2/2nd W.R.Field Ambulance.~~
17. 1st ~~Lowland~~ Highland Brigade.
18. Captain R.G.A.DICKSON.
19. R.T.O., DUREN.,
20. D.A.P.M., Highland Division.
21-22. War Diaries.
23. File.

3rd Highland Brigade.

Train	Unit and Composition of Train	No. of Animals.	No. of Axles.	Remarks.
No. 1 Personnel	H.Q., 3rd Highland Brigade. R.E. Detachment. 'A' Battalion (less one Company). 3rd Highland Lt.T.M.Battery.,	-	-	Personnel to arrive at Station one hour before the scheduled time of departure.
No. 2 Personnel.	'B' Battalion. Supply Section, 528 Coy., R.A.S.C.,	-	-	ditto.
No. 3 Personnel.	'C' Battalion (less one Company).	-	-	ditto.
No. 1 Omnibus.	1 Company 'A' Battalion. Bde H.Q., 3 G.S.Wagons, 2 L.G.S. Wagons, 1 Maltese Cart, 1 Mess Cart, 10 Riders.	26	12	Company Loading and Unloading parties to be not less than 2 Officers and 100 Other Ranks.
	Transport 'A' Battalion. 10 L.G.S. Wagons, 4 Cookers, 2 Water Carts, 1 Mess Cart, 1 Maltese Cart, 2 Baggage Wagons, 11 Riders, 7 Pack animals, 3 spare animals.	59	36	Personnel for transport and Stores to be at station three hours before scheduled time of departure. Horses will be watered before entrainment.
	T.M.B., 1 L.G.S.Wagon.	4	2	Units must provide ropes for tying up horses in the trucks.
	'B' Battalion. 2 Baggage Wagons Blankets, surplus kit and rations of Bde H.Q., 'A' Battalion and 3rd Highland L.T.M.Battery. 'C' Battalion, 2 Baggage Wagons.	8	8	Horses will be unharnessed, harness stacked in the middle of each truck and two men must travel in each truck.

Train No.	Unit and Composition of Train.	No. of Animals	No. of Axles.	Remarks.
No. 2 Omnibus,	1 Company 'C' Battalion. Transport 'B' Battalion. 10 L.G.S. wagons, 4 Cookers, 2 Water Carts, 1 Maltese Cart, 1 Mess Cart, 11 Riders, 7 Pack Animals, 3 spare animals, Blankets, Rations and Surplus Kit.	55	32	As per No. 1 Omnibus Train.
	Transport 'C' Battalion, 10 L.G.S wagons, 4 Cookers, 2 Water Carts, 1 Maltese Cart, 1 Mess Cart, 11 Riders, 7 Pack Animals, 3 spare animals, Blankets, Rations and surplus kit.	55	32	

MESSAGE

In		Recd.		Army Form C 2128.
CALL	v	At	By	(pads of 100)
Out	v	Sent At	By	

PREAMBLE

Date Stamp

M.M. Offices | Delivery | Origin | v

PREFIX | Words

TO

FROM & Place: 3rd Highland Brigade.

Originator's Number	Day of Month	In reply to Number
BM 830	29	

~~Reference para 2 of 3rd Highland Brigade~~
Order No2 dated 25th instant AAA AS YOU
WERE AAA "A" day is to-morrow June 30th AAA.
~~Units of Brigade Group to Acknowledge AAA~~
Addsd all recipients of Order No 2.

Time of Origin 11.45

Time of Handing in (For Signal use only)

Originator's Signature (Not Telegraphed)

Capt. I.B.W. Clear.
Brigade Major.

(6315) Wt. W5622/G1276 502,500 pads. 10/18 H.W.V.Ld. (E. 3830.)

CLEAR CIPHER

Original.

Confidential.

War Diary

of

3rd Highland Brigade.

From 1st June 1919 to 30th June 1919.

(Volume III)

Instructions regarding War Diaries and Intelligence Summaries are contained in F. S. Regs., Part II. and the Staff Manual respectively. Title pages will be prepared in manuscript.

WAR DIARY
or
~~INTELLIGENCE SUMMARY.~~

Army Form C. 2118.

~~(Erase heading not required.)~~ 3rd HIGHLAND BRIGADE.

Place	Date	Hour	Summary of Events and Information	Remarks and references to Appendices
	1919 June 1.		B.G.C. attended Church Parade of 8th Black Watch at MAUBACH, and visited 1/4th Seaforths at BRUCK afterwards.	
	2.		Units rehearsing ceremonial parade to be held to-morrow for H.M. The King's Birthday.	
	3.		H.M. The King's Birthday - Units held individual ceremonial parades in the morning - B.G.C. was present at that of 8th Black Watch at MAUBACH.	
	4.		Corps Commander inspected the billets, institutions and ordinary routine of 8th Black Watch and 1/4th Seaforths. Orders received that C.in C. would inspect 8th Black Watch and 1/4th Seaforths at MAUBACH on 6th instant.	
	5.		Addenda and Corrigenda to 3rd Highland Brigade Warning Order No.2 issued to all concerned with 2 Maps attached. Conference of C.O!s at Brigade Headquarters reference C.in C.'s inspection on 6th inst.	Appendix "A"
	6.		C.in C. inspected 8th Black Watch at MAUBACH - B.G.C. inspected 1/4th Seaforths at BRUCK as preliminary to inspection by the C.in C. next week.	
	7.		Units Training.	
	8.		Church Parades - B.G.C. attended that of 8th Black Watch.	
	9.		Whit Monday - Observed as holiday by all troops - Staff Captain to MALMEDY.	
	10.		B.G.C. and Staff proceeded to MALMEDY to present Colours to 9th Seaforths. After the ceremony the 6th Black Watch detachment at HERBERTSTHAL was visited.	
	11.		Divisional Commander and B.G.C. inspected training of 8th Black Watch.	
	12.		B.G.C. and Brigade Major inspected training of 1/4th Seaforths - Remaining personnel of	

A7092. Wt. W128 9/M1293 750,000. 1/17. D. D & L., Ltd. Forms/C2118/14.

Army Form C. 2118.

Instructions regarding War Diaries and Intelligence Summaries are contained in F. S. Regs., Part II. and the Staff Manual respectively. Title pages will be prepared in manuscript.

WAR DIARY
or
~~INTELLIGENCE SUMMARY.~~ 3rd HIGHLAND BRIGADE.

(*Erase heading not required.*)

Place	Date	Hour	Summary of Events and Information	Remarks and references to Appendices
	1919 June 12.		Remaining personnel of 9th Seaforths relieved at MALMEDY by 6th Black Watch and distributed to units of the Division - Capt. A.E.Preedy arrived from 51st Devons to take over duties of Staff Captain.	
	13.		B.G.C. president of G.C.M. at DUREN. Units training - Capt. H.J.Impson, C.B.E., M.C., Norfolk Regiment, late Staff Captain left to take up duties of D.A.Q.M.G. Lancashire Division at BONN - Capt. A.E.Preedy, Devonshire Regiment took over duties of Staff Captain.	
	14.		B.G.C. and C.O., 6th Black Watch visited Cookery School at COLOGNE - Units Training - Brigade Major visited training Coys. of 6th Black Watch.	
	15.		Church Parades - B.G.C. and Brigade Major visited that of 1/4th Seaforths at BRUCK. Warning Order received from Division that J day will be 20th June, and Brigade to be ready to move on J - 3 day.	
	16.		Warning Order issued to Units of Brigade to be ready to concentrate round DUREN on 17th June prior to moving forward on J - 2 day - B.G.C. and Brigade Major visited training of 8th Black Watch.	Appendix B.
	17.		Orders to move forward to BENRATH Area received from Division at 0500 hours. Repeated to Units at 0515 hours. Brigade H.Q. moved from MAUBACH to DUREN - 8th Black Watch from MAUBACH to BIRKESDORF - 1/4th Seaforths from BRUCK to DUREN BARRACKS - 3rd Highland T.M.Battery from UDINGEN to BIRKESDORF - Moves completed by 1500 hours.	
	18.		Brigade Transport Column left by road for MUNGERSDORF - Conference of C.O.s at Brigade H.Q. at 0930 hours - Brigade moved by rail from DUREN Area to BENRATH Area and were accommodated Brigade H.Q. BENRATH, 3rd Highland T.M.B. BENRATH, 6th Black Watch HILDEN, 8th Black Watch BENRATH, 1/4th Seaforths OHLIGS, 528th Coy. R.A.S.C. HILDEN.	

A7092. Wt. W125 9/M1293 750,000. 1/17. D. D & L. Ltd. Forms/C2118/14.

Instructions regarding War Diaries and Intelligence Summaries are contained in F. S. Regs., Part II. and the Staff Manual respectively. Title pages will be prepared in manuscript.

Army Form C. 2118.

WAR DIARY
or
~~INTELLIGENCE SUMMARY.~~ 3rd HIGHLAND BRIGADE.

(Erase heading not required.)

Place	Date	Hour	Summary of Events and Information	Remarks and references to Appendices
	1919 June 19.		8th Black Watch and 1/4th Seaforths took over all guards, duties, etc from Units of Lowland Division in accordance with orders previously issued - B.G.C. visited Perimeter Posts of 3rd Lowland Brigade in company with B.G.C. 3rd Lowland Brigade.	
	20.		J day indefinitely postponed - B.G.C. visited 8th Black Watch perimeter posts with O.C. 8th Black Watch, II Corps Commander and Highland Divisional Commander visited B.G.C. in morning.	
	21.		B.G.C. visited perimeter posts of 1/4th Seaforths - Civil Administration of BENRATH - OHLIGS Area taken over by B.G.C. 3rd Highland Brigade - 6th Black Watch took over two right-posts of 8th Black Watch at KEMPERDICK and DICKHAUS - Visit of Dr. Wallace Williamson from Edinburgh to this Brigade.	appendix "C."
	22.		Church Parades held by each Battalion which Dr. Wallace Williamson attended in turn, accompanied by B.G.C. and ladies of Scottish Churches Hut. 3rd Highland Brigade Warning Order No.3 issued, reference probable return of Brigade to MAUBACH Area.	appendix D.
	23.		Lowland Divisional Commander visited H.Q. of 1/4th Seaforths at OHLIGS and then visited some of the 8th Black Watch perimeter posts, accompanied by B.G.C.- Lowland Divisional Order No4 received, intimating that J day would be to-morrow 24th inst. and Zero Hour 0315 - 3rd Highland Brigade Order No. 1 issued to Units giving instructions for concentration of Units after Lowland Divisional Troops have passed the perimeter - B.G.C. with O.C. 8th Black Watch visited HIMMELGEIST Posts in afternoon. Information received shortly before 1900 hours to the effect that the Germans had official promised to sign and that the advance into Germany on J day was cancelled.	appendix E.
	24.		B.G.C. visited posts - Warning Order received from Division that in the event of Peace being signed, the Brigade would return to MAUBACH Area on B day, date of which to be notified later - Administrative Instructions issued by the Staff Captain giving details of entrainment, transport etc for return journey to MAUBACH - Commander in Chief visited Brigade H.Q.	appendix F appendix G.

(A7092). Wt. W12839/M1293. 750,000. 1/17. D. D. & L., Ltd. Forms/C.2118/14.

Army Form C. 2118.

Instructions regarding War Diaries and Intelligence Summaries are contained in F. S. Regs., Part II. and the Staff Manual respectively. Title pages will be prepared in manuscript.

WAR DIARY
or
INTELLIGENCE SUMMARY.

(Erase heading not required.)

3rd HIGHLAND BRIGADE.

Place	Date	Hour	Summary of Events and Information	Remarks and references to Appendices
	1919 June 25.		Brigade Order No.2 issued with reference to the return of the Brigade to MAUBACH Area - B.G.C. visited out-posts.	Appendix H.
	26.		B.G.C. to COLOGNE - IV Corps Commander visited Brigade H.Q. and HOLTHAUSEN BARRIER out-post.	
	27.		B.G.C. visited Seaforths' H.Q. and out-posts.	
	28.		PEACE TREATY SIGNED AT VERSAILLES - Orders received from Lowland Division that "A" day would be June 30th and this Brigade would return to MAUBACH Area on July 1st - Units informed.	
	29.		Order issued to Units that 3rd Highland Brigade Order No 2 comes into operation from June 30th "A" day - B.G.C. attended Church Parade of 8th Black Watch at BENRATH - B.G.C. visited 6th Black Watch and 1/4th Seaforths in afternoon.	Appendix I
	30.		B.G.C. inspected Perimeter Out-posts prior to relief of them by Lowland Division Troops, Relief of all posts, guards, etc completed by 1800 hours and Battalions concentrated in billets prior to entrainment to-morrow.	

Brigadier General,
Commanding 3rd Highland Brigade.

(A7092). Wt. W12839/M1293. 750,000. 1/17. D. D. & L., Ltd. Forms/C.2118.14.

Appendix A

[illegible] Copy No. 24.

ADDENDA AND CORRIGENDA TO 3rd HIGHLAND BRIGADE
Warning Order No. 2 dated May 26th 1919.

- - - - - - - - - - - - - - - - - - - -

5th June 1919.

1. Cancel para. 10 and substitute :-

"10. On arrival in the new area battalions will take over on J - 1 day the following out-posts, guards, etc at present found by battalions of the 2nd and 3rd Lowland Brigades :-

1/4th Bn. Seaforth Highlanders at OHLIGS.

Nature of Duty.	Location.	Offs.	O.Rs.
No. 1 Perimeter Post	GRUITEN	-	9
No.2 do	On Railway at K.88.07	-	12
No.3 do	ELP	1	22
No.4 do	KELLERTHOR	1	24

8th Bn. The Black Watch at BENRATH.

Nature of Duty.	Location.	Offs.	O.Rs.
No. 5 Perimeter Post	KEMPERDICK	1	21
No. 6 do	DICKHAUS	1	19
No. 7 do	REISHOLZ	1	32
No. 8 do	HOLTHAUSEN	2	37
No. 9 do	FRIEDHOF	1	16
No.10 do	HIMMELGEIST	2	24
Guard on ~~Railway~~ RHENANIA Petroleum Works.		1 platoon minimum	
Guard on Electric Power Station close to above		1 platoon	
∅ Examining Post.	HILDEN Rly. Station	3	29
∅ Examining Post.	REISHOLZ Rly. Stn.	4	26

∅ It is possible that in the near future these two latter duties will be found by the Allied Railway Commission.

The Numbers given above are merely intended as a guide, for it must be clearly understood that only complete units are to be detailed for these detached duties.

A Map 'A' showing approximate locations of all Perimeter Posts, guards, etc. in the new area is attached (to battalions only)."

2. Cancel para. 12 and substitute :-

"12. 3rd Highland Brigade Headquarters will close at UNT MAUBACH at 1200 hours on J - 3 day and will re-open at the same hour at 34 SCHOELLERSTRASSE, DUREN. On J - 2 days Brigade Headquarters will close at DUREN at an hour to be notified later and will re-open at BAHNHOF HOTEL, BENRATH, on arrival."

3. Cancel Tables 'A' and 'B' and substitute the attached.

4. Add the following paragraphs :-

"17. The Highland Division will take over from the Lowland Division and II Corps Troops the area shown on the attached Map 'B'. (To battalions and L.T.M.Battery only).

The boundaries of the Brigade area are provisional and do not concern the civil administrative areas, ~~w~~which will be notified separately.

"18. (a) On J - 2 days a set of tactical trains will be at the disposal of the 3rd Highland Brigade and will be composed as follows :-

3 personnel trains - accommodation 1,000 each.
2 'Omnibus' type trains, each 1 coach, 30 covers, 17 flats.

(b) Entraining Station - DUREN
Detraining Station - HILDEN.

(c) All other details regarding entrainment, detrainment, etc. have been issued in Administrative Instructions.

"19. Cadres of units remaining in the present Highland Divisional area will pass to the command of IX Corps at 1800 hours on J day.

"20. (a) The Divisional School will remain at LANGENBROITCH, the Educational School at NIEDERAU and the Agricultural School at BOISDORF FARM, LENDERSDORF, for the present.

(b) There will be certain cadres, installations and units of the Lowland Division remaining in the new Highland Divisional area for a few days. These must not be interfered with.

"21. All troops of the Highland Division entering their new area xxxx prior to noon on J day will come under orders of the G.O.C. Lowland Division.

"22. Command of 3rd Brigade area shown on the attached Map 'B' will be taken over by the Brigadier General Commanding 3rd Highland Brigade at 1800 hours on J day.

"23. (a) On receipt of orders from Divisional Headquarters that the advance is to take place, the code word "CONCENTRATE" will be sent by wire to all concerned. On receipt of this order the moves shown on Table 'A' will be put into operation and the Brigade will concentrate in the vicinity of DUREN on J - 3 days.

(b) A second code-message "MOVE" will be sent. This message will also notify 'J' day.
In notifying J day by telegram the following code will be employed -

4th June ... K
5th June ... L.
6th June ... M
7th June ... N
8th June ... O
etc.
etc.

Thus if J day were the 6th June the following wire would be sent "Reference 3rd Highland Brigade Warning Order No. 2 AAA J day will be M"
On receipt of this wire the above orders will be put in force and the moves carried out as from J - 3 day".

5. ACKNOWLEDGE.

McCallum
Captain.
Brigade Major.
3rd Highland Brigade.

Issued through signals at 10.30 hours
to all recipients of 3rd Highland Brigade Warning Order No.2.

Table 'A' issued with 3rd Highland Brigade Warning Order No. 2 dated May 26th 1919.

Serial No.	Date.	Unit.	From.	To.	How Moving.	Remarks.
1.	J - 3 day.	6th Black Watch	Remain at LENDERSDORF			
X 2.	do	8th Black Watch	MAUBACH	BIRKESDORF	Train for Personnel March route for transport	Personnel entrain at MAUBACH
X 3.	do	1/4th Seaforths	BRUCK	BUREN BARRACKS	Train for personnel. March route for transport.	Personnel entrain at NIDEGGEN
X 4.	do	3rd Highland T.M.B.	UDINGEN	BIRKESDORF	Train for personnel. March route for transport.	Personnel entrain at MAUBACH
X 5.	do	3rd Highland Bde H.Q.	UNT MAUBACH	SCHOELLERSTRASSE, DUREN.	Train for personnel. March route for Transport.	Personnel entrain at MAUBACH.
6.	do	R.E.Detachments of 461 Field Coy. R.E.	FRAUWULLERSHEIM	DUREN.	March Route	To join 3rd Highland Bde H.Q.
7.	do	528 Coy. R.A.S.C.	Remain at DISTELRATH.			

X Arrangements are being made for lorries to convey surplus kit, blankets, etc. on J - 3 days.

Table 'b' issued with 3rd Highland Brigade Warning Order No. 2 dated 26th May 1919.

Serial No.	Date.	Unit.	From	To.	How Moving.	Entraining Stn.	Relieving.	Remarks.
1.	J - 2 day	3rd Highland Bde Headquarters.	DUREN	BENRATH	Train	DUREN	3rd Lowland Bde	
2.	do	3rd Highland T.M.B.	BIRKESDORF	BENRATH	Train	do	----	
3.	do	6th Black Watch	LENDERSDORF	HILDEN	Train	do	8th Scot. Rifles & 4th Royal Scots.	To be Reserve Battalion.
4.	do	8th Black Watch	BIRKESDORF	BENRATH	Train	do	9th Scot. Rifles.	To be left forward battalion.
5.	do	1/4th Seaforths	DUREN Barracks.	OHLIGS.	Train	do	5/6th Royal Scots	To be right forward battalion and to take over also Perimeter posts found by 11th Royal Scots in HAAN.
6.	do	R.E. detachments of 461 Field Coy. R.E.	DUREN	BENRATH	Train	do	--	To remain with Brigade H.Q. until fetched by Lowland Div. R.E.
7.	do	528 Coy. R.A.S.C.	DISTELRATH	HILDEN	Train	do	No.4 Coy. Lowland Divn. Train.	Only such personnel as are not required to proceed with transport

Table 'B' continued.

8.	J - 2 day	Units transport Brigaded, plus transport of 62nd Bn. M.G.C.	DUREN area	BENRATH area	Road	---	---	Such portion as in unable to proceed by train. Transport of units will rendezvous at junction of MERZENICH and main DUREN - COLOGNE Road at 0900 hours and proceed to MUNGERSDORF via Main COLOGNE Rd.
9.	do J - 1 day	do	MUNGERSDORF	OPLADEN	do	----	---	Keep North of COLOGNE and cross RHINE by bridge of boats at RIEHL.
10.	J day.	do	OPLADEN	Units respective billetting areas.	do	----	---	By shortest routes to respective billetting areas.

(a) Brigade Transport Column will move as one column under Capt. R.G.A.Dickson, The Black Watch.

(b) Accommodation for transport staging will be obtained from H.Q. 42nd Bn. M.G.C. at FORT for MUNGERSDORF, at OPLADEN from Civil Administrator.

(c) Train arrangements will be notified later.

(d) Arrangements are being made for lorries to convey surplus kit, blankets, etc. to entraining Station on J - 2 day.

Appendix B

War Diary

3rd Highland Bde No. BM/35

SECRET.

16th June 1919.

1. Reference 3rd Highland Brigade Warning Orders Nos. 1 and 2 dated 23.5.1919 and 26.5.1919 respectively, and amendments thereto, the following additional amendments will be made :-

(a) As Capt. R.G.A.Dickson is now acting Civil Staff Captain, the Brigaded Transport Column will march under orders of O.C. 528 Coy. R.A.S.C. on J - 2 day and subsequent days.

(b) Lieut. J. BLACK, 8th Bn. The Black Watch will be detailed as Brigade Entraining Officer at DUREN Station on J - 2 day. He will carry out the duties previously assigned to Capt. R.G.A.Dickson in Administrative Instructions dated May 29th.

(c) Reference para. 23 (b) of 3rd Highland Brigade Warning Order No. 2, the code for notifying J day should the latter fall on or after 20th June 1919, will be as follows :-

20th June	...	A
21st June	...	B
22nd June	...	C etc. etc.

2. (a) The Company of 6th Bn. The Black Watch, now working on the Divisional Musketry Range, will rejoin its battalion on J - 3 day, prior to entraining on J - 2 day.

(b) The detachment of the 6th Bn. The Black Watch at MALMEDY will be relieved by the WESTERN Division on a date to be notified later.

(c) The HERBERTSTHAL detachment will be relieved by the 2nd Midland Brigade on J - 1 day.

Further orders will be issued reference thex reliefs of (b) and (c).

3. ACKNOWLEDGE.

A McCallum
Captain.
Brigade Major.
3rd Highland Brigade.

Issued through Signals at 1300 hours.

To all recipients of 3rd Highland Brigade Warning Order No. 2.

Appendix C

SECRET.

3rd Highland Brigade.No.BM/35.

21st June 1919.

1. J. Day has been postponed until further notice.

2. Troops of the Highland Division now in XI Corps Area are under the orders of G.O.C. Lowland Division for tactical and civil administration purposes until G.O.C. Highland Division arrives in Lowland Division Area. The IV Corps administers the Highland Division.

3. The Lowland Division is responsible for civil administration duties in Lowland Division Area, Corps Heavy Artillery Sub-Area, and Corps Headquarters Sub-Area until taken over by G.O.C. Highland Division.

4. The civil administration of the BENRATH--OHLIGS Area will be taken over by the B.G.C. 3rd Highland Brigade at 18.00 hours to-day. The present Lowland Divisional civil administration staff will, however, remain until J Day to assist 3rd Highland Brigade Staff in the performance of its new duties.

5. 3rd Highland Brigade Sub-Area is as shown on Map "B" issued with Addenda and Corrigenda to 3rd Highland Brigade Warning Order No. 2 dated May 26th, 1919.

6. ACKNOWLEDGE.

Al. Preedy. Capt.
for Captain,
Brigade Major,
3rd Highland Brigade.

Issued through Signals
at 12.30 hours.

Copies to -

6th Bn The Black Watch.
8th Bn The Black Watch,
1/4th Bn Seaforth Highrs.
3rd Highland T.M.B.
528th Coy. R.A.S.C.
1st Highland Brigade.
2nd Highland Brigade.
2nd Lowland Brigade.
3rd Lowland Brigade.
Staff Captain.
Staff Captain for Civil Duties.

Appendix D

War Diary

SECRET.

Copy No. 15

3RD HIGHLAND BRIGADE WARNING ORDER NO.3.

22nd June 1919.

1. The following instructions are issued as a warning and a guide as to the course of action should the Germans sign the Peace Treaty.

2. Notice for the return of troops to their original stations may be short, and it is probable that orders for the first days moves will be issued on the prevéous evening only.

3. Should the troops be ordered to return to their original stations as occupied before J - 3 day, Moves and reliefs will be in the reverse order, i.e., 3rd Highland Brigade will entrain and move on the second day after the order "as you were" is issued.

4. Troops of 3rd Highland Brigade will entrain at HILDEN Station.

Reliefs of 3rd Highland Brigade troops by Lowland Division troops will be carried out on the first day after receipt of the order "as you were", in order that units may be concentrated ready to move on the second day. Times of departure of trains will be notified later.

5. Further orders regarding the move of Transport will be issued.

6. Acknowledge.

7. Units will be prepared to send on billeting parties to DUREN Staging Area on first day.

D. McCallum Captain.
Brigade Major. 3rd Highland Brigade.

Issued through Signals at 1730 hours.

Copies to:-

No. 1 6th Bn. Black Watch
2 8th Bn. Black Watch
3 1/4th Bn. Seaforth Highrs.
4 3rd Highland Bde.L.T.M.B.
5. Highland Division.
6. 2nd Lowland Brigade.
7. 3rd Lowland Brigade.
8. 461st Field Coy., R.E.
9. 528th Coy., R.A.S.C.,
10 & 11. Civil Staff Captain.
12. B.G.C.
13. Brigade Major.
14. 62nd Bn. M.G.C.
15 & 16. War Diary.
17. Staff Captain.

Appendix E

War Diary

SECRET.

Copy No. 21....

3RD HIGHLAND BRIGADE ORDER NO. 1.

23rd June, 1919.

1. All preparations will be made to commence moves laid down for J Day at 0315 hours (Zero hour) on 24th June.

2. No troops will cross the perimeter until receipt of the following Urgent Operations Priority Message -

"CROSS PERIMETER ZERO HOUR 24TH AAA ACKNOWLEDGE".

Possibly this message may not be sent out from Lowland Divisional Headquarters before 2200 hours on the 23rd June, 1919.

From receipt of this Order onwards an Officer must be on duty in the Orderly Room of each Unit.

3. As soon as the troops of the Lowland Division have passed the present perimeter posts all sentries, examining posts and patrols will be withdrawn (except Sentries over arms) and the garrison of the posts will be concentrated in the billets attached to their respective posts ready to move at very short notice to rejoin their Battalions.

4. On receipt of the Order mentioned in para. 2 above, the precautionary measures detailed in 3rd Highland Brigade No. B.M/35 D of 17th June, 1919, reference guarding of railways, bridges, importants works and buildings, patrolling the OPLADEN - VOHWINKEL Railway etc., will be put into force immediately.

5. Contact aeroplanes of the 7th Squadron R.A.F., will fly a yellow and red streamer from their tails and will also carry black flaps attached to the rear edge of the lower plane, one on each side of the body.

6. 3rd Highland Brigade Headquarters will remain at BAHNHOF Hotel, BENRATH, until further orders.

7. All Officers are to be warned that they are not to leave their units until further orders.

8. ACKNOWLEDGE.

D M McCallum.
Captain,
Brigade Major.
3rd Highland Brigade.,

Issued through Signals at 1550 hours.

Copies to -

No. 1 6th Bn. Black Watch.
2. 6th Bn. Black Watch.
3. 4th Bn. Seaforth Hrs.
4. 3rd Hd. L.T.M.Battery.
5. 528 Coy., R.A.S.C.,
6. 461st Field Coy.,R.E.,
7. Highland Divn. (Adv. 'G').
8. Highland Division.
9. Lowland Division.
10. 2nd Lowland Brigade.
11. 3rd Lowland Brigade.
12. 1st Highland Brigade.

No. 13. 2nd Highland Bde.
14. 62nd Bn. M.G.Corps.
15. B.G.C.,
16. Brigade Major.
17. Staff Captain.
18. Staff Captn. for Civil (Duties
19. Brigade Signal Officer
20. P.R.O.,
—21. War Diary.
—22. ditto.
23. File.

Appendix F

War Diary

SECRET.

Copy No. 16

ADDENDA NO.1 TO 3RD HIGHLAND BRIGADE WARNING ORDER NO.3

24th June 1919.

1. Reference para. 4 of 3rd Highland Brigade Warning Order No.3 of 22nd instant, the times of trains from HILDEN Station will be:-

First Train	(personnel)	load 14.00 hours.	depart	14.30 hours.
Second "	(")	" 14.30 "	"	15.00 "
Third "	(")	" 15.00 "	"	15.30 "
Fourth "	(omnibus)	" 15.00 "	"	18.00 "
Fifth "	(")	" 18.00 "	"	21.00 "

The journey to DUREN takes about 3 hours to complete.

2. Units will entrain in the various personnel trains as under:-

First Train - 3rd Highland Brigade Headquarters, 6th Bn The Black Watch, 3rd Highland L.T.M.Battery.
March from DUREN to MAUBACH, LENDERSDORF and WINDEN.

Second Train - 8th Bn The Black Watch, plus Supply Section 528th Coy. R.A.S.C.
8th Bn The Black Watch will march from DUREN to BIRKESDORF for one night.

Third Train - 1/4th Bn Seaforth Highlanders, plus R.E. detachment.
1/4th Bn Seaforth Highlanders will march from DUREN Station to DUREN BARRACKS for one night.

3. Further orders will be issued regarding march of transport; also regarding move of 8th Bn The Black Watch and 1/4th Bn Seaforth Highrs. from DUREN Staging Area to MAUBACH and BRUCK.

4. ACKNOWLEDGE.

A McCallum
Captain,
Brigade Major,
3rd Highland Brigade.

Issued through Signals at 17.30 hours.

To all recipients of 3rd Highland Brigade Warning Order No. 3.

Appendix G

SECRET.

Copy No. 20

3rd Highland Brigade.

ADMINISTRATIVE INSTRUCTIONS ISSUED IN CONJUNCTION WITH 3RD HIGHLAND BRIGADE WARNING ORDER No. 3, DATED 22ND JUNE, 1919 AND ADDENDA No. 1, DATED 24TH JUNE, 1919.

-+-+-+-+-+-+-+-+-+-+-+-+-+-+-+-+-+-+-

25th June, 1919.

1. ENTRAINMENT.

Units will entrain in accordance with the attached Train Table. Train times have been notified in the above Addenda.

Major S.F.SHARP, M.C., 4th Bn. Seaforth Highlanders will act as Entraining Officer of the Brigade Group for the Personnel trains, and on completion of entrainment will proceed by the last personnel train.

Lieut. T. BRODIE BROWN M.C., 8th Bn. The Black Watch (R.H.)., will act as Entraining Officer for the Transport of the Brigade Group and on completion of duty will proceed by No. 2 Omnibus Train.

Units will each detail one Entraining Officer to report to Major S.F.SHARPE M.C., 4th Bn. Seaforth Hlders., at HILDEN half an hour before the hour specified for personnel to arrive.

He will be in possession of an Entraining State in duplicate showing -

No. of Officers.
No. of Other Ranks.
No. of Animals.
No. of two wheeled vehicles.
No. of four - ditto -

to be entrained.

'A' Battalion will be 6th Bn. The Black Watch (R.H.).,
'B' Battalion will be 8th Bn. The Black Watch (R.H.).,
'C' Battalion will be 4th Bn. Seaforth Highlanders.,

The Officer Commanding 'B' Battalion will detail one Company to load No. 1 Omnibus Train at HILDEN, proceed with train and unload same at DUREN.

The Officer Commanding 'C' Battalion will similiarly detail one Company to load and unload No. 2 Omnibus Train.

An Officer of these Companies will report to the Brigade Representative half an hour before scheduled time for loading.

Two baggage wagons and two L.G.S.Wagons per Battalion will proceed by road under instructions to be notified later.

2. SUPPLIES.

(a) The unconsumed portion of the day's rations will be carried on the men.

Rations for the two following days will be taken on t[illegible] Personnel Train for troops travelling by rail.

(b) Transport moving by road will carry the unexpended portion of the day's rations on the man and the two following da[illegible] rations and forage on the vehicles.

(c) Representatives of Units will report to the Brigade Supply Officer at 1000 hours at the Brigade Entraining Station and take over two days' rations for the whole of their unit. They will then split up their rations into two parts, viz -

(i) For that portion proceeding by rail. This will be kept there until unit arrives to entrain when it will be loaded under unit's arrangements.

(ii) For that portion proceeding by road. This will be reloaded on to the Supply wagons (which will be at entraining station from 0900 hours). These wagons will then proceed to the end of the first staging area under orders of the Officer Commanding, 528th Company, R.A.S.C., Delivery of rations to the road portion of units will be made at the end of each days march.

The third day's rations will be drawn by First Line Transport at DISTELRATH at 1300 hours. The fourth day's rations by First Line Transport at 0900 hours at DISTELRATH,

3. LORRIES.

Lorries will report to Units at 0800 hours on Entraining day as follows -

Brigade Headquarters	-	1.
6th Black Watch (R.H).	-	2.
8th Black Watch (R.H).	-	3.
4th Seaforth Hlders.,	-	3.
3rd Highland T.M.Btty.	-	1.

On detraining at DUREN -

Brigade Headquarters	-	1.
6th Black Watch (R.H).	-	4.
8th Black Watch (R.H).	-	2.
4th Seaforth Hlders.,	-	2.
3rd Highland T.M.Btty.	-	1.

On Entraining day at DUREN for final destination -

8th Black Watch (R.H).	-	5.
4th Seaforth Hlders.,	-	5.

4. DAY FOLLOWING STAGING.

A Tactical train to accommodate 1600 will run on the day following staging at DUREN from DUREN to HEIMBACH loading at 1015 hours and departing at 1045 hours to convey personnel of 8th Bn. The Black Watch (R.H.)., and 4th Bn. Seaforth Highlanders to UNTER MAUBACH and NIDEGGEN.

An Entraining Officer will be detailed to report to the Brigade Representative half an hour before entrainment.

All transport will proceed by road.

5. AREA STORES ETC.,

All Area Stores taken over in the Lowland Divisional Area will be left in situ.

6. ACKNOWLEDGE by Units of Brigade Group only.

A.C. Purdy
Captain.
Staff Captain, 3rd Highland Brigade.

Issued through Signals at 1730 hours.

3rd Highland Brigade.

Train.	Unit and Composition of Train.	No. of Animals.	No. of Axles.	Remarks.
No. 1 Personnel.	H.Q., 3rd Highland Brigade. 'A' Battalion. 3rd Highland Lt. T.M.Battery.,	-	-	Personnel to arrive at Station one hour before the scheduled time of departure.
No. 2 Personnel.	'B' Battalion (less one Company). Supply Section, 528 Coy.,R.A.S.C.,	-	-	- ditto -
No. 3 Personnel.	'C' Battalion (less one Company).	-	-	- ditto -
No. 1 Omnibus.	1 Company 'B' Battalion. Bde H.Q., 3 G.S.Wagons, 2 L.G.S. wagons, 1 Maltese Cart, 1 Mess Cart, 10 Riders.	26	12	Company Loading and Unloading parties to be not less than 2 Officers and 100 Other Ranks.
	Transport 'A' Battalion, 8 L.G.S. wagons, 4 Cookers, 2 Water Carts, 1 Mess Cart, 1 Maltese Cart, 11 Riders, 7 Pack animals, 3 spare animals.	55	28	Personnel for transport and Stores to be at station three hours before scheduled time of departure. Horses will be watered before entrainment.
	T.M.B., 1 L.G.S. Wagon.	4	2	Units must provide ropes for tying up horses in the trucks.
	4 Cookers of 'B' Battalion. Blankets surplus kit and rations of Brigade H.Q., 'A' Battalion and 3rd Highland L.T.M.Battery.,	8	8	Horses will be unharnessed, harness stacked in the middle of each truck and two men must travel in each truck.

Train No.	Unit and Composition of Train.	No. of Animals	No. of Axles.	Remarks.
No. 2 Omnibus.	1 Company 'C' Battalion. Transport 'B' Battalion. 8 L.G.S. wagons, 2 Water Carts, 1 Maltese Cart, 1 Mess Cart, 11 Riders, 7 Pack Animals, 3 spare animals, Blankets, Rations and Surplus kit and 5 L.G.S.Wagons Divisional H.Q 1 Officer and 50 Other Ranks.	69	30	As per No. 1 Omnibus Train.
	Transport 'C' Battalion, 8 L.G.S. Wagons, 4 Cookers, 2 Water Carts, 1 Maltese Cart, 1 Mess Cart, 11 Riders, 7 Pack Animals, 3 spare animals, Blankets, Rations and surplus kit.	51	28	

Copies to -

No. 1. G.O.C.,
2. Brigade Major.
3. Staff Captain.
4. Staff Captain for Civil Duties.
5. Brigade Signal Officer.
6. 6th Bn. The Black Watch (R.H.)
7. 8th Bn. The Black Watch (R.H.).
8. 4th Bn. Seaforth Highlanders.,
9. 3rd Highland Lt.T.M.Battery.,
10. 461st Field Company, R.E.,
11. Brigade Entraining Officer.
12. 528 Company, R.A.S.C.,
13. O. i/c Supplies, 3rd Hd Bde.
14. Highland Division 'Q'.,
15. 2nd Lowland Brigade.
16. 3rd Lowland Brigade.
17. R.T.O., DUREN.,
18. D.A.P.M., Highland Division.
19. War Diary.,
20. War Diary.
21. File.

appendix "H" War Diary.

SECRET.

Copy No...16...

3RD HIGHLAND BRIGADE ORDER NO.2.

25th June 1919.

1. In confirmation of 3rd Highland Brigade Warning Order No.3 dated 22nd June, 1919, in the event of Peace being signed without any further advance taking place, orders may be expected for all troops to resume their normal dispositions, and the organisation of areas and Civil Administration that existed prior to J - 3 Day would be resumed.

2. On receipt of such orders from advanced Highland Division, the order "As you were" will be wired out from these Headquarters and the arrangements forecasted in these orders will come into force. This wire will also give the date of "A" day. The reliefs will then be carried out as laid down below and the move in accordance with the attached table.

3. (a). On "A" day all perimeter posts, guards, detached duties etc. at present being found by Battalions of the 3rd Highland Brigade will be relieved and taken over again by Battalions of the 2nd and 3rd Lowland Brigades. Reliefs to be complete by 18.00 hours on "A" day.

On completion of the reliefs, Battalions of the 3rd Highland Brigade will concentrate in billets in BENRATH, HILDEN, and OHLIGS respectively ready to march to the entraining station on "B" day.

(b). Similarly, the Civil Administration duties of the present No.3 Sub-Area will be handed back to the Civil Administration Staffs of the 2nd and 3rd Lowland Brigades. This relief to be complete by 18.00 hours on "A" day.

(c). Completion of reliefs will be reported by wire to these Headquarters.

(d). All details of reliefs will be arranged direct between Commanding Officers concerned.

4. In connection with the above reliefs, applications for Trams for concentrating personnel will be made to the Civil Staff Captain, No. 3 Sub-Area.

5. On arrival in the MAUBACH Area, Units of the 3rd Highland Brigade will take over the same Guards and Detachments as they found prior to J - 3 day. Reliefs to be complete by 12.00 hours on "D" day, with the exception of the MALMEDY and HERBERTSTHAL detachments, orders concerning which, are being issued separately to the 6th Bn The Black Watch. Completion of these reliefs will be reported to Brigade Headquarters at MAUBACH.

6. (a). On "B" day, Units' transport proceeding by road, will march independently by the shortest route to billets in OPLADEN, where all transport of the Brigade Group will be concentrated by 15.00 hours on "B" day. O.C., 528th Coy. R.A.S.C., will make arrangements to have guides to meet Units' transport at the road-junction ½ mile North of the N in OPLADEN. (reference Map, GERMANY, Sheet 2K, 1/100.000).

(b). Transport of the Brigade Group proceeding by road will be Brigaded on "C" day and march under orders of O.C., 528th Coy.R.A.S.C., who will ensure that strict march discipline is maintained en route.

7. Troops will move in "Marching Order".

8. While on the line of march, particular attention will be paid to march discipline and the keeping of the proper intervals laid down in G.H.Q. pamphlet dated 22nd May, 1919.

9. Instructions re entraining, supplies, lorries etc., are being issued in Administrative Instructions.

10. Command of No.3 Sub-Area will revert to Brigadier-Generals Commanding 2nd and 3rd Lowland Brigades at 18.00 hours on "A" day.

11. 3rd Highland Brigade Headquarters will close at BENRATH at 12.00 hours on "B" day and will re-open at UNT-MAUBACH on arrival.

12. ACKNOWLEDGE.

Captain,
Brigade Major,
3rd Highland Brigade.

Issued through Signals at 08.00 hours on 26th June 1919, to all recipients of 3rd Highland Brigade Warning Order No.3.

Table issued with 3rd Highland Brigade Order No.3 dated 25th June 1919.

Serial No.	Date.	Unit.	From.	To.	How Moving.	Remarks.
1.	"B" Day.	3rd High.Bde.H.Q.	BENRATH.	UNT-MAUBACH.	Train.	
2.	"	3rd High,L.T.M.B.	"	WINDEN.	"	
3.	"	6th Black Watch.	HILDEN.	LENDERSDORF.	"	
4.	"	8th Black Watch.	BENRATH.	BIRKESDORF.	"	
5.	"	1/4th Seaforth Hrs.	OHLIGS.	DUREN BARRACKS.	"	
6.	"	Supply Section 528th Coy.R.A.S.C.	HILDEN.	DISTELRATH.	"	
7.	"	Units Transport proceeding by road.	BENRATH Area.	OPLADEN.	Road.	See para 6 (a) of attached order.
8.	"C" Day.	do.	OPLADEN.	MUNGERSDORF.	"	See para 6 (b) of attached order- Cross RHINE by BRIDGE of BOATS and keep N. of COLOGNE.
9.	"	8th Black Watch.	BIRKESDORF.	MAUBACH.	Train.	Entrain at DUREN STATION, detrain at MAUBACH.
10.	"	1/4th Seaforth Hrs.	DUREN BARRACKS.	BRUCK.	"	Entrain at DUREN STATION, detrain at NIDEGGEN.
11.	"D" Day.	Units Transport proceeding by road.	MUNGERSDORF.	Units respective billeting areas.	Road.	To march brigaded as far as DUREN, thence by shortest route to billets

(a). Entraining Station on "B" day, HILDEN -- Detraining Station on "B" day, DUREN.
(b). Accommodation for transport staging will be obtained from Civil Administration at OPLADEN; from Headquarters, 42nd Battalion Machine Gun Corps at FORT for MUNGERSDORF.
(c). Transport proceeding by train on "B" day will proceed direct from detraining station to final destinations as soon as unloaded from omnibus trains.

Confidential

War Diary

~of~

3rd. Highland Brigade.

From. 1st. July. 1919 ~ To ~ 31st. July. 1919.

Original.

Volume. No. IV.

(6414) Wt. W3906/P1607 2,500,000 7/18 McA & W Ltd (E 3591) Forms W3091/4.

Army Form W.3091.

Cover for Documents.

Nature of Enclosures.

Notes, or Letters written.

Instructions regarding War Diaries and Intelligence Summaries are contained in F. S. Regs., Part II. and the Staff Manual respectively. Title pages will be prepared in manuscript.

WAR DIARY
or
INTELLIGENCE SUMMARY. 3rd HIGHLAND BRIGADE.
(*Erase heading not required.*)

Army Form C. 2118.

Place	Date	Hour	Summary of Events and Information	Remarks and references to Appendices
	1919 July 1		Units of the Brigade entrained at HILDEN Station and returned to DUREN area, detraining at DUREN. On night of July 1st/2nd the Brigade was disposed as follows:- Brigade Headquarters - UNT-MAUBACH; 3rd Highland L.T.M.Battery - WINDEN; 6th Black Watch - LENDERSDORF; 8th Black Watch - BIRKESDORF; 1/4th Seaforth Highrs - DUREN BARRACKS.	Dew
	2		Brigade completed return to MAUBACH area, 8th Black Watch and 1/4th Seaforth Highrs entraining at DUREN and proceeded to UNT-MAUBACH and NIDEGGEN respectively.	Dew
	3		Units settling in again and cleaning up. 6th Black Watch took over all guards etc previously found by this Brigade in this area.	Dew
	4		Units Training.	Dew
	5		Kit and billet inspections by all Units.	Dew
	6		Church Parades with all Units - B.G.C. attended that of 8th Black Watch.	Dew
	7		Units training - Lt.Col. Green, D.S.O., Colour parties of 6th Black Watch and 1/4th Seaforth Highrs, also massed pipe-bands left for COLOGNE to join the troops proceeding to PARIS to take part in Victory March.	Dew
	8		Holiday throughout IV Corps to celebrate signing of peace. Football Match and Aquatic sports held by Brigade Headquarters personnel. B.G.C. and Brigade Major visited sports of 6th and 8th Black Watch in the afternoon.	Dew
	9		Units Training.	Dew
	10.		Units Training.	Dew
	11.		Commander-in-Chief inspected billets, institutions etc of 8th Black Watch.	Dew

T2134. Wt. W708-776. 500000. 4/15. Sir J. C. & S.

Instructions regarding War Diaries and Intelligence Summaries are contained in F. S. Regs., Part II. and the Staff Manual respectively. Title pages will be prepared in manuscript.

WAR DIARY
or
INTELLIGENCE SUMMARY. 3rd HIGHLAND BRIGADE.
(*Erase heading not required.*)

Army Form C. 2118.

Place	Date	Hour	Summary of Events and Information	Remarks and references to Appendices
	1919 July 12		Divisional Commander addressed the 8th Black Watch in Y.M.C.A., UNT-MAUBACH.	
	13.		Church Parades by Units - B.G.C. attended that of 8th Black Watch.	
	14		Units Training.	
	15		B.G.C. attended Conference at IV Corps Headquarters reference Torchlight Tattoo to be held near NIDEGGEN about Aug.16th. 1/4th Seaforth Highrs Sports Meeting (First Day) at BRUCK - B.G.C. and Brigade Major were present.	
	16		2nd day of 1/4th Seaforth Higrs Sports Meeting - B.G.C. and Staff attended. Trench Mortar demonstration at BILSTEIN by 3rd Highland L.T.M.Battery witnessed by 8th Black Watch.	
	17		Units Training.	
	18		Meeting of Brigade Sports Committee at Brigade Headquarters. Units training. 1/4th Seaforth Highrs. relieved guards and other duties of 6th Black Watch, prior to taking over as "Duty" Battalion on 19th inst.	
	19		B.G.C. attended Conference at IV Corps Headquarters reference Torchlight Tattoo. 6th Black Watch moved from LENDERSDORF to BRUCK. 1/4th Seaforth Highrs. moved from BRUCK to LENDERSDORF to relieve 6th Black Watch as "Duty" Battalion. Day observed as a holiday.- Peace Day at home.	
	20		B.G.C., Staff Captain and Education Officer attended Church Parade at 8th Black Watch at 10.30 hours.	
	21		B.G.C. visited Range at NIDEGGEN, saw Civil Staff Captain re Billets for Tattoo Contingent in NIDEGGEN, and visited 6th Black Watch. Conference of "B" Sub-Committee for Brigade Sports at Headquarters, 8th Black Watch, at 13.30 hours. Battalions carried out training and education.	

T.134. Wt. W708-776. 500000. 4/15. Sir J. C. & S.

Instructions regarding War Diaries and Intelligence Summaries are contained in F. S. Regs., Part II. and the Staff Manual respectively. Title pages will be prepared in manuscript.

WAR DIARY
or
INTELLIGENCE SUMMARY. 3rd HIGHLAND BRIGADE.
(Erase heading not required.)

Army Form C. 2118.

Place	Date	Hour	Summary of Events and Information	Remarks and references to Appendices
	1919 July 22		B.G.C. visited Agricultural School at BOISDORF in forenoon. Brigade Transport Competition held at 14.30 hours in bad weather - G.O.C. Divisionacted as principal judge. 6th Black Watch won. Meeting of "A" Sub-Committee, Brigade Games, at Brigade Headquarters at 17.15 hours	appx "A" DMcC
	23		B.G.C. attended Meeting of Tattoo Committee at Corps Headquarters at 10.00 hours. Brigade Major attended Lecture on Pay and Mess Book at Corps Cinema at 11.00 hours.	DMcC
	24		B.G.C. attended Tactical Scheme of "C" and "D" Companies of 8th Black Watch at UNT-MAUBACH.	DMcC
	25		Units Training. Sports Committee Meetings during afternoon at Brigade Headquarters.	DMcC
	26		Units Training.	DMcC
	27		Church Parades held by each Unit - B.G.C. attended that of 8th Black Watch.	DMcC
	28		B.G.C. attended Conference at Corps Headquarters reference Torchlight Tattoo. 8th Black Watch carrying out Shooting Competition.	DMcC
	29		Units Training. Highland Division Horse Show in afternoon at HAUSEN.	DMcC
	30		First Day of 8th Black Watch Sports.	DMcC
	31		Second Day of 8th Black Watch Sports - B.G.C.attended them.	DMcC

D McCallum Capt
for Brigadier General.
Commanding. 3rd Highland Brigade.

T2134. Wt. W708-776. 500000. 4/15. Sir J. C. & S.

Appendix A

3rd Highland Brigade.

TRANSPORT COMPETITION.

1. A 1st Line Transport Competition will be held on Tuesday 22nd. inst. Location of Ground will be notified later. This Competition is for the Units of the 3rd Highland Brigade.

2. CONDITIONS.

(a) Regomental 1st Line Transport will be paraded as follows:-

3 Cookers per Battalion.
4 L.G.Limbers "
2 Water Carts "

4 S.A.A. Limbers per Battalion.
1 Tool Limber " "
1 Maltese Cart " "
1 Mess Cart. " "

6 Pack Mules per Battalion
1 Spare H.D.Horse "

2 spare L.D.Animals per Battalion
1 spare Pack Mule " "

(b) Dress.- Full Marching Order. Steel Helmets to be worn. No F.S.Caps to be carried.

(c) Detachments.- 1 Driver and 1 Brakesman to each vehicle.
1 Driver and 1 Cook to each Cooker.
1 man to each Pack animal.

(d) Harness.- Steelwork to be burnished. Packing ropes of pack animals not to be whitened.

(e) Loads.- Lewis Gun Limbers will be loaded. Other Limbers will not be loaded. All Limbers will be paraded with covers. Pack animals will be loaded with empty ammunition boxes.

(f) Marks will be allotted according to the following scale:-

General Appearance	20%
Cleanliness of Harness	15%
Fitting of Harness	5%
Condition of Animals (not shape)	20%
Grooming of Horses	5%
Mens Clothing and Equipment.	10%
Turn out of carriages etc.	10%
Completeness of Equipment	10%
Packing Equipment	5%
	100%

Fractions will not be awarded in giving marks.

R McCallum.

Captain,
Brigade Major. 3rd Highland Brigade.

13th July, 1919.

Confidential.

War Diary

of

3rd Highland Brigade

from 1st August 1919 to 31st August 1919.

Original.

Volume No. V.

17

(6[illegible]) Wt. W3906/P1607 2,500,000 7/18 McA & W Ltd (E 3591) Forms W3091/4. Army Form W.3091.

Cover for Documents.

Nature of Enclosures.

Notes, or Letters written.

3rd Highland Brigade B.M./57.A.
12th ~~2nd~~ September 1919.

Headquarters.

Highland Division.

Herewith War Diary for month ending 31st August 1919.

C H Gotto Captain

for Brigadier-General.
Commanding, 3rd Highland Brigade.

Instructions regarding War Diaries and Intelligence Summaries are contained in F. S. Regs., Part II. and the Staff Manual respectively. Title pages will be prepared in manuscript.

WAR DIARY
or
~~INTELLIGENCE SUMMARY~~. 3rd Highland Brigade.
(Erase heading not required.)

Army Form C. 2118.

Place	Date	Hour	Summary of Events and Information	Remarks and references to Appendices
Maubach. Germany.	1919 Aug. 1.		First day of 6th Bn. The Black Watch Sports. - B.G.C. to COLOGNE.	CHG
	2.		Second day of 6th Bn. The Black Watch Sports - B.G.C. attended.	CHG
	3.		B.G.C. to COBLENZ - Units held Church Parades.	CHG
	4.		Bank Holiday - No training by Units.	CHG
	5.		Preparations for Brigade Sports.	CHG
	6.		First day of Brigade Sports at GERMANIA Sports Ground DUREN.	CHG
	7.		Brigade Sports at GERMANIA Sports Ground. - An excellent meeting large number of guests attended - Prizes were presented by Lady Godley.	CHG
	9th		Brigade Group moved into DUREN preparatory to entraining for ENGLAND.	Appendix A CHG
	10.		6th and 8th Bn. The Black Watch, 3rd Highland L.T.M.Btry., and Brigade Headquarters entrain. - 8th Bn. The Black Watch marched to the Station the Colours unfurled.	Appendix B CHG
	11.		4th Bn. Seaforth Highlanders, 528th Coy. R.A.S.C., 461st Field Coy R.E., and 62nd. M.G. Battn. entrain - B.G.C. and Brigade Major proceeded by BOULOGNE - COLOGNE Express.	CHG
England. Folkestone.	12.		Troops arrive at FOLKESTONE and are despatched to CANNOCK CHASE detraining at BROCTON station on early morning of 13th August.	CHG
Brocton.	13.		Brigade Group arrive BROCTON CAMP less 461st Field Coy R.E. and 528th Coy R.A.S.C.	CHG

T.134. Wt. W708-776. 500000. 4/15. Sir J. C. & S.

Instructions regarding War Diaries and Intelligence Summaries are contained in F. S. Regs., Part II. and the Staff Manual respectively. Title pages will be prepared in manuscript.

Army Form C. 2118.

WAR DIARY
or
~~INTELLIGENCE SUMMARY~~. 3rd Highland Brigade.

(Erase heading not required.)

Place	Date	Hour	Summary of Events and Information	Remarks and references to Appendices
	1919. Aug. 14.		461st Field Coy R.E. arrive BROCTON CAMP - 528th Coy R.A.S.C. go to CLIPSTONE.	CHG
Brocton. England.	15.		Brigade held a short Route March and returned to Camp about 12.30 hours having marched past the Major General Commandingthe Centre. - Brigade Group came under the orders of Cannock Chase Centre.	Appendix "C" CHG
	16.		Inspections and general clean up.	CHG
	17.		Church Parades - B.G.C. proceeded on leave.	CHG
	18.		Ordinary Training and Education commences. - Meeting of Cannock Chase Horse Show Committee at Officers Club RUGELEY.	CHG
	21.		G.O.C. Highland Division payed a flying visit to the Brigade. -	CHG
	22.		First batch of week-end men proceed.	CHG
	24.		2nd. Bn. Kings Liverpool Regiment left camp for service abroad - Escorted to the station by the 6th & 8th Bn.The Black Watch Pipe Bands.	CHG
	25.		2 Coys from each Battalion proceed on 14 days leave about 900 men in all.	CHG
	26.		Usual Training continued	CHG
	28.		Over 400 men left the Brigade for Demobilisation - These men had joined the colours prior to July 1916.- A very wet day.	CHG.

T.134. Wt. W708-776. 500000. 4/15. Sir J. C. & S.

Instructions regarding War Diaries and Intelligence Summaries are contained in F. S. Regs., Part II. and the Staff Manual respectively. Title pages will be prepared in manuscript.

WAR DIARY
or of
~~INTELLIGENCE SUMMARY.~~ 3rd Highland Brigade.

(*Erase heading not required.*)

Army Form C. 2118.

Place	Date	Hour	Summary of Events and Information	Remarks and references to Appendices
	1919 Aug.			
Brocton. England.	31.		Church Parades as usual.	CHG

C H Gotto Captain
for Brigadier General.
Commanding, 3rd Highland Brigade.

T2134. Wt. W708–776. 500000. 4/15. Sir J. C. & S.

APPENDIX. "A".

SECRET.

Copy No..17.....

3rd Highland Brigade.

ADMINISTRATIVE INSTRUCTIONS CONCERNING DEPARTURE OF

EQUIPMENT TRAINS.

7th August 1919.

1. A schedule of Equipment Trains is attached. The times will be notified later.

TRANSPORT. 2. Transport is to be parked in Sugar Factory, DUREN by tonight.

LOADING PARTIES. 3. O.C., 4th Bn. Seaforth Highlanders will detail a loading party strength not less than 100 other ranks with a proportion of Officers to load vehicles of Brigade Group. This party to report to R.T.O., at station 3 hours before scheduled time of departure of Equipment Trains, Unloading parties at ANTWERP will be provided by Base Commandant.

MULES. 4. Ten pairs of Mules have been lent to this Brigade to draw vehicles from Sugar Factory to Station. They will be accomodated in lines vacated by 4th Gordon Highrs. Supply Officer will arrange forage for these animals.
2nd Brigade are detailing an Officer and 2 N.C.Os. to organise the work of those animals and the transport of vehicles from the Sugar Factory to the Station. Units will get in touch with this officer and let him know their requirements. On arrival at Sugar Factory harness will be packed in transport.
Division are endeavouring to arrange for the Mules of Units to remain at DUREN and be despatched from there.

GUARD. 5. A guard of one officer and 4 other ranks per unit will remain with the transport and accompany it to ANTWERP. When the vehicles are embarked the guards will be despatched by Base Commandant, ANTWERP to rejoin their units in ENGLAND. Inventories in triplicate of all vehicles and stores will be handed to Base Commandant on arrival at ANTWERP by the officer in charge of unit equipment etc.
This officer will also hand to the R.T.O., at Entraining station an entrainment statement showing,

No. of Vehicles 4 wheeled limbered.
" " " 4 " (non limbered).
" " " 2 "

MARKING OF VEHICLES. 6. All vehicles will be properly marked by each Unit.

SUPPLIES. 7. Two days rations and the unconsumed portion of the days ration will be taken in the train. Two days hard ration will be issued at DUREN Station.
Forage will be taken with mules in case of despatch from DUREN.

Units of Brigade Group to ACKNOWLEDGE.

Al. Preedy.
Captain.
Staff Captain. 3rd Highland Brigade.

(Issued through Signals at 1200 hours on 7-8-1919.)

Appendix. A.

EQUIPMENT TRAINS.

8th August 1919.

		AXLES	Nos. of Trains
M.B.6.	457th Field Coy, R.E.	34	2.
M.B.7.	53rd Gordon Highlanders.	40	
M.B.8.	6th Royal Highlanders.	36	
M.B.9.	3rd Brigade H.Qrs.	11	
M.B.10.	3rd Brigade Signal Section.		
M.B.11.	8th Royal Highlanders.	36	3.
M.B.12.	4th Seaforth Highrs.	36	
M.B.13.	461st Field Coy.	34	
M.B.14.	No. 3 Coy, Train.	31	4.
M.B.15.	No.4. Coy Train.	31	
M.B.16.	460th Coy R.E.	34	

Copies to :-

No.1. B.G.C.
2. 6th Royal Highlanders.
3. 8th Royal Highlanders.
4. 1/4th Seaforth Highlanders.
5. 3rd Highland T.M.B.
6. 528 Coy R.A.S.C.
7. 461st Field Coy, R.E.
8. 62nd Machine Gun Battn.
9. Highland Division 'G'.
10. Highland Division 'A'.
11. 1st Highland Brigade.
12. 2nd Highland Brigade.
13. Brigade Major.
14. Staff Captain.
15. Staff Captain for Civil Duties.
16. Brigade Signal Offr.
17. War Diary.
18. Ditto.
19. File.

Appendix A.

War Diary

SECRET.

Copy No. .....

3RD. HIGHLAND BRIGADE ORDER NO. 3.

7th August 1919

1. The Highland Division will move by rail and boat to United Kingdom commencing 8th August.

2. The 3rd Highland Brigade Group will be known as "B" Group and entrain at DUREN Station on 9th and 10th August.

3. "B" Group will be composed as under :-

   3rd Highland Brigade H.Q.
   3rd Highland T.M.B.
   6th Royal Highlanders.
   8th Royal Highlanders.
   1/4th Seaforth Highlanders.
   62nd Machine Gun Battalion.
   461 Field Coy. R.E.
   528 Coy. R.A.S.C.

4. The following Units of "B" Group will concentrate in DUREN Area on 9th August.

   3rd Highland Brigade H.Q. Signal Section.) Take over billets at present occupied by 2nd Highland Brigade H.Q.

   6th Royal Highlanders, 8th Royal Highlanders, 3rd Highland T.M.B.) DUREN BARRACKS.

   Trains have been asked for to convey these troops to DUREN.
   Billetting parties should be sent forward by above Units.

   1/4th Seaforth Highrs. 62nd Machine Battalion 461 Field Coy. and 528 Coy. R.A.S.C., will proceed direct from present billets to Station on day of entrainment.

5. Personnel trains will possibly run as follows 10th August.

   No. 5. A.O. 129. 6th Royal Highlanders) 3rd Highland T.M.B.) O.C. Train. Lieut. Col. W. Green D.S.O.

   No. 6. A.O. 130 8th Royal Highrs.) A.O. 131. 3rd High. Brigade H.Q.) A.O. 132. Brigade Signal Section.) O.C. Train, Maj. R.E. Anstruther M.C.

   On 11th August.
   No. 7. A.O. 133. 1/4th Seaforth Highrs.) A.O. 134. 528 Coy R.A.S.C.) O.C. Train. Lieut. Col. S.F. Sharp M.C.
   8. A.O. 135. 62nd Machine Gun Battn. A.O. 136. 461 Field Coy. R.E.) O.C. Train. Lt. Col. Birkett D.S.O

   1st Train each day will probably leave about 06.00 hours.
   Destination of train. CALAIS or BOULOGNE.
   Staff Officers of Brigade will meet trains on arrival at above stations.

6. Orders re. Transport and Administrative Instructions are being issued separately.

7. Arrival of Units in DUREN Area will be reported to Brigade H.Q..

Appendix A.

(2)

8. 3rd Highland Brigade H.Q. will close at MAUBACH at 15. 00 hours. on August 9th. and reopen at DUREN 16.00 hours same date.

9. Units of Brigade Group to acknowledge.

C H Gotto.

Captain.
Brigade Major.
3rd Highland Brigade.

Issued through Signals at 10.30 hours.

Copies to:-

No.1. B.G.C.
2. 6th Royal Highlanders.
3. 8th Royal Highlanders.
4. 1/4th Seaforth Highlanders.
5. 3rd Highland T.M.B.
6. 528 Coy. R.A.S.C.
7. 461 Field Coy. R.E.
8. 62nd Machine Gun Battn.
9. Highland Division "G"
10. Highland Division. "A".
11. 1st Highland Brigade.
12. 2nd Highland Brigade.
13. Brigade Major.
14. Staff Captain.
15. Staff Captain for Civil Duties.
16. Brigade Signal Officer.
17. War Diary.
18. Ditto.
19. File.

Appendix. "B"

SECRET.

Copy No....17....

3rd Highland Brigade.

ADMINISTRATIVE INSTRUCTIONS ISSUED IN CONJUNCTION WITH 3RD HIGHLAND BRIGADE ORDER NO.3. dated 7th August 1919.

8th August 1919.

ENTRAINMENT. 1. Times of departure will be notified.

PERSONNEL TRAINS.

Personnel with arms, personnel with equipment, Lewis Machine Guns complete will proceed by above trains.
Composition of train 47 covers, 1 coach, 2 brakes.
Length of journey by RAIL about 36 hours.

ADVANCE PARTIES. 2. One Officer and fifteen Other Ranks per Battalion will proceed by personnel train on 9th instant.
Instructions have been issued separately.

ENTRAINING STATION. 3. The O.C., Unit or detachment will on arrival at entraining station hand the R.T.O., an entraining state showing :-

(a) Number of Officers and Other Ranks.
(b) Amounts of baggage in tons, stores etc., (other than in vehicles.)

All packages etc., are to be clearly marked with name of unit and contents and securely packed.

TIMES OF ARRIVAL AND DEPARTURE. 4. Units will arrive at station one hour before scheduled time of departure and will entrain half an hour before departure.

LOADING AND UNLOADING PARTIES. 5. Units will provide suitable parties to load and unload their own stores etc.,

POLICING. 6. D.A.P.M., is arranging for policing of entraining and detraining stations.

TRANSPORT. 7. Following will report :-

8 lorries to 6th Black Watch on 9th instant.
8 " " 8th " " " "
2 " " Brigade Hqrs. " " "
1 " " 3rd H'd.Bde.T.M.B." " "
8 " " 4th Seaforth Hrs. on 11th instant.

to convey stores, kits, etc., to Station. O.Cs. Units will arrange to mount guards over their kits, stores etc., on the Station.

SUPPLIES. 8. The unconsumed portions and two days rations will be taken on the train. Haltes repas have been arranged at HUY, CHARLEROI, CHISLENGHEN, and MERRIS. Hot meals will be provided. Each Officer and other rank will carry the Iron Ration.
Until day of entrainment rations will be delivered to Units. On day of entrainment two days rations will be delivered on the train.

TENTAGE. 9. Marquees and Tents will be struck on 9th instant. Four lorries will report to 6th Black Watch, and 8th Black Watch and 2 to the Company at BOCHEIM at 1000 hours on Saturday, to convey Tents to O.C. IV Corps troops direct.

Appendix "B"

Sheet No.2.

STORES. 10. All requisitioned stores (including R.E.) will be given in charge of nearest Burgermeister, through Civil Staff Captain, No. 3. Sub-Area, NIDEGGEN, and receipts obtained. All stores and equipment surplus to A.F.G. 1098 will be handed in to D.A.D.O.S.

BLANKETS. 11. One blanket per man to be taken.

AMMUNITION. 12. SIXTY rounds S.A.A. per man and THIRTY-TWO drums per gun, filled, to be taken. Balance of S.A.A. and all GRENADES to be sent to VOCHEM.

CANTEENS ETC. 13. All Canteens and outstanding accounts are to be settle by Units before departure.

Units of Brigade Group to ACKNOWLEDGE.

A.E. Priddy
Captain,
Staff Captain. 3rd Highland Brigade.

(Issued through Signals at 1200hours on 8th August 1919).

Copies to all recipients of Brigade Order No. 3.

Appendix "C"   War Diary

Copy No........

3RD HIGHLAND BRIGADE ORDER NO.4.

14th August 1919.

Reference Map CANNOCK CHASE $\frac{1}{63360}$

1. There will be a Brigade Route March to-morrow, 15th August.

2. Starting Point:-

3rd Highland Brigade Headquarters on BROCTON Road.

Route:- BROCTON - MILFORD - WALTON - thence left-handed by N of WALTON to road junction ¾ mile S.W. of WALTON - thence left-handed - NEWTOWN - BROCTON - Camp.

3. Order of March .-

Brigade H.Qrs. and Signal Section will pass Starting Point at 0930 hr						
6th Royal Highlanders	"	"	"	"	"	0931 "
8th Royal Highlanders	"	"	"	"	"	0934 "
1/4th Seaforth Highlanders	"	"	"	"	"	0937 "
3rd Highland T.M.Battery	"	"	"	"	"	0940 "

4. Intervals.-

100 Yards interval will be maintained between Battalions.

10 Yards between Companies.

Usual halts will be observed at 10 minutes to each clock hour.

5. Dress.-

Drill Order.

6. Correct time will be sent out from Brigade Headquarters by D.R. leaving at 08.00 hours.

7. Acknowledge.

CHGotto.

Captain,
Brigade Major,
3rd Highland Brigade.

Copies to:-
No.1. B.G.C.
2. 6th Royal Highlanders.
3. 8th Royal Highlanders.
4. 1/4th Seaforth Highrs.
5. 3rd Highland T.M.Battery.
6. Brigade Major.
7. Staff Captain.
8. Brigade Signal Officer.
9. CANNOCK CHASE Centre H.Qrs. (for information).

BEF

HIGHLAND DIV formerly
62 DIV

2 HIGHLAND Bde

1/4 BN GORDONS

1919 MAY TO 1919 AUG

FROM 51, 154 BDE

NO BOX

Secret. ORIGINAL.

a07.0

2 Bde

Confidential

War Diary

of

1/4 Batt. The Gordon Highlanders

From 1st May 1919. To 31st May 1919.

[signature]

Lieut. - Col.
Commanding 1/4th Bn. The Gordon Highlanders

(6414) Wt. W3906/P1607 2,500,000 7/18 McA & W Ltd (E 3591) Forms W3091/4.

Army Form W.3091.

Cover for Documents.

Nature of Enclosures.

Notes, or Letters written.

Army Form C. 2118.

1/4th. Bn. The Gordon Highlanders.

WAR DIARY
or
INTELLIGENCE SUMMARY.
(Erase heading not required.)

ORIGINAL.

Instructions regarding War Diaries and Intelligence Summaries are contained in F. S. Regs., Part II. and the Staff Manual respectively. Title pages will be prepared in manuscript.

Place	Date	Hour	Summary of Events and Information	Remarks and references to Appendices
DUREN	1/5/19.		Parades in accordance with Programme. Classification of employed men under Educational Scheme. Captain Drummond on Audit Board of Canteen.	A D Capt
	2nd.		Wet day. Training in Billets. Coys paid. Cinema performance 'Whatsoever a man Soweth', Subject : Venereal Disease. 1 Platoon ('A' Coy) attended.	A D Capt
	3rd.		Commanding Officer inspected billets of Transport, B.A.D.C. Coys.	A D Capt
	4th.		Church Parades. Pres. in Corps Cinema at 10.00 hrs. Lt.J.J.Ogston appointed A/Adjt. and is transferred to Headquarter Company.	A D Capt
	5th.		'A' & 'B' Coys attended Education Classes. The opening of Education Scheme. Battalion Reading Room opened in STADT SCHOOL. 13.30 - 14.30 hrs. 16.00 - 21.30 hrs.	A D Capt
	6th.		'C' & 'D' Education. New Routine for Band. In future they will play Reveille on Mondays and Tuesdays; Retreat on Tuesdays and Fridays; Tattoo on Wednesdays.	A D Capt
	7th.		Battalion Route March. Warm and Dusty.	A D Capt
	8th.		Lecture by Viscount Broome at 10.00 in Corps Cinema entitled 'The Navy'. Very good. The men appeared to like it very much. After Lecture Coy drill was carried out.	A D Capt
	9th.		Baths. Coys paid out.	A D Capt
	10th.		Baths. Very good. New Leave train for men started, leaving DUREN 15.15 hrs. and reaching CALAIS 06.00 hrs.	A D Capt
	11th.		Church Parade. 10.00 hrs. in Corps Cinema. From this day onwards no B.Os. will be issued on Sundays.	A D Capt
	12th.		Pleasure Trip on Rhine. 3 Officers and 80 men from 'A' Coy went. 'D' Coy proceeded to HURTGEN.	A D Capt
	13th.		Rehearsal for C. in C's. Inspection, Battle Order. Battalion paraded 08.15 hrs and marched to Inspection Ground near DUREN Barracks. Dull and Wet. Battalion Football practiced 17.15 hrs.	A D Capt
	14th.		Battalion Parade. Very hot and dry.	A D Capt
	1tth.		Inspection by C. in C. Gen. Sir W.Robertson on Ground in front of Aerodrome, near DUREN. C. in C. arrived a few minutes after 10.00 hrs. All troops in DUREN on parade. The C. in C. made a careful inspection of each Unit, after which Units marched past in fours. Capt.P.V.Mulvey i/c of Battalion Lieut.Colonel. P.W.Brown,C.M.G. D.S.O. being in temporary command of 2nd Highland Brigade. Battn. Football Team practice 17.15 hrs.	A D Capt
	16th.		Baths and Training.	A D Capt
	17th.		Guard of Honour. 3 Officers 2 N.C.Os.100 O/Ranks. at Duren Station with Regtl.Colours to receive Marshal Foch at 09.00 hrs.	A D Capt

A6945 Wt. W11422/M1160 350,000 12/16 D. D. & L. Forms/C./2118/14.

1/4th. Bn. The Gordon Highlanders

Army Form C. 2118.

ORIGINAL.

WAR DIARY
or
INTELLIGENCE SUMMARY.

(Erase heading not required.)

Instructions regarding War Diaries and Intelligence Summaries are contained in F. S. Regs., Part II. and the Staff Manual respectively. Title pages will be prepared in manuscript.

Place	Date	Hour	Summary of Events and Information	Remarks and references to Appendices
DUREN	17/5/19 (cont)		Captain J.Jefferson in Command, Lieut.G.T.McCulloch Subaltern of the Guard and Lt.P.M.Small carrying the Regtl. Colours Marshal Foch congratulated the Guard on their smart and Soldier like bearing and upon their steadiness on parade. Battalion Team beat 1/5th Gordon Highrs. at Association Football at BIRKESDORF : 2 gls. 1 gl.	A.D. Capt.
	18th.		Church Parade 10.00 hrs. No padre arrived to take the service.	A.D. Capt.
	19th.		Training & Education.	A.D. Capt.
	20th.		Lecture by Mr. J.Saxon Mills "Railway developement of the Future": good.	A.D. Capt.
	21st.		Battalion Route March. BINSFELD - GIRBELSRATH. Very hot and fine.	A.D. Capt.
	22nd		Lecture by Lt.Col. Tyshan on "Bolshevism" at Corps Cinema. (good) at 15.00 hours. Temporary curtailment of leave owing to uncertainty as to whether Germans will sign Peace Treaty.	A.D. Capt.
	23rd.		Precautionary measures taken in preparation for possible move forward in event of Germans not signing Peace Treaty. Lewis Guns kept packed & parked in front of KLEIN TIVOLI. Baths.	A.D. Capt.
	24th.		Baths. C.O.'s Inspection "C" Coy's Kit. "D" Dinners. 12.15 hours.	A.D. Capt.
	25th.		Church Parade. 2/Lt. P.M.Small appointed Scout Officer.	A.D. Capt.
	26th.		Scheme for Officers of "A" & "B" Coys.	A.D. Capt.
	27th.		Scheme for Officers of "C" & "D" Coys. Range on W. side of JOHANN BRIDGE ready for use.	A.D. Capt.
	28th.		Ordinary training carried out, including a demonstration of Advance Guards & Outposts for "A" & "D" Companies.	A.D. Capt.
	29th.		Weather very fine, warm and dry. Ordinary training carried out including 2 Coys. Education.	A.D. Capt.
	30th.		Lecture given on "Warfare on the Italian Front" to 3 Coys. Very Good.	A.D. Capt.
	31st.		Kit Inspection and Recreational Training carried out. Captain Brodie, M.C. Adjutant, appointed Staff Captain of 1st Highland Brigade. Many Officers & O/Ranks attended 51st Bn. Gordon Highlanders' Sports which were very successful.	
			Captain A. Drummond appointed Acting Adjutant. Lieut. A.W. Gregor assumes command of "A" Company.	A.D. Capt.

[signature]

Lieut.-Colonel,
Cmdg. 1/4TH BN. THE GORDON HIGHLANDERS.

A6945 Wt. W11422/M1160 350,000 12/16 D. D. & L. Forms/C./2118/14.

Army Form C. 2118.

WAR DIARY or INTELLIGENCE SUMMARY.

(Erase heading not required.)

1/4th. Bn. The Gordon Highlanders,

ORIGINAL.

Instructions regarding War Diaries and Intelligence Summaries are contained in F. S. Regs., Part II. and the Staff Manual respectively. Title pages will be prepared in manuscript.

NOMINAL ROLL OF OFFICERS AS AT 31/5/19.

Lt. Col.	Brown.	P.W.,C.M.G.,D.S.O.	Commanding Officer.
Major	Gordon	J.H.,M.C.	2nd in Command.
Captain	Brodie	B.C.,M.C.	
Captain	Giles	R.J.	Adjt.,Div.School.
Captain	Drummond	A.	Adjutant.
~~Captain~~	~~Mulvey~~	~~P.V.~~	~~O.C."B" Company.~~
Lieut (handwritten) Captain	Jefferson	J.	O.C."C" Company.
~~Captain~~	~~Seton~~	~~Sir H.H.~~	
Captain	Neay	T.	Quartermaster.
Lieut.	Milne	D.J.	O.C."D" Company.
~~Lieut.~~	~~Ogston~~	~~J.J.~~	~~Assistant Adjutant.~~
Lieut.	Robertson	A.W.	Education Officer.
Lieut.	Henry	R,	Signalling Officer.
Lieut.	Semple	J.W.	Transport Officer.
Lieut.	Gregor	A.W.	O.C."A" Company.
Lieut.	McCulloch	G.T.	
Lieut.	Cruickshank	G.G.	
Lieut.	Marshall.	R.R.,M.M.	Attached T.M.B.
Lieut.	Cranston	S.,M.C.	Attached T.M.B.
Lieut.	Walshaw	R.	
Lieut.	Matthews	D.A.	Lewis Gun Officer.
2/Lieut.	Scott	J.McD.,	Attached T.M.B.
2/Lieut.	Harold	W.	
2/Lieut.	Robertson	A.	
2/Lieut.	Flint M.	M.C.W.	
2/Lieut.	Fowler	J.J.	Course at Newmarket.
2/Lieut.	Grant	R.F.	
2/Lieut.	Murdoch	J.F.	
2/Lieut.	Davidson	C.	
2/Lieut.	Lawson	A.G.	Scout Officer.
2/Lieut.	Small	P.M.	
2/Lieut.	Allan	H.M.	
2/Lieut.	Miller	A.	
2/Lieut.	S.J. Cox.		
2/Lieut.	Leys.	J.M.	

ATTACHED.

Lieut.	Breakey	S.F.	Medical Officer.
Captain	Lamb	J.	Chaplain.
Captain	Shields	J.A.	Chaplain.

POSTED - NOT YET JOINED.

Lieut.	Wilson	N.J.	152nd Inf. Bde Course.
Lieut.	Somerville	S.E.	

Effective Strength		Detached		Ration Strength.	
Off.	O/R	Off.	O/R	Off.	O/R
39	909	10	362	29	547

[signature] Capt

A6945 Wt. W11422/M1160 350,000 12/16 D. D. & L. Forms/C./2118/14.

Secret. Original.

War Diary

of

1/4th Battalion The Gordon Highlanders

From 1st June To 30th June

1919.

(Volume LIII)

[illegible]

Lieut. Colonel,
Commanding 1/4th Battalion The Gordon Hrs.

Instructions regarding War Diaries and Intelligence Summaries are contained in F. S. Regs., Part II. and the Staff Manual respectively. Title pages will be prepared in manuscript.

WAR DIARY
or
INTELLIGENCE SUMMARY.
(Erase heading not required.)

Army Form C. 2118.

Place	Date	Hour	Summary of Events and Information	Remarks and references to Appendices
DUREN.	1919. 2/6/19.		Birthday of H.M. The King observed by short Battalion Ceremonial Parade on GERMANIA Sportsground. A "feu de joie" was fired by the Battalion and the Battalion marched past in Column of Companies. Remainder of the day was observed as a holiday.	[initials]
	3rd.		Usual training carried out including Education, Musketry, Physical Training &c.	[initials]
	4th.		Battalion attended a Lecture in the Y.M.C.A. building "Amongst Big Game in Wildest Africa" by Mr. Joseph Best, illustrated by films. Very good lecture and well received by the men. Usual Training carried on.	
			Military funeral of No. 40914 A/Sergt. Denoon D. (from No. 11 Stationary Hospital), formerly Scout Sergt. of the Battalion.	[initials]
	5th.		Ordinary training carried out. Education and Musketry.	[initials]
	6th.		"B" Company proceeded to HURTGEN to complete digging on Rifle Range for Battalion. Scout Class and Lewis Gun Class accompanying it to carry out training in the country.	[initials]
	8th.		In the afternoon preliminary heats of football 5 a side for Battalion Sports, took place.	[initials]
	9th & 10th.		Ordinary training took place, including Education, Musketry and one Coy. Tactical Scheme.	[initials]
	11th.		Battalion Sports took place. A large number of Officers & O/Ranks of other units attended and the Sports were very successful. "C" Company scored the highest number of points and Lieut. G.T. McCulloch won the Commanding Officer's Cup for best individual competitor.	
			A lecture on the System of Pay & Mess Books was given by the Command Paymaster, COLOGNE, in the Divisional Theatrê, DUREN. Battalion Imprest Holder, O.C. Companies & Coy.Q.M.S's attended.	
			Captain Sir John Seton, Bart, was appointed to command of "D" Company, and Lieut. D.J. Milne to command of "B" Company.	[initials]
	12th,		Usual training carried out including Education, Musketry, Coy. Tactical Scheme.	[initials]
	13th & 14th.		Many Officers & O/R's attended 5th Battalion The Gordon Highlanders Sports on 13th instant, and 53rd Battalion The Gordon Highlanders Sports on 14th.	[initials]
	16th.		Considerable doubt as to whether the Germans will sign the Peace terms, and warning was received that Battalion may have to move forward to SOLINGEN on very short notice.	[initials]
DUREN. SOLINGEN.	17th & 18th.		At about 05.00 hours 17/6/19, notice was received for Battalion to move forward by train to SOLINGEN. Entrained at 15.30 hours and arrived SOLINGEN about 20.00 hours. Transport &	[initials]

(A9475) Wt W2358/P360 600,000 12/17 D. D. & L. Sch. 52a. Forms/C2118/15.

Instructions regarding War Diaries and Intelligence Summaries are contained in F. S. Regs., Part II. and the Staff Manual respectively. Title pages will be prepared in manuscript.

2.

WAR DIARY
or
INTELLIGENCE SUMMARY.

(Erase heading not required.)

Army Form C. 2118.

Place	Date	Hour	Summary of Events and Information	Remarks and references to Appendices
			Baggage did not arrive till about 02.00 hours on 18th. Everybne billeted on evening of 17th.	[initials]
SOLINGEN.	19th, 20th & 21st.		Training carried out including Musketry & P.T.	[initials]
	23rd.		Warning received that Battalion may have to continue the advance on 24th June., this being the latest date allowed to the German delegates to sign the peace terms.	
			All battle arrangements made for an advance to REMSHEID. At about 19.30 hours, a 'phone message was received from 2nd Highland Brigade that there would be no advance.	[initials]
	24th.		Lieut. A.W. Robertson takes over command of "B" Company from Lieut. D.J. Milnes who is posted to "C" Company. 2/Lieut. J.J. Fowler is appointed Battalion Educational Officer vice Lieut. A.W. Robertson. Training carried out. Captain J. Lamb, C.F., proceeded to U.K. for Demobilization.	[initials]
	25th & 27th.		Usual training carried out including Close Order Drill, Musketry, P.T. On 25th, Captain P.W. Lilley C.F., joined the Battalion for attachment.	[initials] [initials]
	28th.		Notified by phone from 2nd Highland Brigade about 18.00 hours that Peace had been signed by the German delegates. Orders regarding Fraternizing cancelled. There was no public demonstration.	[initials]
	30th.		Education & Training carried out.	[initials] Capt

[signature] Lt. Colonel,
Commanding
1/4th Batt. The Gordon Highlanders.

(A9475) Wt W2358/P360 600,000 12/17 D. D. & L. Sch. 52a. Forms/C2118/15.

1/4TH BATTALION THE GORDON HIGHLANDERS.

NOMINAL ROLL OF OFFICERS AS AT 20/8/1919.

Commission.	Rank. Sub.	Rank. Temp.	Rank. Act.	Name.		Regt. if attached.	Remarks.
Reg.	Major.	Bt.Lt.Col.		Brown	P.W., C.M.G., D.S.O.	Gordon Hrs.	Commanding Officer.
T.F.	Capt.			Gordon	J.M., M.C.		Second in Command.
Temp.	Capt.			Wilson.	R.J.	1st Gordon Hrs.	Adjt. Divisional School.
T.F.	Lieut.		Captain.	Drummond	A.	7th A. & S. Hrs.	Adjutant.
Temp.	Lieut.		Captain.	Jefferson	J.	1st Gordon Hrs.	O.C. "C" Company.
Perm.	Capt.			Seton	Sir J.H.,	6th Gordon Hrs.	O.C. "D" Company.
Temp.	Capt.			Keay	T.	37th Lancs. Fus.	Quartermaster.
T.F.	Capt.			Hall	J.H., M.C.		Quartermaster.
T.F.	Lieut.			Milne	D.J.	6th Gordon Hrs.	
Temp.	Lieut.			Ogston	J.J.	1st Gordon Hrs.	Assistant Adjutant.
T.F.	Lieut.			Robertson	A.W.	9th Gordon Hrs.	O.C. "B" Company.
T.F.	Lieut.			Henry.	R.		Signalling Officer.
Temp.	Lieut.			Semple	J.W.	8th Gordon Hrs.	Transport Officer.
T.F.	Lieut.			Gregor	A.W.	7th Gordon Hrs.	O.C. "A" Company.
T.F.	Lieut.			McCulloch	G.T.		
T.F.	Lieut.			Cruickshank	G.G.		
T.F.	Lieut.			Marshall	R.B.	12th H.L.I.	Attached T.M.B.
T.F.	Lieut.			Cranston	G., M.C.	7th Scot. Rifles.	Attached T.M.B.
T.F.	Lieut.			Matthews.	C.A.	5th Gordon Hrs.	
T.F.	2/Lieut.			Harold	W.	5th Gordon Hrs.	
T.F.	2/Lieut.			Robertson	A.	6th Gordon Hrs.	
Temp.S.R.	2/Lieut.			Flint	H.C.W.	3rd Gordon Hrs.	
Temp.	2/Lieut.			Fowler	J.J.	1st Gordon Hrs.	Education Officer.
Temp.	2/Lieut.			Grant	R.F.	1st Gordon Hrs.	
T.F.	2/Lieut.			Murdoch	J.F.	6th Gordon Hrs.	
T.F.	2/Lieut.			Davidson	G.	6th Gordon Hrs.	
T.F.	2/Lieut.			Lawson	A.G.		
T.F.	2/Lieut.			Small	P.M.		Scout Officer.
Temp.	Lieut.			Miller	A.	1st Gordon Hrs.	
Temp.	2/Lieut.			Cox	S.J.	1st Gordon Hrs.	
Temp.	2/Lieut.			Rae	A.		

Commission.	Rank. Sub.	Rank. Temp.	Rank. Act.	Name.		Regt. if attached.	Remarks.
ATTACHED.							
	Lieut.			Bronkey	S.F.	R.A.M.C.	Medical Officer.
	Capt.			Shields.	J.A.		Chaplain.
	Capt.			Lilley	P.W.		Chaplain.
		POSTED NOT YET JOINED.					
T.F.	Lieut.			Wilson	M.J.		152nd Inf. Bde.
TEMP.	Lieut.			Somerville	A.C.		1st Army Inf. School.

A.D. Capt.

STRENGTH.

Effective Strength :-	33	Officers	907	O/Ranks.
Attached :-	3	"	3	"
	36	"	910	"
Detached :-	9	"	208	"
Ration Strength :-	27	"	702	"

A.D. Capt.

Secret. Original.

War Diary.

of

1/4th Battalion The Gordon Highlanders.

From 1st to 31st July 1919.

Volume 54.

[signature]

Lieut. Colonel,
Commanding 1/4th Battalion The Gordon Highlanders.

Army Form C. 2118.

Instructions regarding War Diaries and Intelligence Summaries are contained in F. S. Regs., Part II. and the Staff Manual respectively. Title pages will be prepared in manuscript.

WAR DIARY
or
INTELLIGENCE SUMMARY.
(Erase heading not required.)

Place	Date	Hour	Summary of Events and Information	Remarks and references to Appendices
SOLINGEN&	July	1st.	Nothing of importance took place, Batt. training in the morning, the rest of the day being spent in all forms of sport.	JJO. Lt.
		2nd.	The Batt. received orders to return to DUREN by train, A.B.&C, Coys & H.Qrs. left with the personnel train leaving SOLINGEN at 14.30 hrs. "D" Coy being left behind to assist with the loading of the Transport, baggage etc. and then travelled down on the baggage train, along with the Transport section. The personnel train was due to arrive at DUREN about 17.30 hrs. which it did, and the weather being very good at the time every one enjoyed the trip very much. The baggage train did not leave SOLINGEN until 21.00 hrs. and arrived at DUREN about 03.00 hrs. when the detraining commenced. Everything went smoothly and the work was finished about 05.00 hrs. on the morning of the 3/7/19. The whole Battalion took o ver the Billets they occupied before moving to SOLINGEN.	JJO. Lt.
DUREN.		3rd.	"A" Coy proceeded to HUERTGEN by Motor Lorries to continue the construction of the Rifle Range. The men seemed very pleased to go there, as it is situated in the Hills amidst lovely scenery. The remainder of the Batt. was busy getting everything in their billets put in good order.	JJO. Lt.
		4th, 5th, & 6th.	Nothing of importance took place in that period. The Batt. carried out a Route March on the 5th. The remainder of the time was mostly devoted to Interplatoon competitions.	JJO. Lt.
		7th.	In view of the Victory March to be held in Paris on 14th July, the party representing this Batt. Lt.Col.P.W.Brown, C.M.G., D.S.O., ~~etc.~~, Lt.J.J.Ogston, 2/Lt.P.M.Small, D.C.M., 209343.C.Q.M.S.McCombie, D.C.M., M.M., 22583.Sgt.Ferrier, M.M., 269196.Sgt.Linley, M.M., 201648.Sgt.Davidson, Croix de Guerre, with the Kings and Regimental Colours, proceeded to COLOGNE prior to proceeding to PARIS for the March.	
		8th, 9th.	Training was carried out as laid down in Training Programme for those dates, along with the running off of the preliminary heats of several events to take place at Bgde Sports on 11th inst.	JJO. Lt.
		10th.	The Battalion attended a Lecture by Maj.Gen.Sir D.Campbell, K.C.B. Comdg. Highland Division, on Demobilization, Discipline etc. It was very much appreciated by the men as the subjects were of an instructive nature to all.	JJO. Lt.
		11th.	The 2nd Highland Brigade Group held their Sports in GERMANIA SPORTS GROUND, DUREN, the day being observed as a Holiday for all men in the Brigade. The Batt. was very well represented in the events, winning both "Tug-of-war" events; 1st for best Cooker and Watercart and 2nd for Limber; in the athletic events the Batt. won 2nd place in the Brigade, the 53rd Gordon Hrs. being the winners. After the sports the whole of the evening was devoted to various amusements, after which there was a Torchlight procession, headed by the Mass Bands of the Brigade.	JJO. Lt.
		12, 13-14th.	Nothing of importance took place on these dates.	JJO. Lt.

D. D. & L., London, E.C. (A8001) Wt. W1771/M2031 750,000 5/17 Sch. 52 Forms C2118/14

Army Form C. 2118.

Instructions regarding War Diaries and Intelligence Summaries are contained in F. S. Regs., Part II. and the Staff Manual respectively. Title pages will be prepared in manuscript.

WAR DIARY
or
INTELLIGENCE SUMMARY.
(Erase heading not required.)

Place	Date	Hour	Summary of Events and Information	Remarks and references to Appendices
DUREN.	JULY	15TH.	5 Officers and 200 men of the Battalion went on a pleasure trip up the River Rhine, which was very much appreciated by all ranks: the weather being good added to the enjoyment of the trip.	[illegible]
		16th.	Batt. attended a Lecture given on "PHOTOGRAPHING"OVER THE WORLD" illustrated by films, given by Capt.Cherry Kearton. This Lecture was much appreciated by all ranks.	[illegible]
		17th.	Nothing of importance took place on this date. The party returned from VICTORY MARCH at PARIS.	[illegible]
		18th.	Competitors from the Batt.proceeded to the 52nd Hordon Hrs.Sports,and succeeded in carrying off several prizes.	[illegible]
		19th.	This day was selected for the Peace celebrations of the British Empire and was observed by every one as a Holiday. No demonstrations of any kind took place by the troops.	[illegible]
		20,21st.	Nothing of importance took place on these dates,sports etc. took place by Platoons.	[illegible]
		22nd.	The Batt. carried out usual training,including sports etc. in the afternoon. Competitors from the Battalion went to the 10th A. & S.Hrs.Sports and succeeded in carrying off some prizes.	
		23/27th.	Nothing of importance happened in that period,usual sports etc.being taken part in by the men. At the Games of the 5th Bn.Cameron Highrs.at HAUSEN the 1st and 2nd prizes for Highland Dancing were won by Pte.Cuthbertson & L/C.Morrison of the Battalion.	[illegible]
		28th.	Batt. attended a Lecture on "VENEREAL DISEASE"by Rev.G.H.HEASLETTE,B.A. and gained much information on the subject.	[illegible]
		29th.	Highland Divisional Horse Show took place at HAUSEN: the Batt. did very well,winning five 1st. prizes and one 2nd prize. 1st Prizes : (best Officers charger,Water Cart,Mess Cart,best pair of Mules and the Mule Race;)2nd prize :- was for the best Cooker.	[illegible]
		30th.	The day was spent in playing off most of the Interplatoon Tug-of war, Football Matches etc.	[illegible]
		31st.	Nothing of importance took place.	[illegible]

[signature]

Lt. Colonel,
Commanding
1/4th Batt. The Gordon Highlanders.

D. D. & L., London, E.C.
(A8003) Wt. W1771/M2031 750,000 5/17 Sch. 52 Forms/C2118/14

1/4TH BATTALION THE GORDON HIGHLANDERS.

NOMINAL ROLL OF OFFICERS AS AT 30/7/19.

Commission.	Rank. Sub.	Rank. Temp.	Rank. Act.	Name.		Regt. if attached.	Remarks.
Reg.	Major.	Bt.Lt.Col.		Brown	P.W., C.M.G., D.S.O.	Gordon Hrs.	Commanding Officer.
T.F.	Capt.	Major.		Gordon	J.H.McI., M.C.		Second in Command.
Temp.	Capt.			Giles	R.J.	1st Gordon Hrs.	Adjt. Divl.School.
T.F.	Lieut.		Capt.	Drummond	A.	7th A. & S.Hrs.	Adjutant.
Temp.	Lieut.		Capt.	Jefferson	J.	1st Gordon Hrs.	O.C. "C" Coy.
Perm.	Capt.			Seton	Sir J.H. Bart.	6th Gordon Hrs.	O.C. "D" Coy.
T.F.	Lieut.		Capt.	Robertson	A.W.	7th Gordon Hrs.	O.C. "B" Coy.
T.F.	Lieut.		Capt.	Gregor	A.W.	7th Gordon Hrs.	O.C. "A" Coy.
T.F.	Capt.			Hall	J.H., M.C.		Quartermaster.
T.F.	Lieut.			Milne	D.J.	6th Gordon Hrs.	
Temp.	Lieut.			Ogston	J.J.	1st Gordon Hrs.	Asst. Adjutant.
T.F.	Lieut.			Henry	R.		Signalling Officer.
Temp.	Lieut.			Semple	J.H.	8th Gordon Hrs.	
T.F.	Lieut.			McCulloch	G.T.		
T.F.	Lieut.			Cruickshank	G.G.		
T.F.	Lieut.			Watthews	O.A.	5th Gordon Hrs.	
T.F.	2/Lieut.			Harold	W.	5th Gordon Hrs.	
T.F.	2/Lieut.			Robertson	A.	6th Gordon Hrs.	
Temp.S.R.	2/Lieut.			Flint	M.C.W.	3rd Gordon Hrs.	
Temp.	2/Lieut.			Fowler	J.J.	1st Gordon Hrs.	Education Officer.
Temp.	2/Lieut.			Grant	R.F.	1st Gordon Hrs.	
T.F.	2/Lieut.			Murdoch	J.F.	6th Gordon Hrs.	
T.F.	2/Lieut.			Davidson	C.	6th Gordon Hrs.	
T.F.	2/Lieut.			Lawson	A.G.		
T.F.	2/Lieut.			Small	P.M.		Scout Officer.
Temp.	Lieut.			Miller	A.	1st Gordon Hrs.	
Temp.	2/Lieut.			Cox	S.J.	1st Gordon Hrs.	Transport Officer.

Commission.	Rank. Sub.	Rank. Temp.	Rank. Act.	Name.		Regt. if attached.	Remarks.
ATTACHED.							
	Lieut.			Breakey	S.F.	R.A.M.C.	Medical Officer.
	Capt.			Shields	J.A.		Chaplain.
	Capt.			Lilley	P.W.		Chaplain.
		POSTED NOT YET JOINED.					
T.F.	Lieut.			Wilson	M.J.		152nd Infantry Brigade.

...

STRENGTH. 31ST JUKY.1919.

	Offs.	O/Rs.
Effective	28	851
Attached	3	18
Total	31	869
Detached	9	233
Ration Strength	22	636

Lieut. Colonel,
Commanding 1/4TH BATTALION THE GORDON HIGHLANDERS.

Secret

Original.

Vol. 55.

War Diary

of

1/4th Bn The Gordon Highlanders

August 1st – 31st, 1914.

James H. Gordon. Major.

Cmdg 1/4th Bn The Gordon Hrs.

Secret.

4th Bn. The Gordon Highlanders Original

WAR DIARY
or
INTELLIGENCE SUMMARY.
(*Erase heading not required.*)

Army Form C. 2118.

Instructions regarding War Diaries and Intelligence Summaries are contained in F. S. Regs., Part II. and the Staff Manual respectively. Title pages will be prepared in manuscript.

Place	Date 1919.	Hour	Summary of Events and Information	Remarks and references to Appendices
DUREN.	Aug.1		Training carried out as usual.	
	" 2.		Information received the Battalion shortly moving to England.	
	" 4.		Training suspended for Bank Holiday. Inter-Platoon Matches, Tug-of-War, Football etc.,	
	" 5.		Training carried out as usual.	
	" 6.		Packing up for move to England.	
	" 7.		'A' Coy. move from HURTGEN and are billeted under canvas in STADTPARK. Information received that Battalion will move tomorrow.	
	" 8.		Crowds pf Germans lined the streets and seemed to show regret at our Leaving. Battalion entrained at DUREN Station at 13.44 hours. Baggage train having been loaded in the early morning leaving DUREN at 10.29 hours. A halt was made at HUY about 23.00 hours where a meal was served.	
	" 9.		Train proceeded through battle area of ARMENTIERES and BAILLEUL. Reach CALAIS at 19.30 hours where Battalion proceeded to No. 5 Camp and stayed for the night.	
CALAIS.	"10.		Embarked for England at 08.30 hours, disembarked Folkstone at 11.00 hours where a meal was served. First train with "A", "B", & "D" Coy's. left for Clipstone Camp, Notts., at 13.30 hours. 2ndTrain with "C" Ccy. left 16.30 hours, arriving Clipstone 01.00 hours. 11/8/19.	
CLIPSTONE CAMP	" 11.		Battalion parade to check number of complete equipments.	
	" 12.		Training carried out - Arm Drill.	
	" 13.		Late Passes granted to Battalion up to 10% to proceed to MANSFIELD. No. 19792 Pte. O'Lone J., 'C' Company, was drowned while bathing. 2/Lieut. R.F. Grant appointed Battalion Messing Officer. No. 280051 Sgt. Towner appointed Battalion Messing N.C.O.	
	" 14.		Training - Coy. Inspection of Arms and Equipment. Coy., Bathing parades. Lieut. G.T.McCulloch appointed Battalion Musketry Officer. All H.Q. Details rejoin their Companies.	
	" 15.		Training - "A" & "B" Coy. Platoon & Coy. Drill. "C" & "D" Coy. Elementary Musketry - Standard Tests.	
	" 16.		Lieut. J.J. Ogston takes over command of "A" Coy., A/Capt. A.W. Gregor reverts to Lieut., and is transferred to "B" Company. Lieut. J.H. Semple from "C" to "A"., 2/Lt. A. Robertson from 'A' to 'C'. Photographs of Company Groups taken after Church Parade.	
	" 17.		Training - 'C' & 'D' Coys. commence General Musketry Course. "A" & "B" Coys., Gas Training, Elementary Musketry & Bathing Parade. Lieut. G.T.McCulloch appointed Assist/Adjutant vice Lieut. J. J. Ogston.	
	" 18.		Dental Inspection for all O/Ranks. Investments in War Savings Assoc. 'A' Coy. £4. 13/9d. 'B' £6., 'C' £7. 18/6d. 'D' Nil.	

D. D. & L., London, E.C.
(A8004) Wt. W1771/M2031 750,000 5/17 Sch. 52 Forms/C2118/14

Secret.

4th Bn Gordon Highlanders

Original

Army Form C. 2118.

Instructions regarding War Diaries and Intelligence Summaries are contained in F. S. Regs., Part II. and the Staff Manual respectively. Title pages will be prepared in manuscript.

WAR DIARY
or
INTELLIGENCE SUMMARY.

(Erase heading not required.)

Place	Date 1919.	Hour	Summary of Events and Information	Remarks and references to Appendices
CLIPSTONE CAMP.	Aug. 19.		Training - P.T. & Games. Baths. 'C' & 'D' Coys. Range.	
	" 20.		Training - 'C' & 'D' Coys. Range. 'A' & 'B' Coys. Baths.	
	" 21.		Usual Training, 'C' & 'D' Coys. Range. Details of 'A' Coy. P.T. & Games. 'B' Coy. Elem.Musketry.	
	" 22.		'A' Coy. proceeded on leave.	
	" 23.		Battalion contributed £14. 19. 3d. to War Savings Association for week ending 23/8/19.	
	" 24.		Volunteers called for for service in General Denikin's Army in South Russia.	
	" 25.		Usual Training - 'C' Coy. only at Range, 'D' Coy. supply Butts party.	
	" 26.		'B' Coy. proceeded on leave. 'C' Coy. at Range.	
	" 27.		'C' Coy. at Range. 2/Lieut. R.F.Grant appointed Unit Salvage Officer.	
	" 28.		General Musketry Course continued.	
	" 29.		Baths. Demobilization started. 81 O/Ranks proceed to Dispersal Stations.	
	" 30.		'C' Coy. continue G.M.C.,	

James H. Gordon.
Major,
Commanding, 1/4TH BATTALION THE GORDON HIGHLANDERS.

14TH SEPTEMBER 1919.

D. D. & L., London, E.C. (A8004) Wt. W1771/M2031 750,000 5/17 Sch. 52 Forms/C2118/14

1/4TH BATTALION THE GORDON HIGHLANDERS.

STRENGTH ON 31/8/19.

---*----

	OFFICERS	O/RANKS.
EFFECTIVE	27	758
ATTACHED	3	Nil.
TOTAL	30	758.
DETACHED	11	447
RATION STRENGTH	19	311

HIGHLAND (62nd) DIVISION

3rd HIGHLAND BDE

8th ROYAL HDRS (BLACK WATCH)

1919 MAR – 1919 AUG

(from 9 DN 26 BDE)

Original

Confidential

War Diary

of

8th Bn The Black Watch (R.H.)

1st March to 31st March 1919

(Volume)

From 9 DIV 26 BDE

62 / 187 Bde

XLI

M.47

(6114) Wt. W3906/P1607 2,500,000 7/18 McA & W Ltd (E 3591) Forms W3091/4.

Army Form W.3091.

Cover for Documents.

Nature of Enclosures.

Notes, or Letters written.

8th (S) Battalion The Black Watch (R.H.)

Instructions regarding War Diaries and Intelligence Summaries are contained in F. S. Regs., Part II. and the Staff Manual respectively. Title pages will be prepared in manuscript.

WAR DIARY
or
~~INTELLIGENCE SUMMARY.~~

(Erase heading not required.)

Army Form C. 2118.

Place	Date	Hour	Summary of Events and Information	Remarks and references to Appendices
	1919.			
SOLINGEN	1st March		Battalion moved by train from SOLINGEN to MECHERNICH departing from SOLINGEN STATION at 15 10 hours, and arriving at MECHERNICH approximately at 24 00 hours. The band of the 5th CAMERON HIGHLANDERS played the Battalion to SOLINGEN Station, and the massed pipes and drums of the 7th SEAFORTH HIGHLANDERS and the 5th CAMERON HIGHLANDERS played a farewell to the battalion before the train steamed out – on the occasion of the departure of the Battalion from the 9th Division.	
BURVENICH	2nd March.		Battalion proceeded from MECHERNICH Station by march route to BURVENICH where they were billeted; coming under orders of the 187th Infantry Brigade.	WJ
	3rd March		COMMANDING OFFICER inspected draft which joined Battalion on 28th ulto. Usual Battalion parades.	
	4th March		Usual Battalion parades. Baths.	
	5th March		Usual Battalion parades.	
	6th March		Usual Battalion parades	
MERZENICH	7th March		Battalion moved by route march from BURVENICH to ZULPICH, by rail ZULPICH to DUREN, and by route march DUREN to MERZENICH, where battalion was billeted	WJ

A7092. Wt W128 9/M1293 750,000. 1/17. D. D & L., Ltd. Forms/C2118/14.

Army Form C. 2118.

WAR DIARY

~~INTELLIGENCE SUMMARY.~~

(Erase heading not required.)

Instructions regarding War Diaries and Intelligence Summaries are contained in F. S. Regs., Part II. and the Staff Manual respectively. Title pages will be prepared in manuscript.

Place	Date	Hour	Summary of Events and Information	Remarks and references to Appendices
MERZENICH	1919 March 8th.		Usual Battalion Parades.	
	9th March		Divine Service. One Company Relieved guard of 2/20th London Regt at MALMEDY.	WJ
	10th March.		Three Companies marched to DUREN + relieved 2/20th London Regt taking over duties as Staff of Second Army Demobilisation Camp (two Companies) Other Company on railway guard duties at DUREN Station	
	11th March		Two Companies on Staff of Second Army Demobilisation Camp, DUREN One Company on guard at Malmedy + One Company on railway guard at DUREN STATION	WJ
	12th March		Two Companies on staff of Second Army Demobilisation Camp DUREN, One Company on guard at Malmedy + one Company on railway guard at DUREN Station	
	13th March		Two Companies on Staff of Second Army Demobilisation Camp DUREN, One Company on guard at MALMEDY + one Company on railway guard at DUREN Station	
	14th March		Two Companies on Staff of Second Army Demobilisation Camp DUREN. One Company on guard at MALMEDY + one Company on railway guard at DUREN Stn.	WJ

A7092. Wt. W128 9/M1293 750,000. 1/17. D. D & L., Ltd. Forms/C. 18/14.

Army Form C. 2118.

Instructions regarding War Diaries and Intelligence Summaries are contained in F. S. Regs., Part II, and the Staff Manual respectively. Title pages will be prepared in manuscript.

WAR DIARY

or

~~INTELLIGENCE SUMMARY.~~

(Erase heading not required.)

Place	Date	Hour	Summary of Events and Information	Remarks and references to Appendices
GERMANY MALMEDY & DUREN.	15th March.		Two Companies on Staff of Second Army Demobilisation Camp DUREN. One Company on guard at MALMEDY & one Company on railway guard at DUREN Station.	
	16th March		Two Companies on Staff of Second Army Demobilisation Camp DUREN. One Company on guard at MALMEDY & one Company on railway guard at DUREN Station	[initials]
	17th March		Two Companies on Staff of Second Army Demobilisation Camp. DUREN. One Company on guard at MALMEDY & one Company on railway guard at DUREN Station	
VETTWEISS & MALMEDY	18th March.		One Company on guard at MALMEDY. Remainder of Battalion moved from DUREN by route march to VETTWEISS where they were billeted	[initials]
	19th ~~March~~		undernoted officer joined this date. Lieut A MORRISON	
	19th March		One Company on guard at MALMEDY. Remainder of Battalion usual parades.	
	20th March		One Company on guard at MALMEDY. Remainder of Battalion Usual parades. The under-mentioned are awarded Meritorious Service Medals: supplement to London Gazette 17/-1819 S/3596 Cpl J McINTYRE. M.M. S/16267 Sgt W STEVENSON S/7265 L/Cpl. J. FOTHERINGHAM	[initials]

(A9175) Wt W2359/P360 600,000 12/17 D. D. & L. Sch. 52a. Forms/C2118/15.

Instructions regarding War Diaries and Intelligence Summaries are contained in F. S. Regs., Part II. and the Staff Manual respectively. Title pages will be prepared in manuscript.

WAR DIARY

~~or INTELLIGENCE SUMMARY~~.

(Erase heading not required.)

Army Form C. 2118.

Place	Date	Hour	Summary of Events and Information	Remarks and references to Appendices
VETTWEISS + MALMEDY	21st March.		One Company on guard at MALMEDY. Remainder of Battalion Usual parades.	
			Draft of 93 Other ranks joined from 13th (Scottish Horse) Battn The Black Watch (R.H.)	
			Undernoted Officers joined this date:	
			Capt A.F. ROBERTSON	
			2/Lieut C. F. FOSTER	WJ
			2/Lieut T. PRICE.	
	22nd March		One Company on guard at MALMEDY Remainder of Battalion Usual parades.	
	23rd March		One Company on guard at MALMEDY. Remainder of Battalion Divine Service.	
			Draft of 95 Other ranks joined from 14th (Fife & Forfar Yeomanry) Batt. The Black Watch (RH)	WJ
			Undernoted Officers joined this date	
			Lieut G. D. M. BEARD.	
			2/Lieut J. E. RIDDELL.	
	24th March		One Company on guard at MALMEDY. Remainder of Battalion Usual parades.	WJ

(A9175) Wt W2358/P360 600,000 12/17 D. D. & L. Sch. 52a. Forms/C2118/15.

Instructions regarding War Diaries and Intelligence Summaries are contained in F. S. Regs., Part II, and the Staff Manual respectively. Title pages will be prepared in manuscript.

WAR DIARY
or
~~INTELLIGENCE SUMMARY~~.
(Erase heading not required.)

Army Form C. 2118.

Place	Date	Hour	Summary of Events and Information	Remarks and references to Appendices
VETTWEISS + MALMADY	25th March		One Company on guard at MALMADY. Remainder of Battn usual parades. Draft of 127 Other ranks joined from 4/5th Battn The Black Watch (RH)	WJ
	26th March		One Company on guard at MALMEDY. Remainder of Battalion usual parades	
	27th March		One Company on guard at MALMEDY. Remainder of Battalion usual parades. Baths. The following BELGIAN decorations have been awarded:- CHEVALIER de l'ordre de la COURONNE and CROIX de GUERRE: CAPTAIN A. L. MILROY M.C. DECORATION MILITAIRE 2nd Class + CROSS de GUERRE No. 29,000 Sgt W. WALKER	WJ
	28th March		One Company on guard at MALMEDY. Remainder of Battalion usual parades	WJ

(A9175) Wt W2358/P360 600,000 12/17 D. D. & L. Sch. 52a. Forms/C2118/15.

Army Form C. 2118.

Instructions regarding War Diaries and Intelligence Summaries are contained in F. S. Regs., Part II, and the Staff Manual respectively. Title pages will be prepared in manuscript.

WAR DIARY
or
~~INTELLIGENCE SUMMARY.~~

(Erase heading not required.)

Place	Date	Hour	Summary of Events and Information	Remarks and references to Appendices
VETTWEISS + MALMEDY	29th March		One Company on guard at MALMEDY. Remainder of Battalion Usual Parades.	
			Undernoted Officer joined this date	
			2/Lieut J. ROSS.	
	30th March		One Company on guard at MALMEDY. Remainder of Battalion Divine Service.	
			Draft of 21 Other ranks joined this date from 13th (Scottish Horse) Battn The Black Watch (R.H.)	
	31st March		One Company on guard at MALMEDY. Remainder of Battalion Usual parades.	
			APPENDIX "A" EDUCATION	
			APPENDIX "B" DEMOBILISATION	
			APPENDIX "C" SPORT.	
			D. French [illegible] Lieut Colonel	
			Commanding 8th (S) Battn The Black Watch (R.H.)	

(A9175) Wt W2358/P360 600,000 12/17 D. D. & L. Sch. 52a. Forms/C2118/15.

Army Form C. 2118.

Instructions regarding War Diaries and Intelligence Summaries are contained in F. S. Regs., Part II, and the Staff Manual respectively. Title pages will be prepared in manuscript.

WAR DIARY
or
INTELLIGENCE SUMMARY.
(*Erase heading not required.*)

EDUCATION
APPENDIX "A"

Place	Date	Hour	Summary of Events and Information	Remarks and references to Appendices
			EDUCATION.	
	31/3/19		During the month of March very little "Education" was done in this Battalion, owing mainly to Battalion movements. At the beginning of the month the battalion left the 9th Division to join the 63rd, consequently students at the 9th Divisional College were recalled, and unit and Brigade classes were temporarily suspended. Men, however, attending courses at Army Workshops & at the Base continued their respective courses of instruction.	
			The results of the examinations for Army School Certificates classes 2 and 3 are now published. All the candidates from this Battalion sat the 2nd class examination. Four candidates were successful at this examination, that is about one-third of the number from this unit competing.	
			[signature] Lieut Colonel Commanding 8th (S) Battn The Black Watch (R.H.)	

(A9175) Wt W2358/P360 600,000 12/17 D. D. & L. Sch. 52a. Forms/C2118/15.

March, 1919.

Instructions regarding War Diaries and Intelligence Summaries are contained in F. S. Regs., Part II. and the Staff Manual respectively. Title pages will be prepared in manuscript.

WAR DIARY or ~~INTELLIGENCE SUMMARY~~.

(Erase heading not required.)

DEMOBILISATION Army Form C. 2118.

APPENDIX "B".

Place	Date	Hour	Summary of Events and Information	Remarks and references to Appendices
			8th Bn. The Black Watch – DEMOBILIZATION.	
GERMANY.	1919. March.		Demobilization in the battalion was suspended from Feb. 14, ~~of~~ owing to the ration strength having fallen to 500. With the arrival of drafts in March, however, it would have been possible to release all the men who were not "volunteers" or "retainables", but only 54 men were demobilized, owing to the small number of vacancies that could be obtained. Ten of these were "demobilizers" and four were sent home on leave, having re-engaged for service in the Regular Army.	
			200078 Pte John Troup was the longest service man released during March, having been overseas upwards of four years.	
			J. F. Calder Lieut. Demobilisation Officer	
			W. Lauk Lieut Col. Commanding 8th (S) Batt The Black Watch (RH)	

A7092 Wt. W128 9/M1293 750,000 1/17 D. D. & L., Ltd. Forms/C2118/14.

Instructions regarding War Diaries and Intelligence Summaries are contained in F. S. Regs., Part II. and the Staff Manual respectively. Title pages will be prepared in manuscript.

WAR DIARY or ~~INTELLIGENCE SUMMARY.~~

(Erase heading not required.)

SPORT

APPENDIX "C"

Army Form C. 2118.

Place	Date	Hour	Summary of Events and Information	Remarks and references to Appendices
VETTWEISS GERMANY	31st March 1919		Football On march 3rd the 3rd round of 9th Div. cup was played at Bismarck Strasse Solingen We were unfortunate in losing a player in the first few minutes but won the game by 1 goal to nil. Opponents 9th Bn. M.G.C. On march 8th we played the semifinal at WALD and beat 9th Scottish Rifles 2 goals to nil. The final was played at HILDEN on March 13th when we beat 9th Seaforth H^rs by 3 goals to 2 after playing extra time. We had a bye into corpscup. Final which was played at MULHEIM on March 18th when we beat 1st Lanc. Fus. by 3 goals to nil A bye again brought us into 2nd Army Semi-Final which was played at COLOGNE P+R.T. ground on 24th March where we beat 5th Dragoon Guards (1st Cav. Div.) by 3 goals to 1. The Final was played at Blucher Park COLOGNE on 28th mar. when we were beaten by 1st Cameron H^rs by 2 goals to 1. winning goal scored in the last second. The month was devoted mostly to Football and nothing of importance occurred in Boxing Running, or other sports. An attempt was made to introduce Ruby and it is hoped to have a team in the near future	

W. French Lieut Colonel
Commanding 8th (S) Batt The Black Watch (R.H.)

(A9175) Wt W2358/P360 650,000 12/17 D. D. & L. Sch. 52a. Forms/C2118/15.

War Diary

File

O.C.,

8th. Bn. The Black Watch (R.H.)

187th. Inf. Bde. BM/57(d).

8th. March 1919.

187th. Inf. Bde. Warning Order No. BM/411 dated 7th. March is confirmed.

1. The following guard at present found by 2/20th. London Regt. at MALMEDY will be taken over by 8th. Bn. The Black Watch (R.H.) on 9th. March 1919.

5 Officers 122 O.Rs. (with 1 Cooker and Lewis Gun Limber).

2. This party will leave DUREN Station by special train at 0907 hours arriving MALMEDY 1447 hours.

Party to report to R.T.O. DUREN 0800 hours.

3. The above numbers include all cooks, orderlies, officers servants etc.

4. The train conveying 8th. Bn. The Black Watch (R.H.) is reloaded at MALMEDY with the troops of 2/20th. London Regt. relieved by your Battalion.

5 Rations for and up to consumption on 11th inst. will be taken.

[signature]

Capt.

Bde. Major,

187th. Inf. Bde.

War Diary

SECRET.

187th. Inf. Bde. BM/57(c).

1st. March 1919.

To Units of Brigade Group.

WARNING ORDER.

1. The 187th. Infantry Brigade is to be transferred to the area occupied at present by the 8th. Infantry Brigade, 3rd. Division.

2. The move will be made by train from ZULPICH Station, commencing 5th. March, 1919.

3. Detailed instructions will be issued later.

4. ACKNOWLEDGE.

File

J.K. Newbigging.
Capt.
Bde. Major,
187th. Inf. Bde.

SECRET. Copy No..1......

187th. (Highland) Infantry Brigade
Warning Order No. 1. 2.3.1919.

---

1. The 62nd. Division is being transferred from the IX Corps to the VI Corps.

2. The 187th. (Highland) Infantry Brigade Group will move by train to the area at present occupied by the 8th. Infantry Brigade, 3rd. Division.

3. The following is a forecast of the moves. Further details will be issued.

Date.	Unit	Entraining Station.	Detraining Station.	Accommodated in
Mar.5th.	1/4th. The Gordon Highlanders.	ZULPICH	BUIR	BUIR
Mar.6th.	1/4th. The Seaforth Highlanders.	-do-	BUIR or DUREN	GOLZHEIM.
-do-	8th. Royal Highlanders.	-do-	DUREN	MERZENICH

4. Dates of entrainment of remainder of units of Brigade Group are not yet settled. Probable destinations are as follows :-

Brigade Headquarters.	BINSFELD.
187th. T. M. B.	BINSFELD.
2/3rd. Field Ambulance.	GIRBELSRATH.
461st. Field Coy. R.E.	FRAUWULLESHEIM.
528th. Coy. R.A.S.C.	ESCHWEILER.

5. Advance Parties from Battalions will proceed by train from ZULPICH to DUREN 48 hours previous to date of entrainment. On arrival they will report at Headquarters 8th. Infantry Brigade, BINSFELD for accommodation. Two days' rations will be carried.

6. Battalions of 187th. (Highland) Infantry Brigade to ACKNOWLEDGE.

J.K. Dunlop [signature]
Capt.
Bde. Major,
187th. Inf. Bde.

Issued through Signals at 1100 hours.

Copies to -
1. 8th. Royal Highlanders.
2. 1/4th. Bn. The Seaforth Highlanders.
3. 1/4th. Bn. The Gordon Highlanders.
4. 187th. T.M.B.
5. 2/3rd. Field Ambulance.
6. 528th. Coy. R.A.S.C.
7. 461st. Field Coy. R.E.
8. Office.

1 officer + 1 NCO for HQ
1 NCO for TM
~~1 NCO for ...~~

1 officer + 1 NCO per Coy

on 4/3/19

[initials]

O.C., Units of Brigade Group
plus 62nd Division 'G'
185th Inf. Bde.

187th Inf. Bde. No. BM/57 (b)

10th March 1919.

1. Reference 187th Infantry Brigade No. BM/57 (e) dated 8th March (sent to 8th Bn. The Black Watch (R.H.) only) the move of the 8th Bn. The Black Watch (R.H.) to DUREN will take place on 12th March.

2. On arrival the Battalion will take over accommodation now occupied by 2/20th London Rgt, together with the duties found by that battalion as already detailed in 187th Inf. Bde, BM/53(e)

3. The move will be carried out under battalion arrangements. the 8th Bn. The Black Watch (R.H.) will be clear of MERZENICH by 1200 hours 12th March.

4. A rear party of 8th Bn. Black Watch will be left behind to hand over billets, stores, etc to advanced party of 6th Bn. The Black Watch (R.H.)

5. On completion of relief of 2/20th London Rgt. 8th Bn. The Black Watch (R.H.) will come under orders of G.O.C. 186th Inf. Bde

War Diary
file

[signature]
Capt.
Bde Major.
187th Inf. Bde.

187th. Inf. Bde. BM/57(e).

O.C.,
8th. Bn. The Black Watch (R.H.)

8th. March 1919.

The following forecast of moves of your Battalion is forwarded for information :-

1. 1/6th. Bn. The Black Watch (R.H.) entrain MECHERNICH on 12th. March, detrain DUREN and take over billets at present occupied by your Battalion.

2. ~~8th. Bn. The Black Watch (R.H.)~~ move to DUREN, either on the 11th. or 12th. March taking over accommodation now occupied by 2/20th. London Regt. together with the duties found by this Battalion.

3. The move of 8th. Bn. The Black Watch (R.H.) to DUREN will be carried out concurrently with the move of the 2/20th. London Regt. who go to the 29th. Division on relief.

4. On completion of the move of the 8th. Bn. The Black Watch (R.H.) to DUREN the Battalion comes under the orders of G.O.C. 186th. Infantry Brigade, under whose orders they will remain until the arrival of the 51st. Bn. The Gordon Highlanders, when the Battalion will be transferred to the 185th. Infantry Brigade.

5. The following is an approximate summary of the duties at present found by 2/20th. London Regt.:-

(a) O.C. Battalion in charge of the Second Army Demobilization Camp, DUREN Barracks.

(b) 12 Officers, 200 O.Rs., Staff for Demobilization Camp.

(c) 8 Officers 36 O.Rs. - Railway duties at DUREN.

(d) 5 Officers, 122 O.Rs. - Supply Guard MALMEDY(Orders already issued).

6. In order to facilitate the move of 8th. Bn. The Black Watch (R.H.) to DUREN, the O.C. Battalion should get into touch with O.C. 2/20th. London Regt. (H.Q. DUREN Barracks) for the purpose of obtaining details regarding accommodation, duties, rations etc.

[illegible signature]
Capt.
Bde. Major,
187th. Inf. Bde.

8th Black Watch.

I am sorry not to have had an opportunity of saying Goodbye personally to the Battalion before it left the Brigade, and to express my thanks for the splendid work the Battalion has done while under my command.

During the 7 months that I have had the privilege of being your Brigadier the Battalion has in all respects enhanced the magnificent reputation which it already possessed, and the dash which it showed during the advance from YPRES to the SCHEIDT, the determination to get on at all costs, and the skill by which the Germans were manouvered out of position after position, showed, during those five weeks of continuous fighting, a spirit and state of efficiency of which any regiment might justly be proud.

The marching of the Battalion from the SCHEIDT to the COLOGNE Bridgehead was a remarkable display of march discipline and endurance, and the exemplary behaviour of the Battalion while in Germany, in difficult circumstances and in spite of many temptations - reflect the greatest credit on all ranks.

It will always remain a proud memory to me to have had under my command such a Battalion under such conditions.

You are carrying with you to the Highland Division a record which few Battalions can equal, and none can surpass, and in bidding you farewell I am confident that you will worthily uphold this record in the days to come.

SEEN	
C.O.	
2 i/c.	
Adj.	
Q.M.	
T.O.	
S.O.	
[illegible]	

SEEN	
"A" Coy	
"B" Coy	
"C" Coy	
"D" Coy	
[illegible]	
[illegible]	

P. Hore-Ruthven.

Brigadier-General.,
Commanding 26th Infantry Brigade.,

Solingen.,
Germany.,
16th March 1919.,

To/
ALL UNITS,
9th (Scottish) Division.

The time has come for me to say farewell to my comrades of the 9th (Scottish) Division.

Whilst tendering them my heartfelt thanks I wish to express my great admiration for the Officers, N.C.Os. and Men who by their pride in the Division, their devotion to duty and their valour have made so glorious the imperishable name of the 9th Division.

The 3 years I have served with you have been the most memorable of my life; and that I have had the honour of commanding you for a year will ever be my proudest thought. By your constant support and friendship you have made my task a happy one. I have always been supremely confident that you are invincible in defence and matchless in attack.

Goodbye and good luck.

H.H. TUDOR,
Major-General,
Commanding 9th (Scottish) Division.

17/3/19.

War Diary

SEEN	
C.O.	
2 i/c.	
Adj.	
Q.M.	
[illegible]	
[illegible]	
[illegible]	

SEEN	
"A" Coy	
"B" Coy	
"C" Coy	
"D" Coy	
H.Q.	
[illegible]	

Original

Confidential

War Diary

of

8th Bn. The Black Watch

From 1st May 1919 to 31st May 1919.

M.45

(6392) Wt. W6192/P875 1,500,000 4/18 McA & W Ltd (E 2815) Forms W3091/4. Army Form W.3091.

Cover for Documents.

Nature of Enclosures.

Notes, or Letters written.

May

Army Form C. 2118.

Instructions regarding War Diaries and Intelligence Summaries are contained in F. S. Regs., Part II, and the Staff Manual respectively. Title pages will be prepared in manuscript.

8th (Service) Battalion WAR DIARY or INTELLIGENCE SUMMARY. THE BLACK WATCH.

(Erase heading not required.)

Place	Date	Hour	Summary of Events and Information	Remarks and references to Appendices
BUIR.	1/5/19.	09.30-12.30	Company and Platoon Training.	[initials]
do	2/5/19.	09.30-12.30	Do Do.	[initials]
do	3/5/19.	09.30-12.30	Do Do.	[initials]
do	4/5/19.	10.00	Church Parade to Y.M.C.A. Hut.	[initials]
do	5/5/19.	09.30-12.30	Company and Platoon ~~Exit~~ Training.	[initials]
do	6/5/19.	09.30-12.30	Do Do.	[initials]
do	7/5/19.	09.30-12.30	Do Do.	[initials]
do	8/5/19.	09.30-12.30	Do Do.	[initials]
BUIR-MAUBACH.	9/5/19.	09.00	Battalion Personnel moved off (by train) to MAUBACH, near DUREN. Transport by road	[initials]
MAUBACH.	10/5/19.		Day spent in settling down in new billets.	[initials]
do	11/5/19.	10.00	Church Parade to Y.M.C.A. Hut.	[initials]
do	12/5/19.	09.30-12.30	Company and Platoon Training.	[initials]
do	13/5/19.	09.30-12.30	Do Do.	[initials]
do	14/5/19.		Do Do, Working Party at BOGHEIM isolated.	[initials]
do	15/5/19.		Unit Registers ("A","B" & "D" Coys, MALMEDY) inspected.	[initials]
do	16/5/19.	09.30-12.30	Company and Platoon Training.	

(A9175) Wt W2358/P360 600,000 12/17 D. D. & L. Sch. 52a. Forms/C2118/15.

8th (Service) Battalion   Page 2   The B L A C K W A T C H.   Army Form C. 2118.

WAR DIARY
or
~~INTELLIGENCE SUMMARY~~.
(Erase heading not required.)

Instructions regarding War Diaries and Intelligence Summaries are contained in F. S. Regs., Part II, and the Staff Manual respectively. Title pages will be prepared in manuscript.

Place	Date	Hour	Summary of Events and Information	Remarks and references to Appendices
MAUBACH.	17/5/19.	09.30-12.30	Company and Platoon Training.	AWJ
do	18/5/19.	10.00 ~~09.30-12.30~~	Church Parade to Y.M.C.A. Hut.	AWJ
do	19/5/19	09.30-12.30	Company and Platoon Training.	AWJ
do	20/5/19.	09.30-12.30	Do Do.	AWJ
do	21/5/19.	09.30-12.30	Do Do.	AWJ
do	22/5/19.	09.30-12.30	Do Do.	AWJ
do	23/5/19.	09.30-12.30	Do Do.	AWJ
do	24/5/19.		"D" Coy arrive from MALMEDY.	AWJ
			Messing Committee formed consisting of 1 representative from each Coy& Headqrs.	AWJ
do	25/5/19.	10.00	Church Parade to Y.M.C.A. Hut.	AWJ
do	26/5/19.	09.30-12.30	Company and Platoon Training.	AWJ
do	27/5/19.		"D" Company commence a week's progressive training.	AWJ
			Education Classes commence.	AWJ
do	28/5/19.	09.30-12.30	Company and Platoon Training under Coy arrangements.	AWJ
do	29/5/19.		"B" & "C" Coys Kit Inspection & reorganization of Platoons	AWJ
do	30/5/19		Divisional Commander inspected Transport. Coy & Plat. Training	AWJ
do	31/5/19		Working Party at BOCHHEIM rejoined Battn. Subalterns & NCOs under Adjutant	

V M Fortune
LIEUT.-COLONEL
COMMANDING 8th BATTALION THE BLACK WATCH

(A9175) Wt W2358/P360 600,000 12/17 D. D. & L. Sch. 52a. Forms/C2118/15.

Appendix "A"

Army Form C. 2118.

Instructions regarding War Diaries and Intelligence Summaries are contained in F. S. Regs., Part II, and the Staff Manual respectively. Title pages will be prepared in manuscript.

WAR DIARY or INTELLIGENCE SUMMARY.

8th (S) Battalion The BLACK WATCH.

DEMOBILIZATION.

(Erase heading not required.)

Place	Date	Hour	Summary of Events and Information	Remarks and references to Appendices
BUIR-MAUBACH.	MAY.		During May, 60 N.C.O.s and men were demobilized from this Battalion. Early in the month G.H.Q. definitely ordered the release of all "Pivital" men, irrespective of age and service and fifty of these were despatched. The great majority were ploughmen who enlisted in 1918	
			Two men were released on Compassionate Grounds.	
			Major I.W.W. SHEPHERD, M.C. was demobilized on 7th May, after serving over two years and a half with the 8th Battalion The BLACK WATCH.	
			No less than 39 applications for release on Compassionate Grounds were dealt with during May but after investigations only four of these were found to be sufficiently extreme cases for forwarding to Higher Authorities.	
			The "Unit Register" of the Battalion was made up during the month to include the names of all the new drafts.	AW
			(Sgd) H.F.CALDER, Lieut Demobilization Officer, 8th (S) Battalion The BLACK WATCH.	

(A9175) Wt W2358/P360 600,000 12/17 D. D. & L. Sch. 52a. Forms/C2118/15.

Appendix "B"

Army Form C. 2118.

Instructions regarding War Diaries and Intelligence Summaries are contained in F. S. Regs., Part II. and the Staff Manual respectively. Title pages will be prepared in manuscript.

WAR DIARY or ~~INTELLIGENCE SUMMARY.~~

8th (Service) Battalion The BLACK WATCH.

(*Erase heading not required.*)

Place	Date	Hour	Summary of Events and Information	Remarks and references to Appendices
			EDUCATION.	
BUIR-MAUBACH.	MAY.		During May, Education has re-commenced in the Battalion.	
			Men have enrolled in most of the Groups indicated in the Schedule of Subjects, Elementary and Intermediate (see War Office Letter 2176 of 20th Novr., 1919.) Classes are being conducted in the "A" Group. Subjects in which the men show a keen interest.	
			A good supply of Text Books and Stationery has been received, and, given the necessary accomodation for holding classes, good progress in Education will be made in the near future.	
			(Sgd) J. BLACK, Lieut Education Officer, 8th (S) Battalion The BLACK WATCH.	[initials]

(A9175) Wt W2358/P360 600,000 12/17 D. D. & L. Sch. 52a. Forms/C2118/15.

Original.

Confidential.

War Diary

of

8th. Bn. The Black Watch. (R.H.).

From 1st. June 1919 To 30th. June 1919.

(Volume VI)

Army Form C. 2118.

Instructions regarding War Diaries and Intelligence Summaries are contained in F. S. Regs., Part II. and the Staff Manual respectively. Title pages will be prepared in manuscript.

8th (Service) Battalion The B L A C K W A T C H.

WAR DIARY
or
~~INTELLIGENCE SUMMARY.~~
(*Erase heading not required.*)

J U N E. 1 9 1 9.

Place	Date	Hour	Summary of Events and Information	Remarks and references to Appendices
MAUBACH.	1st		Church Services in Y. M. C. A. Hut.	A.G.
Do	2nd		Ceremonial Practice Parade.(near MAUBACH Station.)	A.G.
Do	3rd		Ceremonial Parade at MAUBACH Station for H.M. The KING'S Birthday. Remainder of the day, holiday.	A.G.
Do	4th		Company and Platoon Training.	A.G.
Do	5th		Do Do.	A.G.
Do	6th		C-in-C inspected the Battalion. The turn-out of both Men and Transport was most creditable	A.G.
			to all concerned and the March Past, very good.	
Do	7th		Company and Platoon Training.	A.G.
Do	8th		Church Services in the Y. M. C. A. Hut.	A.G.
Do	9th		Company and Platoon Training. Lieut W. F. MACRAE joined the Battalion from 5th Cameron Highlanders	A.G.
			and posted to "B" Coy.	
Do	10th		Company and Platoon Training.	A.G.
Do	11th		Divisional Commander visited the Battalion and inspected all the Companies in Training,	A.G.
			commencing with "C" Company at 10.00 hours.	
Do	12th		Company and Platoon Training.	A.G.
Do	13th		Company Commanders Conference. It was decided that Officers Servts etc employed in Headqrs Mess	
			attend Educational Classes two days per week / 13th	

(A9175) Wt W2358/P560 600,000 12/17 D. D. & L. Sch. 52a. Forms/C2118/15.

Instructions regarding War Diaries and Intelligence Summaries are contained in F. S. Regs., Part II. and the Staff Manual respectively. Title pages will be prepared in manuscript.

Army Form C. 2118.

8th (Service)Battn WAR DIARY The B L A C K W A T C H.
Continued. INTELLIGENCE SUMMARY.

(*Erase heading not required.*)

J U N E. 1 9 1 9.

Place	Date	Hour	Summary of Events and Information	Remarks and references to Appendices
MAUBACH.	13th		Company and Platoon Training.	A.S.
Do	14th		Do Do.	A.S.
Do	15th		Church Services in Y. M. C. A. Hut.	A.S.
Do	16th		Company and Platoon Training. Captain GLEN, M.C.(O.C. "B" Coy)took over Command of the Battalion	A.S.
			whilst Lieut-Colonel FORTUNE, D.S.O. on leave to U.K.	
Do	17th		Battalion- less 1 Officer and 14 O.R.s- left MAUBACH,by train, enroute for BENRATH.	A.S.
			The Battalion, on arrival at DUREN, marched to BIRKESDORF(3 Kilos) and remained there overnight.	
			releiving 5th Gordon Highlanders who proceeded to - -	A.S.
Do.BIRKS-	18th	15.15	Battalion left BIRKESDORF and marched to DUREN Station, where they entrained at 18.30 hours	A.S.
-DORF-BENRATH.			for HILDEN. HILDEN was reached at 21.30 hours, thereafter the Battalion marched to BENRATH a	
			distance of 3-4 Kilos, and were billeted there. Transport left DUREN at 22.00 hours and arrived	
			at BENRATH at 04.00 hours.	A.S.
BENRATH.	19th		Posts named below, held by the 9th Scottish Rifles, were taken over by the following Coys:-	

POST.	Relieved by	POST.	Relieved by	POST.	Relieved by.
DICKHAUS	"A" Coy	KEMPERDICK	"A" Coy.	MEIDE.	"A" Coy.
HOLTHAUSEN.	"B" "	HIMMELGUIST	"C" "	BENRATH.	"D" "
REISHOLZ	"D" "	FRIEDHOF	"B" "	DAMSTEIG	"D" "

A.S.

(A6475) Wt W2358/P360 600,000 12/17 D. D. & L. Sch. 52a. Forms/C2118/15.

Army Form C. 2118.

Instructions regarding War Diaries and Intelligence Summaries are contained in F. S. Regs., Part II, and the Staff Manual respectively. Title pages will be prepared in manuscript.

8th (Service) WAR DIARY Battn The BLACK WATCH. Continued. ~~INTELLIGENCE SUMMARY.~~

JUNE. (Erase heading not required.) 1919.

Place	Date	Hour	Summary of Events and Information	Remarks and references to Appendices
BENRATH	19th		Lieut-COLONEL V.M. FORTUNE, D.S.O. recalled fro leave.	A.G.
BENRATH.	20th		Normal Routine- Examining Posts, etc.	A.G.
Do	21st		Do. Do.	A.G.
Do	22nd		Church Services in Scottish Churches' Hut- The Very Revd Dr WALLACE WILLUAMSON, D.D. M.V.O.	A.G.
			conducted the Service (representative of Churches in Scotland)	
Do	23rd	06.50	Telegram received that Germans intended to sign the Peace Treaty. Firing at Posts ceased.	A.G.
Do	24th		Posts visited by the Commander-in-Chief.	A.G.
Do	25th		Normal Routine.	A.G.
Do	26th		Do.	A.G.
Do	27th		Do.	A.G.
Do	28th	18.45	Telegram received that Germans had signed the Peace Treaty. There was no demonstration by the	
			Troops.	A.G.
Do	29th		Church Services in Scottish Churches' Hut.	A.G.
Do	30		Advance Parties left for Billeting purposes at BIRKESDORF & UNT-MAUBACH. Normal Routine	A.G.
			Companies relieved by Troops of the Lowland Division.	

A.G.[illegible] Captain
for Lieut-Colonel,
Commanding, 8th (S) Battalion The BLACK WATCH.

attached (a) Demobilization. (b) Education.

(A9175) W: W2358/P360 600,000 12/17 D. D. & L. Sch. 52a. Forms/C2118/15.

Appendix "A".

Army Form C. 2118.

8th (Service) Battalion The BLACK WATCH.

WAR DIARY

~~or~~

DEMOBILIZATION. ~~INTELLIGENCE SUMMARY~~.

Instructions regarding War Diaries and Intelligence Summaries are contained in F. S. Regs., Part II. and the Staff Manual respectively. Title pages will be prepared in manuscript.

J U N E. (*Erase heading not required.*) 1 9 1 9.

Place	Date	Hour	Summary of Events and Information	Remarks and references to Appendices
MAUBACH.			During the month of JUNE, thirteen men were sent fordispersal, including Staff Armourer Sergeant J. WOOD who had served with the Battalion for over four years.	
			Numerous applications for release on Compassionate Grounds were dealt with, none of which however came within the meaning of Army Council Instructions 287 of 1919, which definitely lay down the grounds upon which claims for release on extreme Compassionate Grounds are to be considered.	A.G.

Appendix 'B'

Army Form C. 2118.

8th(S) Battalion The BLACK WATCH.

WAR DIARY

~~or~~

~~INTELLIGENCE SUMMARY.~~

(Erase heading not required.)

Instructions regarding War Diaries and Intelligence Summaries are contained in F. S. Regs., Part II. and the Staff Manual respectively. Title pages will be prepared in manuscript.

EDUCATION.

J U N E. 1 9 1 9.

Place	Date	Hour	Summary of Events and Information	Remarks and references to Appendices
MAUBACH.			During the month of June all the available N.C.O.s and Men of the Battalion attended classes in Group "A" Subjects (English and Arithmetic -Elementary, Intermediate and Advanced.)	
			In addition, a voluntary class in French has been started and is being exceedingly well attend-ed.	
			~~Further, for the purpose of giving men who desire it the opportunity of training in a Trade~~ Men have been attached to the Regimental Tailor for Tailoring, to the Regimental Shoemaker for Shoemaking, to the Pioneers for Joinery and Painting, to the Gardener for Gardening and Agric-ulture, and to the Poultry Farm for Poultry rearing.	A.S.

(A9175) Wt W2358/P360 600,000 12/17 D. D. & L. Sch. 52a. Forms/C2118/15.

Confidential

War Diary

of

8th Bn. Black Watch (R.H.)

From 1st July 1919 ~ To ~ 31st July 1919.

Original.

Volume IV

(14) Wt. W3906/P1607 2,500,000 7/18 McA & W Ltd (E 3591) Forms W3091/4.

Army Form W.3091.

Cover for Documents.

Nature of Enclosures.

Notes, or Letters written.

Army Form C. 2118.

WAR DIARY or ~~INTELLIGENCE~~ ~~SUMMARY~~

8th (S) Battalion The BLACK WATCH.

Instructions regarding War Diaries and Intelligence Summaries are contained in F. S. Regs., Part II, and the Staff Manual respectively. Title pages will be prepared in manuscript.

JULY. 1919.

(Erase heading not required.)

Place	Date	Hour	Summary of Events and Information	Remarks and references to Appendices
BENRATH-	1st	13.00	Battalion marched from BENRATH to HILDEN where they entrained for DUREN at 15.30 hours, arriving	
-BIRKES-			at DUREN at 18.30 hours. On arrival at DUREN, Battalion marched to BIRKESDORF and remained there	
-DORF.			overnight. Transport proceeded direct to UNT-MAUBACH (by Rail) with the exception of Company	
			Cookers which accompanied their respective Companies to BIRKESDORF.	A.S.
BIRKESDORF-	2nd	09.30	Battalion paraded and marched to DUREN Station and entrained for Unt-MAUBACH. Company Cookers	A.S.
-MAUBACH.			went by road. On arrival at MAUBACH at 12.00 hours Companies marched to their new Company Areas	
			and the remainder of the day was spent in settling down in billets etc.	A.S.
MAUBACH.	3rd		Day spent in settling down in billets and organization of Platoons, etc.	A.S.
	4th		Do Do.	A.S.
	5th		Bathing Parades and Clothing and Kit Inspections.	A.S.
	6th		G.O.C. 3rd Highland Brigade inspected Camp after Church Service.	A.S.
	7th		Parades according to Training Programmes.	A.S.
	8th		Do.	A.S.
	9th		Observed as Peace Day in the Army of the Rhine. In the afternoon Company Sports were held and	A.S.
			in the evening a Battalion Concert.	
	10th		Training accordding to Programme.	A.S.

(A9175) Wt W2358/P360 600,000 12/17 D. D. & L. Sch. 52a. Forms/C2118/15.

Instructions regarding War Diaries and Intelligence Summaries are contained in F. S. Regs., Part II, and the Staff Manual respectively. Title pages will be prepared in manuscript.

Army Form C. 2118.

WAR DIARY or ~~INTELLIGENCE SUMMARY~~.

8th (S) Battalion The BLACK WATCH.

(Erase heading not required.)

JULY. 1919.

Place	Date	Hour	Summary of Events and Information	Remarks and references to Appendices
MAUBACH.	11th		~~Company~~ Force ~~Commanders Conference at Brigade Headqrs at 10.30 hours~~. A.S.	
		11.30	Commander-in-Chief visited the Battalion and inspected Camps and Training.	A.S.
	12th		Divisional Commander gave an address in the Y.M.C.A. Hut at 09.30 hours.80 O.R.s from eachCoy	
			30, O.R.s from Headqrs and 15 O.R.s from Transport attended.	A.S.
	13th		Church Services.	A.S.
	14th		Training according to Programme. B.F. & P.T. Class for Officers and N.C.O.s at 14.00 hours	A.S.
	15th		Training according to Programme.	A.S.
	16th		Trench Mortar Demonstration at Quarry, between BOGHEIM and LANGENBROICH.	A.S.
			2/Lt M.J.DEMPSEY, 2/Lt J.B.POLLOCK and 2/Lieut FRASER, M.C. reported ~~from~~ for duty from 53rd	
			Battalion The BLACK WATCH.	
	17th		Training according to Programme.	A.S.
	18th		Corps Commander visited Camps and Cookhouses at 11.00 hours Ordinary Routine not interfered	
			with.	A.S.
	19th		Holiday throughout the Army.	A.S.
	20th		Church Services.	A.S.
	21st		Training according to Programme.	A.S.

(A9275) Wt W2358/P360 600,000 12/17 D. D. & L. Sch. 52a. Forms/C2118/15.

Instructions regarding War Diaries and Intelligence Summaries are contained in F. S. Regs., Part II. and the Staff Manual respectively. Title pages will be prepared in manuscript.

Army Form C. 2118.

8th (S) Battalion The **WAR DIARY** or **INTELLIGENCE SUMMARY.** BLACKWATCH.

(Erase heading not required.)

JULY. 1919.

Place	Date	Hour	Summary of Events and Information	Remarks and references to Appendices
MAUBACH.	22nd		Major R.E.ANSTRUTHER, M.C. having joind., from 3rd Battn The BLACK WATCH, assumed the duties	
			of Second-in-Command of the Battalion.	AG
	23rd	11.00	Rev W.G.HEASLETT lectured in Y.M.C.A. on "Venereal Disease"	AG.
			At Company Commanders Conference it was decided that each Company Commander would receive One	
			Silver and Two Bronze Medals, to be presented to the three best shots in connection with the	
			Shooting Competition, taking place on 28th July.	AG
	~~24th~~		Transport Competition (Brigade) 1st,6th Battn The BLACK WATCH. 2nd;8th(S) Bn The BLACK WATCH	AG.
	24th		Training according to Programme.	AG.
	25th		Do Do	AG.
	26th		Do Do	AG
	27th		Church Services.	AG
	28th		Eliminating Competitions for Shooting Contest.	AG.
	29th		Battalion Shooting Competition.	
			Lt-Colonel V.M.FORTUNE, D.S.O. proceeded to Command Rhine Army School Of Musketry. Major R.E. ANSTRUTHER, M.C. assumed Command of the Battalion vice Lt-Col FORTUNE, D.S.O.	
			Captain A. GLEN, M.C. (O.C. "B" Coy) appointed 2nd-in-Command.	AG.

(A9175) Wt W2358/P360 600,000 12/17 D. D. & L. Sch. 52a. Forms/C2118/15.

Army Form C. 2118.

Instructions regarding War Diaries and Intelligence Summaries are contained in F. S. Regs., Part II, and the Staff Manual respectively. Title pages will be prepared in manuscript.

8th (S) Battalion The **WAR DIARY** B L A C K W A T C H.

~~or INTELLIGENCE SUMMARY.~~

(Erase heading not required.)

Place	Date	Hour	Summary of Events and Information	Remarks and references to Appendices
MAUBACH.	29th	Cont.	Lieut Macrae, 2nd-in-Command, "B" Coy appointed O.C. "B" Coy vice Captn GLEN, M.C.	AG
	30th		Eliminating heats for Regimental Sports.	AG
	31st		Regimental Sports (See Appendix "C" -Sports.	AG
			[signature] Major,	
			Commanding, 8th (S) Battalion The BLACK WATCH.	
			Attached-Appendix "A" "B" & "C"	

(A9175) Wt W2358/P360 600,000 12/17 D. D. & L. Sch. 52a. Forms/C2118/15.

Instructions regarding War Diaries and Intelligence Summaries are contained in F. S. Regs., Part II, and the Staff Manual respectively. Title pages will be prepared in manuscript.

8th (S) Battalion The **WAR DIARY** BLACK WATCH.
or
~~INTELLIGENCE SUMMARY~~.
JULY, 1919.
(Erase heading not required.)

Army Form C. 2118.

Place	Date	Hour	Summary of Events and Information	Remarks and references to Appendices
MAUBACH.			DEMOBILIZATION - Appendix "A".	
			Thirteen men were demobilized during July, 1919 and one man was sent for leave, having re-en-listed for 2 years. Two men were released on Extreme Compassionate Grounds.	
			Sixteen Compassionate cases were dealt with during the month. The majority of these were found after investigation, not to conform to the requirements of Army Council Instructions 287 and 421, but two were put forward for decision.	
			A Return differentiating between "Derby" men and other Retainable men, was among the many returns called for during JULY.	AS

(A9175) Wt W2358/P360 600,000 12/17 D. D. & L. Sch. 52a. Forms/C2118/15.

Instructions regarding War Diaries and Intelligence Summaries are contained in F. S. Regs., Part II. and the Staff Manual respectively. Title pages will be prepared in manuscript.

8th (S) Battalion The BLACK WATCH.

WAR DIARY ~~or~~ ~~**INTELLIGENCE SUMMARY.**~~ (Erase heading not required.)

JULY, 1919.

Army Form C. 2118.

Place	Date	Hour	Summary of Events and Information	Remarks and references to Appendices
			EDUCATION- Appendix "B".	
			Classes. :- During the month of July. Satisfactory progress has been made in Education throughout the Battalion. The compulsory Group "A" Subjects in the Elementary and Intermediate stages are being taken up with increased interest. The following special subjects, German, French, Book-Keeping, Shorthand, Mathematics, and Music are showing good results. These being voluntary subjects, the student is of a better class and more anxious to learn than the type found in Group "A".	
			The stock of Animals, hens and chickens has increased in the Battalion during the month and consequently more men are benefiting by the practical experience of Farming them. Each Company is allotted a portion of land for gardening purposes to which men are attached for instructions.	
			Courses :- The following number of N.C.O.s and Men have been sent to Courses during the month within the Division. General Course School- 13. N.C.O.s 8 Men.	
			Agricultural School. - 12. N.C.O.s	
			Names have been submitted for the Army Technical College, and a full allotment of men are prepared to proceed, on instructions being received. Vacancies in Technical, Commercial and Agricultura, /	

(A0175) Wt W2358/P360 600,000 12/17 D. D. & L. Sch. 52a. Forms/C2118/15.

Instructions regarding War Diaries and Intelligence Summaries are contained in F. S. Regs., Part II, and the Staff Manual respectively. Title pages will be prepared in manuscript.

8th (S) Battalion The **WAR DIARY** ~~or~~ ~~**INTELLIGENCE**~~ **SUMMARY.** BLACK WATCH.

(*Erase heading not required.*)

Army Form C. 2118.

Place	Date	Hour	Summary of Events and Information	Remarks and references to Appendices
			E D U C A T I O N- Appendix "B" Continued.	
MAUBACH.			Agricultural Courses are being eagerly sought after by the men and more liberal allotment in many cases could have been accepted.	
			GENERAL.- The Choir and Orchestra formed some time ago are giving satisfactory results in the various subjects they are called upon to attend. A Circulating library is running con- -junction with the Y.M.C.A. at Battalion Headqrs, Another has been opened in the area belonging to an outlying Company. Both libraries are being largely patronized by all ranks.	AS.

(A9175) Wt W2358/P360 600,000 12/17 D. D. & L. Sch. 52a. Forms/C2118/15.

Army Form C. 2118.

Instructions regarding War Diaries and Intelligence Summaries are contained in F. S. Regs., Part II. and the Staff Manual respectively. Title pages will be prepared in manuscript.

8th (S) Battalion The WAR DIARY BLACK WATCH.

~~INTELLIGENCE SUMMARY.~~

JULY. (Erase heading not required.) 1919.

Place	Date	Hour	Summary of Events and Information	Remarks and references to Appendices
			SPORTS - Appendix "C".	
MAUBACH.			During the early part of the month Battalion was on duty at BENRATH and no opportunity of having any Sports were available. On returning to MAUBACH Company Football League was resumed the first match being "C" coy V "B" Coy. "B" Coy won this match- their first victory in the League.	
	9th		Peace Celebrations were held. Each Coy spent the afternoon in Sports and some very successful results were obtained. A second League match was played in which "B" Coy defeated "A" Coy.	
			Brigade Eliminating trials were held for ALDERSHOT Meeting and 1 Offr and 3 Ors passed into Division Eliminating Contests.	
	28th		An Officers' Badminton Tournament was held and being favoured with very good weather, the play was very good and the final was very closely contested.	
			The greater part of the month was spent in training for The Regimental Sports on 30th & 38st.	
			Battalion Football Match was played against 1/4th Seaforths at LENDERSDORF It was keenly contested game and the O - 0. indicates the play.	

Confidential.

War Diary

of

8th Bn. The Black Watch.

from 1st August 1919 to 31st August 1919.

Original.

Instructions regarding War Diaries and Intelligence Summaries are contained in F. S. Regs., Part II. and the Staff Manual respectively. Title pages will be prepared in manuscript.

Army Form C. 2118.

WAR DIARY
8th (S) Battalion The Black Watch R.H.
or
~~INTELLIGENCE SUMMARY.~~

AUGUST. (Erase heading not required.) 1 9 1 9.

Place	Date	Hour	Summary of Events and Information	Remarks and references to Appendices
MAUBACH, Germany.	1st		Platoon and Company Drill, Handling of Arms.	
	2nd		do. do.	
	3rd		Church Parades.	
	4th		Bank Holiday.-No Training.	
	5th		"C" Company proceeded to DROVE to complete work of burying cables.	
	6th		Platoon & Company Drill, Handling of Arms.	
	7th		Preparing for move to England.-Striking of Tents etc.	
	8th		do do.	
	9th		Major R.E. ANSTRUTHER granted permission to wear the badges of Lieut-Col pending appointment. C.S.M. Hannan, "D" Coy proceeded to England, for duty on Home Establishment.	
	10th		Battalion & Transport moved to DUREN, en route for England. One night was spent at DUREN and left on	
DUREN	11th		for England.	
	12th & 13th		Battalion en route for England. Arrived at CALAIS at 04.00 hours on 13th and marched to No 3. Rest Camp, where two hot meals were served and the Battalion rested until 09.30 hours when orders were received that The Battalion was embarking at 11.00 hours for England. Leaving the Shores of France at 11.30 hours the journey across the Channel took fully 2 hours Arriving at FOLKESTONE shortly after 13.00 hours. The Battalion disembarked and outside the harbour a halt was made and a light refreshment was partaken off. Leaving FOLKESTONE at 14.30 hrs the Battalion marched to SHORNCLIFFE where they entrained for MILFORD & BROCTON. A company left with train leaving SHORNCLIFFE at 18.00 hours and the remainder left at 20.30 hours.	
BROCTON CAMP	14th		Brocton Camp was reached at 04.00 hours and a hot meal was served, afterwards Companies were allotted their lines and the remainder of the day was spent in settling down.	
	15th to 18th		During this period the time was devoted to settling down in billets and cleaning up of the Camp, generally. Brigade Route March on 16th.	
	19th		Training commenced in the Battalion.	
	20th		All ammunition handed into Q.M. Stores.	
	21st		Route March "C" & "D" Coys; "A" & "B" Education.	
	22nd		Route March-"A" & "B" Coys; "C" & "D" Education.	
	23rd		Commanding Officer's Camp Inspection, commencing with "D" Coy. at 10.15 hours.	
	24th		Church Parades. for "B" & "D" Coys. "A" & "C" Coys proceeded on 15 days leave.	
	25th		Training according to Programme.	

D. D. & L., London, E.C. (A8004) Wt W1771/M2031 750,000 5/17 Sch. 52 Forms/C2118/14

Army Form C. 2118.

Instructions regarding War Diaries and Intelligence Summaries are contained in F. S. Regs., Part II. and the Staff Manual respectively. Title pages will be prepared in manuscript.

WAR DIARY
or
INTELLIGENCE SUMMARY.
(Erase heading not required.)

8th (S) Battalion The Black Watch R.H.

AUGUST, 1919.

Place	Date	Hour	Summary of Events and Information	Remarks and references to Appendices
Brocton Camp.	28th		All Derby Men and Men who joined the Colours before 1st July, 1916 proceeded for Demobilization.	
	29th.		"D" Company on Range, "B" Coy on Guard Duties.	
	30th	11.00	Commanding, Officer inspected all Institutes, Cookhouses & Workshops.	
		11.45	Practice Fire Drill	
	31st		Church Parades.	
			R E Anstruther (signature) Lieut-Colonel, Commanding, 8th (S) Battalion The Black Watch R.H.	
			2/9/19.	
			Appendix "A"- Demobilization	
			do "B"- Education.	

D. D. & L., London, E.C.
(A8004) Wt W1771/M2031 750,000 5/17 Sch. 52 Forms/C2118/14

(In lieu A.F.C. 2118.)

8th (S) Battalion The Black Watch R.H.

W A R D I A R Y.

A U G U S T. 1 9 1 9.

Appendix "A".

MAUBACH, Germany

BROCTON CAMP, Staffordshire

One hundred and forty three men were demobilized during August,1919. Of these,seven were released on Extreme Compassionate Grounds,seven under Army Order 55, and the remainder under Army Order 55 as amended by Army Orderrs 245,192,and 298.

Ten Compassionate cases were dealt with during the month,of which three were rejected after investigation, as not conforming to Army Council Instructions 287 and 421.

Seventeen applications put forward on Extreme Compassionate Grounds are at present being investigated.

Three N.C.O.s eligible for demobilization under Army Order 298 have re-engaged for three months.

(Signed) J. POLLOCK,
A/Demobilization Officer,
8th (S) Battalion The Black Watch R.H.

Army Form C. 2118.

Instructions regarding War Diaries and Intelligence Summaries are contained in F. S. Regs., Part II. and the Staff Manual respectively. Title pages will be prepared in manuscript.

WAR DIARY
or
INTELLIGENCE SUMMARY.
(Erase heading not required.)

8th (S) Battalion The Black Watch R.H.

AUGUST. 1 9 1 9 Appendix "B"

Place	Date	Hour	Summary of Events and Information	Remarks and references to Appendices
MAUBACH, Germany. - Brocton Camp, England.			**E D U C A T I O N.** During the month Educational work was carried out in this Unit wherever possible. Owing however to the Battalion moving from Germany to U.K. the Unit Education Syllabus could not be followed. Since arrivibg in the U.K. work under the Education Scheme hastaken the form of courses of Lectures on "The origin and growth of the British Empire", and "Citizenship" by two of the Instructors. This form had to be adopted owing to the lack of Educational material and to Instructors going on leave. It is expected that sufficient Educational Material will be available for the month of Septr., as will enable Instructors to continue teaching Group "A" subjects as well as the above mention-ed subjects. (Signed) W.F. MacLeod C.F. A/ Education Officer, 8th (S) Bn The Black Watch R.H.	[handwritten initials]

D. D. & L., London, E.C.
(A8004) Wt W1771/M2031 750,000 5/17 Sch. 52 Forms/C2118/14

BEF

HIGHLAND DIV formerly
62 DIV

2 HIGHLAND BDE H.Q.

1919 MAY TO 1919 SEPT

NO BOX

Secret. Original.

War Diary

— of —

2nd Highland Brigade H: Qrs:

May 1st 1919 To May 31st 1919.

A. B. Ritchie Brig: Genl:

Comdg: 2nd Highland Brigade.

2nd. Highland Brigade H.Qrs.

ORIGINAL.

Army Form C. 2118.

WAR DIARY

or

~~INTELLIGENCE SUMMARY~~.

(Erase heading not required.)

Instructions regarding War Diaries and Intelligence Summaries are contained in F. S. Regs., Part II. and the Staff Manual respectively. Title pages will be prepared in manuscript.

Place	Date	Hour	Summary of Events and Information	Remarks and references to Appendices
DUREN.	1/5/19.		Lt. Col. Dudgeon commanded the Brigade during the absence on leave of Brigadier-General A.B. Ritchie. C.B. C.M.G. The civilian population held a procession round the town. There were no disturbances.	
	2nd.		Nothing to report. Day wet and cold.	
	3rd.		Nothing to report.	
	4th.		Brigadier-General A.B. Ritchie. CB. CMG. returned from leave and took over command of the Brigade.	
	5th.		Captain I.E. Snell, Brigade Major, proceeded on leave and his duties were taken over by Captain J.S.Aikman. The area in the hills west of Duren allotted to the Brigade for training was reconnoitred.	
	6th.		The 5th. Bn. Gordon Highlanders relieved the 4th. Gordon Highlanders in the duties of finding the " Inlying Picquet ".	Appendix.1
	7th.		G.O.C. visited the 4th. Bn. Gordon Highlanders.	
	8th.		Nothing to report.	
	9th.		Nothing to report.	
	10th.		Nothing to report.	
	11th.		Conference was held at Brigade Headquarters at which the inspection by Sir. W.Robertson, Commander-in-Chief, was discussed.	
	12th.		51st. Bn. Gordon Highlanders relieved the 5th. Bn. Gordon Highlanders in the duties of finding the " Inlying Picquet ".	Appendix.2
	13th.		A rehearsal for the inspection by the Commander-in-Chief was held at the Aerodrome on the Duren-Stockheim Road.	
	14th.		Nothing to report.	
	15th.		The inspection by the Commander-in-Chief was held at 1000 hours.	
	16th.		Nothing to report.	
	17th.		Marshall Foch visited Duren. The G.O.C. 2nd. Highland Brigade welcomed him at Duren Station. The 4th. Bn. Gordon Highlanders provided the Guard of Honour consisting of 100 men.	
	18th.		Nothing to report.	
	19th.		Nothing to report.	
	20th.		G.O.C. attended a conference at Divisional Headquarters.	
	21st.		G.O.C. attended a conference at the Civil & Area Commandants office. A conference was held at Brigade Headquarters at which the C.O's. and Adjutants of the Units were present. A conference was held at Divisional Headquarters on the same day. The matter for discussion at these conferences was the arrangement for a move in the event of an order being received for an advance.	

D. D. & L., London, E.C.
(A8004) Wt W1771/M2031 750,000 5/17 Sch. 52 Forms/C2118/14

Instructions regarding War Diaries and Intelligence Summaries are contained in F. S. Regs., Part II. and the Staff Manual respectively. Title pages will be prepared in manuscript.

Sheet. 2.

WAR DIARY
or
~~INTELLIGENCE SUMMARY~~.
(Erase heading not required.)

2nd. Highland Brigade H.Qrs.

Army Form C. 2118.

ORIGINAL.

Place	Date	Hour	Summary of Events and Information	Remarks and references to Appendices
	22nd.		Warning Order No. 215 was issued.	Appendix.3.
	23rd.		Amendments to Warning Order No.215 were issued.	
	24th.		G.O.C. and Officers of the 2nd. Highland Brigade attended the funeral of R.A.F. Officers who were killed at the Duren Range on Monday the 19th. inst.	
	25th.		Captain I.E.Snell returned from leave and resumed the duties of Brigade Major. Further Amendments to Warning Order No. 215 were issued.	
	26th.		Conference on Sports and an Atheletic Meeting held at Brigade Headquarters.	
	27th.		G.O.C. visited Battalions.	
	28th.		Nothing to report.	
	29th.		Nothing to report.	
	30th.		The 51st. Bn. Gordon Highlanders held the first day of their Battalion Sports.	
	31st.		The 51st. Bn. Gordon Highlanders held the second day of their Battalion Sports. The Divisional Commander and all the Brigadiers in the Division were amongst the spectators.	

A.B. Ritchie
Brigadier-General.
Commanding 2nd. Highland Brigade.

D. D. & L., London, E.C.
(A8204) Wt W1771/M2031 750,000 5/17 Sch. 52 Forms/C2118/14

Appendix. I

2nd HIGHLAND Brigade.

S E C R E T

G 3/1.

Reference DUREN DEFENCE SCHEME.

On Tuesday 6th. inst., the 5th.Bn.Gordon Highlanders will relieve the 4th.Bn.Gordon Highlanders in the duties of finding the "IN-LYING PICQUET". The relief to be carried out by 12.00 hours.

All further details of the relief to be arranged by O.C.'s commanding 4th. and 5th.Gordon Highlanders.

From mid-day on the 5th.instant the responsibility for holding posts in accordance with "APPENDIX 1 DUREN DEFENCE SCHEME " will be as follows :-

4th.Bn.Gordon Highlanders		POSTS:-	1,2,3,11,7.
5th.Bn.	do.	"	4,5,6,14.
51st.Bn.	do.	"	8,9,10,12,13.

4th.5th. and 51st Gordon Highlanders please acknowledge receipt of this Order.

J.E. Snell.
Captain,
Brigade Major,
2nd HIGHLAND Brigade.

4.5.1919.

Minute to:-

4th.Corps H.Q.
Highland Division "G" Branch.
Highland Division "Q" Branch.
Sub-Area Commandant.
G.O.C. R.A. 4th.Corps for R.A.Units.
Commandant,DUREN Barracks for Cavalry.
4th.Bn.Gordon Highlanders.
5th. do.
51st do.
9th. Seaforth do.
Signal Officer.
Staff Captain.
Corps Squadron R.A.F.
527th.Co.R.A.S.C.
457th.Co.R.E.
2/2nd H.R.Field Amb.
D/310 Battery R.F.A.
R.T.O. DUREN.
Camp Commandant 4th.Corps.

Appendix 2

SECRET.

2nd Highland Brigade,
B.M.J. 54

Reference DUREN DEFENCE SCHEME.

On Monday, 12th inst. the 51st Bn.Gordon Hrs. will relieve the 5th Bn.Gordon Hrs. in the duties of finding the "IN-LYING PICQUET." The relief to be carried out by 12.00 hours.

All further details of the relief to be arranged by O.C.s. commanding 5th and 51st Bn.Gordon Highlanders.

From midday on the 12th inst. the responsibility for holding posts in accordance with "Appendix 1, DUREN DEFENCE SCHEME" will be as follows :-

4th Bn.Gordon Highlanders ..... Posts 6, 7, 8, & 9.
5th do. ..... " 1,2,3,4,5,&,11.
51st do. ..... " 10,12,13, & 14.

4th, 5th and 51st Bns. Gordon Highlanders please acknowledge receipt of this order.

J. Aikman.
Lieut.
A/Brigade Major,
2nd HighlandBrigade.

9th May,1919.

Min.to.4th Corps.H.Q.
Highland Div. "G".
do. "Q".
Sub-Area Commandant.
G.O.C.,R.A.,4th Corps,
for R.A.Units.
Commandant, DUREN Barracks
for Cavalry.
4th Bn.Gordon Hrs.
5th do. do.
51st do. do.

Signal Officer.
Staff Captain.
Corps Squadron,R.A.F.
527th Coy.R.A.S.C.
457th F.Coy., R.E.
2/2nd W.R.F.A.
D/310 Battery,R.F.A.
R.T.O., DUREN.
Camp Commandant,
4th Corps.
File.

Appendix 3. War Diary

SECRET. COPY NO. ....

2ND. HIGHLAND BRIGADE WARNING ORDER NO. 215.

1. In the event of the Army of the Rhine being ordered to advance, three days only will be available for preparatory moves and re-distribution of troops, thus if J day is the days on which an advance commences, J minus three days will be the first day on which movements take place.

2. The earliest date on which J minus three can be is 12.00 hours midnight 22/23rd may. From this hour troops of the 2nd. Highland Brigade will be prepared to move by tactical trains and road at a few hours notice.
Three tactical trains have been allotted this Brigade.

1st. train.... 1/4th.Bn.Gordon Hlrs and dismounted personnel of 2/3rd W.R.F.A.
2nd. " .... 2nd.Highland Brigade H.Q. and 1/5th Bn. Gordon Hlrs.
3rd. " .... 51st.Bn.Gordon Hlrs. and 2nd. H.T.M.B.
Entraining Station DUREN, detraining Station SOLINGEN.

All transport of Units of Brigade Group will move by road in one column under O.C. No 3 Coy Train. Suitable intervals will be maintained on the march.
Rendezvous for Transport :- Water Tower COLN PLATZ, DUREN.
The transport will halt at LINDENTHAL on night of J3 & J2 day and OPLADEN on night of J-2 and j-1 day.
Troops of 2nd. Highland Brigade to take over Guards from Lowland Division on arrival.

3. On receipt of the code message "J.3 MOVE" from corps H.Q. the 4th.Corps Cyclist Battalion and 4th. Corps Heavy Artillery are to immediately relieve the guards detailed below, at present found by this Brigade.
Guards will be taken over as follows :-

<u>IV Corps Heavy Artillery.</u>

(a) Electric Power Station WEISWEILER - 1 Officer & 100 O.R. from 53rd.Bn.Gordon Highlanders.
(b) R.A.S.C. Supply Dump BIRGEL - 2 N.C.Os and 6 men from 2nd.Highland Light. T.M.Battery.

<u>IV. Corps Cyclist Battalion.</u>

(c) Railway Station Guard, DUREN.

(1) 1 Officer 2 N.C.Os and 12 men from 5th.Bn.Gordon Hlrs.
(2) 1 Officer 2 N.C.Os and 15 men from 51st.Bn.Gordon Hlrs.
(3) 1 Officer 2 N.C.Os and 15 men from 4th.Bn.Gordon Hlrs.

(d) Captured Vehicle Park, DUREN- 1 N.C.O. and 6 men, from 51st.Bn.Gordon Highlanders.
(e) Railhead Supply and Corps and Divisional Pack Train, DUREN 2 N.C.Os and 12 men. from 51st.Bn.Gordon Hlrs.
(f) Post Office DUREN. 2 N.C.Os and 6 men from 51st.Bn. Gordon Highlanders.

On relief guards of 2nd.Highland Brigade will at once join their Units. Corps Heavy Artillery and 4th.Corps Cyclist Battalion have been ordered to direct Officers to reconnoitre the above mentioned Guards.

4. On receipt of orders that the advance is to take place the code message "CONCENTRATE" will besent by wire and on receipt of this message Units will make ready to entrain.

5. Units to form Dumps of all surplus stores and will detail a Guard of 2 N.C.Os and 6 men to look after same.

6. Administrative instructions :- Trains, supplies ammunition etc. will be issued when received by Brigade.

7. Acknowledge.

J. Aikman

Captain,
A/ Brigade Major,
2nd.Highland Brigade.

22nd. May,1919.

Copies to :-

Highland Division "G"
do. "Q"
4th.Bn.Gordon Highlanders.
5th.Bn.Gordon Highlanders.
51st.Bn.Gordon Highlanders.
2nd.Highland T.M.Battery.
527th.Co. R.A.S.C.
2/3rd. W.R . F.A.
Signal Officer.
Staff Captain.
G.O.C. R.A. 4th.Corps.
4th.Corps Cyclist Battalion.
File.
War Diary
457th Coy R.E

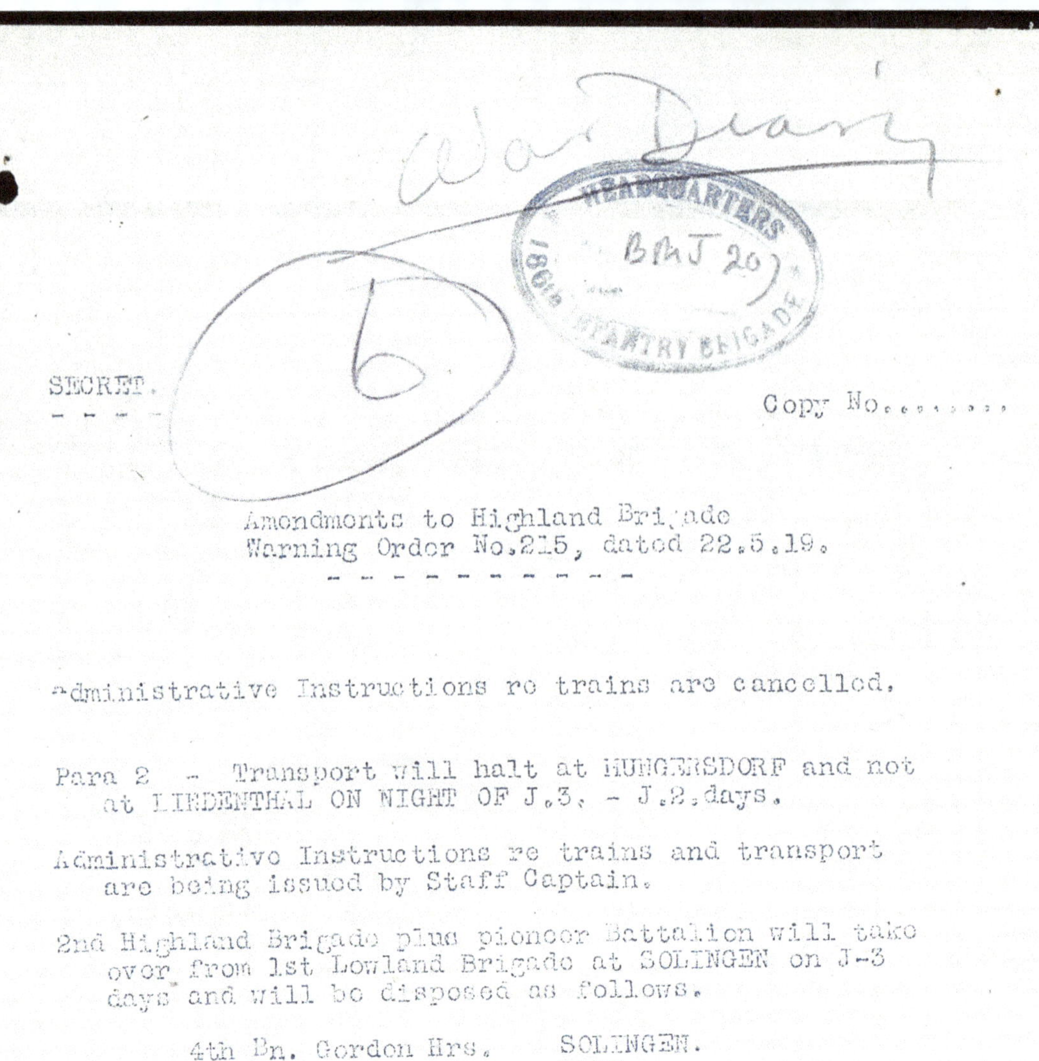

SECRET.

Copy No.........

Amendments to Highland Brigade
Warning Order No.215, dated 22.5.19.

Administrative Instructions re trains are cancelled.

Para 2 - Transport will halt at HUNGERSDORF and not at LINDENTHAL ON NIGHT OF J.3. - J.2.days.

Administrative Instructions re trains and transport are being issued by Staff Captain.

2nd Highland Brigade plus pioneer Battalion will take over from 1st Lowland Brigade at SOLINGEN on J-3 days and will be disposed as follows.

4th Bn. Gordon Hrs.	SOLINGEN.
5th " " "	WALD
51st & 53rd " "	SOLINGEN.

4th Bn. Gordon Highlanders will move forward on J. day and take over REMSCHEID.

J.S. Ackerman,
Captain,
A/Brigade Major,
2nd Highland Brigade.

23rd May, 1919.

Copies to :-

All recipients of 2nd Highland Brigade Warning Order No.215, dated 22-5-19.

SECRET

Copy No....17....

Amendment No.2. to Highland Bde. Warning Order No.215, of 22.5.19.

Para. 3.

Delete in each case "4th Corps Cyclist Battn." and substitute "4th Corps Heavy Artillery."

Captain,
A/Brigade Major,
2nd Highland Brigade.

25th May, 1919.

Copies to :- All recipients of 2nd Highland Brigade Warning Order No.215.

SECRET **ORIGINAL**

WAR DIARY

of

HEADQUARTERS, 2nd HIGHLAND BRIGADE.

From <u>1st June, 1919.</u> To <u>30th June, 1919.</u>

(Volume XXX)

A.B. Ritchie

Major General,
Commanding 2nd Highland Brigade.

ORIGINAL

Army Form C. 2118.

Instructions regarding War Diaries and Intelligence Summaries are contained in F. S. Regs., Part II. and the Staff Manual respectively. Title pages will be prepared in manuscript.

WAR DIARY
or
INTELLIGENCE SUMMARY.

(*Erase heading not required.*)

HEADQUARTERS, 2nd HIGHLAND BRIGADE.

Place	Date	Hour	Summary of Events and Information	Remarks and references to Appendices
	1919.			
DUREN	1st June,		Very hot day. G.O.C. visited 1st Highland Brigade Headquarters in the afternoon.	J.S.
	2nd		The 5th Gordon Highlanders relieved 4th Gordon Highlanders in the duties of finding the In-Lying Picquet.	J.S.
	3rd		Nothing to report.	J.S.
	4th		Orders were issued for the 4th and 5th Gordon Highlanders to send a Company to the Country to build ranges.	Appendix 1 J.S.
			Weather changed and became cold.	J.S.
	5th		Nothing to report.	J.S.
	6th		The 4th and 5th Gordon Highlanders sent one Company each to HURTGEN and GROSSHAU respectively.	J.S.
			Brigade Commander was present as commanding the Division at the Inspection of the 1st and 3rd Highland Brigades by the Commander-in-Chief.	J.S.
	7th		Weather became hot. The G.O.C. attended the Cologne Races. A small camp was started at the Schloss, LAUFENBURG for Brigade Headquarters.	J.S.
	8th		Nothing to report.	J.S.
	9th		The 51st Gordon Highlanders relieved the 5th Gordon Highlanders in the duties of finding the In-Lying Picquet.	Appendix 2 J.S.
			Instructions were received for the withdrawal of certain platoons in the DUREN DEFENCE SCHEME	Appendix 3 J.S.
	10th		Nothing to report.	
	11th		4th Gordon Highlanders held their games at GERMANIA Sports Ground. The G.O.C., and Divisional Commander attended.	J.S.
	12th		A conference was held at Brigade Headquarters on the 2nd Highland Brigade games, and it was decided to have these games on the 20th and 21st June in DUREN.	J.S.
	13th		The 5th Gordon Highlanders held their games at BIRKESDORF. The G.O.C. and Divisional Commander attended.	J.S.
	14th		Nothing to report.	J.S.
	15th		Instructions received that the Infantry Company attached to the 3rd Hussars would be under the Command of the G.O.C., DUREN DEFENCE SCHEME, for the purpose of the Defence of DUREN.	Appendix 4 J.S.
	16th		The 4th Gordon Highlanders relieved the 51st Gordon Highlanders in the duties of finding the In-Lying Picquet.	J.S. Appendix 5
	17th		Orders were received over the telephone at 03.45 hours to the effect that J-3 day (first day of movement to the SOLINGEN area) had commenced, and that all units would entrain in accordance with orders which had been issued on 23rd May. All units of the Brigade Group entrained at DUREN between 15.00 hours, and 20.00 hours, and arrived in SOLINGEN between the hours of 17.00 and 06.00 hours the next morning, taking over billets in SOLINGEN which had been vacated by the 1st Lowland Brigade.	J.S.

D. D. & L., London, E.C.
(A8094) Wt W1771/M2031 750,000 5/18 Sch. 52 Forms/C2118/14

ORIGINAL

Army Form C. 2118.

Instructions regarding War Diaries and Intelligence Summaries are contained in F. S. Regs., Part II. and the Staff Manual respectively. Title pages will be prepared in manuscript.

WAR DIARY
or
INTELLIGENCE SUMMARY.
(Erase heading not required.)

HEADQUARTERS, 2nd HIGHLAND BRIGADE.

Place	Date	Hour	Summary of Events and Information	Remarks and references to Appendices
	1919.			
SOLINGEN	18th	June,	The day was spent settling down in billets. The posts on the perimeter, as previously ordered, were taken over by the 51st Gordon Highlanders and 5th Gordon Highlanders. The Commander-in-Chief visited the Brigade during the afternoon.	
	19th		J-1 day. Brigade Headquarters was moved into the Headquarters occupied by the 1st Lowland Brigade. Information was received that the moves ordered for J day might not be carried out owing to the delay in signing the PEACE terms.	
	20th		Information received that J day had been postponed until further notice. Instructions regarding the maintainance of law and order in the SOLINGEN area were made by G.O.C., 2nd Highland Brigade, and were issued.	Appendix 6 Appendix 7
	21st		Appendix 8, giving instructions for eventual moves was issued.	Appendix 8
	22nd		All units with the exception of the 5th Gordon Highlanders sent a ~~suitable~~ considerable number of men to church parade at 10.15 hours in the LUTHER KIRCHE, SOLINGEN. The G.O.C. attended. The G.O.C. visited posts of the 5th Gordon Highlanders during the afternoon.	
	23rd		Orders issued for preparations to be made to commence the move into GERMANY on 24th June. Later in the day, these orders were cancelled as it was officially announced that the Germans intended to sign the PEACE terms.	Appendix 9.
	24th		Units commenced training on the ground around SOLINGEN.	
	25th		Engaged in training.	
	26th		Orders were issued for the return to DUREN in the event of PEACE being signed in the event of no advance taking place.	Appendix 10.
	27th		Nothing to report. Weather very stormy.	
	28th		PEACE was signed. Information was received that the first day's move back to DUREN would be Monday, 30th June.	
	29th		All Units attended church parade at the LUTHER KIRCHE, SOLINGEN.	
	30th		G.O.C. visited some of the perimeter posts.	

A.B. Ritchie
Major General,
Commanding 2nd Highland Brigade.

D. D. & L., London, E.C. (A8204) Wt W1771/M2031 750,000 5/18 Sch. 52 Forms/C2118/14

Appendix I

2nd. Highland Brigade.

BMJ. 353

O.C. 4th. Gordon Highlanders.
5th. Gordon Highlanders.
51st. Gordon Highlanders. (for Inf.)
457th. Field Coy. R.E. "
Staff Captain. "
O.C. Signals. "

Permission has been received to send troops forthwith to the Training Area. The 4th. and 5th. Gordon Highlanders will send as many men as possible to HURTGEN and GROSSHAU respectively on Friday the 5th. inst. 6

The G.O.C. directs that in the first place these men shall be sent entirely for the purpose of digging the Range and preparing any necessary accomodation to receive further detachments when they can be spared from their duties in DUREN.

As much R.E. assistance as can be spared will be given in the construction of these Ranges. In addition 25 pioneers will be available.

Each man of the party will be required to work at least 4 hours a day on the range and work will be carried out in shifts. By these means the G.O.C. considers that the Range will be prepared for use in one week from the date on which the troops arrive.

The 4th. and 5th. Gordon Highlanders will notify this office as soon as possible the number of men who will proceed to the Training Area and any requirements with regard to tools, transport, etc. which will be required.

Arrangements will be made by the Staff Captain similar to those made the last time the companies were sent out.

J. E. Snell
Capt.
Brigade Major,
2nd. Highland Brigade.

4th. JUNE. 1919.

War Diary Appendix 2.

SECRET.

2nd Highland Brigade.
B.M.J. 390/3.

Reference DUREN DEFENCE SCHEME.

On Monday, June 9th, 51st Bn. Gordon Highlanders will relieve 5th Battalion Gordon Highlanders in the duties of finding the In-Lying Picquet. The relief to be carried out by 12-00 hours.

All further details of the relief to be arranged by O.C's 5th and 51st Gordon Highlanders.

From mid-day, June 9th, the responsibility of holding posts in accordance with "APPENDIX 1, DUREN DEFENCE SCHEME" will be as follows:-

4th Bn. Gordon Highlanders, Posts 6, 7, 8, 9, & 11.
5th " " " " 1, 2, 3, 4, & 5.
51st " " " " 10,12,13,& 14.

4th, 5th and 51st Battalions Gordon Highlanders please acknowledge receipt of this order.

Capt.,
for Brigade Major,
2nd Highland Brigade.

7th June, 1919.

Copies to :-

Recipients of previous orders re In-Lying Picquet.

Appendix 3.

War Diary

2nd. Highland Brigade.

SECRET.

BMJ. 409/3

Reference DUREN DEFENCE SCHEME.

The following amendment will be made to Appendix 1 of 2nd. Highland Brigade DUREN DEFENCE SCHEME. issued on 20th. April 1919.

Serial No. 1
Railway Station. 1 Platoon instead of 2 Platoons.

Serial No. 3
Corps Headquarters. 1 Platoon instead of 2 Platoons.

Serial No. 5
The Church. BIRKERSDORF. 2 Platoons instead of 3 Platoons.

Serial No. 7.
2nd. Highland Bde. H.Q. 1 Platoon instead of 2 Platoons.

ACKNOWLEDGE.

J. E. Snell

Captain,
Brigade Major,
2nd. Highland Brigade.

9th. JUNE. 1919.

Copies to ;- O.C. 4th. Bn. Gordon Highlanders.
5th. Bn. " "
51st. Bn. " "
2nd. Highland Bde. T.M.B.
457th. Field Coy. R.E.
No. 3 Coy. Train.
2/3rd. W.R.F.A.
Civil Administrator.

War Diary. Appendix. IV

2nd. Highland Brigade.

SECRET.

BM. 420/3

Reference DUREN DEFENCE SCHEME.

Under authority of IV Corps No. 117/2/15/G dated 13/6/19 the followings alteration is made in the DUREN DEFENCE SCHEME.

The Company of Infantry attached to the 3rd HUSSARS in DUREN barracks will garrison the following posts of Appendix [illegible] in the event of the DUREN DEFENCE SCHEME coming into force.

Serial No. 10 WATER TOWER, COLN PLATZ..... 1 Platoon
" " 22 FREDRICK PLATZ............... 1 "
" " 13 [illegible] PLATZ............... 1 "

These three posts will be relieved immediately reinforce--ments arrive in the Town.

For purposes of the DUREN DEFENCE SCHEME the above mentioned Infantry Company will therefore come under orders of the G.O.C. Highland Brigade in DUREN, who will issue all necessary instructions.

The O.C. 3rd. Hussars will at once get into touch with the O.C. 51st. Bn. Gordon Highrs. who will give him all information with regard to these three posts.

The Infantry Company attached to the 3rd. Hussars will be prepared to man these posts on and after 1800 hours on Tuesday 17th. inst.

ACKNOWLEDGE

J. L. Snell

Captain
Brigade Major,
2nd. Highland Brigade.

15th. JUNE. 1919.

Copies to all recipients of the DUREN DEFENCE SCHEME and

O.C. 3rd. HUSSARS.

Appendix V

SECRET.

2nd Highland Brigade.
B.M.J.475.

Reference DUREN DEFENCE SCHEME.

On Monday, June 16th, the 4th Battalion, Gordon Highlanders will relieve the 51st Battalion, Gordon Highlanders in the duties of finding the In-Lying Picquet. The relief to be carried out by 12-00 hours.

All further details of the relief to be arranged by O.C's. 4th and 51st Gordon Highlanders.

From mid-day, June 16th, the responsibility 6S holding posts in accordanse with "APPENDIX 1, DUREN DEFENCE SCHEME," will be as follows L-

4th Bn.	Gordon	Highlanders	Posts	3, 6, 7, & 14.
5th "	"	"	"	1, 2, 4, 5, & 11.
51st "	"	"	"	8, 9,10,12 & 13.

The 4th, 5th and 51st Battalions, Gordon Highlanders, please acknowledge receipt of this order.

J. E. Snell

Captain,
Brigade Major,
2nd Highland Brigade.

14th June, 1919.

COPIES TO :-

All recipients of previous orders re

In-Lying Picquet.

Appendix VI   War Diary

SECRET

Copy No. 16 ....

B.M.J.549/3.

2nd Highland Brigade Instructions.

21st June, 1919.

1. "J" Day has been postponed until further notice.

2. Troops of the Highland Division now in II Corps Area are under the orders of the G.O.C., Lowland Division for tactical and civil administration purposes until G.O.C. Highland Division arrives in Lowland Division area.
The IV Corps administers the Highland Division.

3. The Lowland Division is responsible for civil administration duties in Lowland Division Area, Corps Heavy Artillery Sub-area, and Corps Headquarters Sub-area until taken over by G.O.C., Highland Division.

4. ACKNOWLEDGE.

J. E. Snell

Captain,
Brigade Major,
2nd Highland Brigade.

21st June, 1919.

DISTRIBUTION.

1. Highland Division "G"
2. " " Q
3. 4th Gordon Highlanders.
4. 5th " "
5. 51st " "
6. 53rd " "
7. 2nd Highland L.T.M.B.
8. 457th Field Company, R.E.
9. No. 3 Company Train.
10. 2/3rd W. R. Field Amb.
11. Lowland Division.
12. G.O.C.
13. Brigade Major.
14. Staff Captain.
15. Civil Administrator.
16. War Diary.
17. File.
18. Signal Officer.
19. Civil Staff Captain.

S E C R E T

War Diary Appendix VII

Copy No......21......

PROVISIONAL INSTRUCTIONS REGARDING THE MAINTAINANCE OF LAW AND ORDER WITHIN THE 2nd HIGHLAND BRIGADE SUB-AREA.

- -

1. The following inlying picquets will be detailed by each Unit :-

(a) The Battalions holding the perimeter, one platoon of each Company.
(b) The remaining Battalions, each one Company.
(c) Other Unitsin the Sub-Area, 25% of strength.

These picquets will not remain under arms but must be ready to turn out armed and equipped, at short notice any time, day or night. 60 rounds S.A.A. per man will be held ready for issue so as to complete all men armed with a rifle to 120 rounds per man.

Commanding Officers will arrange an alarm post for inlying picquets to fall in on, which is to be made known to all ranks.

2. The following system of Signals has been arranged for in the event of civil disturbance :-

The alarm will be given by three long blasts on the STROMBOS HORNS, repeated at intervals of about a minute, until the call has been heard tohave been taken up by the guards in the neighbourhood who are provided with STROMBOS HORNS.

STROMBOS HORNS will be placed in position at the following Guard Rooms.

2nd Highland Brigade	5 COLNER STRASSE
C/50 Battery Headquarters	HOHSCHIED
457th F.Coy. R.E. H.Q.,	KRAHENHOHE
51st Gordon Hrs.	RESTAURATION, KAISER SAAL
School	SCHWERTZ STRASSE.
Late 16th H.L.I. H.Q.,	OBEN WIDDERT.

The Alarm signal if given in one Sub-Area will be repeated in the other sub-areas.

C.O., 51st Gordon Highlanders will make similar arrangements to warn his Coys stationed in WALD

The following action will be taken on this Alarm Signal sounding :-

(a) All Ranks who are away from their Units will immediately rejoin.
(b) All guards will fall in on their Posts.
(c) The Guards mentioned in Para 4 below will be immediately mounted.
(d) The inlying picquets will fall in on Alarm Posts.
(e) All Units will hold themselves in readiness to turn out fully armed and equipped.

3. On receipt of the message "PRECAUTIONARY ARRANGEMENTS" either by telephone or telegram the following action will be taken:-

(a) Inlying picquets will remain under arms in their Billets.
(b) The posts at MUNGSTEN and KOHLFURTHER will be doubled.
(c) All single sentries on the perimeter will be doubled.
(d) Guards as specified in para 4 below will be detailed.
(e) All troops will remain in the vicinity of their quarters.
(f) No passes will be granted without reference to Brigade H.Q.

4. Battalions will be prepared to mount the following Guards :-

1/4th Gordon Hrs.	1 N§C.O. & 6 men	REICHBANK, 10 BIRKERSTRASSE
- do -	- do -	SPARKASSE BANK, 23 SCHULSTRASSE
- do -	- do -	MITTELDEUTSCHE BANK, KAISER STR and BIRKERSTRASSE
-do-	- do -	BARMER BANK, 22 KOLNER STR§
- do -	2 Sections	EXCHANGE, 54-56 KOLNER STR.
53rd Gordon Hrs.	1 N.C.O. & 6 men.	STOBBE BANK, 11 WUPPER STR.
- do -	- do -	DEUTSCHE BANK, 214, KAISER STR.
5th Gordon Highlanders	- do -	WATER TOWER, WALD.
- do -	- do -	WATER WORKS, GRAFRATH.

All units will mount guards over Ammunition.

5. The Officer commanding the Battalion§ holding the Perimeter must be prepared at all times to hold the line of the Perimeter against the incursion of an armed mob from REMSCHEID or ELBERFELD.

A C K N O W L E D G E§

J. E. Snell

Captain,
Brigad e Major,
2nd Highland Brigade.

20th June, 1919.

D I S T R I B U T I O N

1. Highland Division "G"
2. " " "Q"
3. 4th Gordon Highlanders.
4. 5th " "
5. 51st " "
6. 53rd " "
7. 2nd Highland Light T.M.B.
8. 457th Field Company, R§E§
9 No. 3 Company Train.
10. 2/3rd West Riding F. A.
11. 2nd Southern Brigade. (6 copies)
17 G. O. C.
18. Brigade Major
19. Staff Captain.
20. Civil Administrator.
21. War Diary.
22. File
23 Signal Officer

Appendix VIII

War Diary

S E C R E T

2nd Highland Brigade.
B.M.J.534/1.

The following Lowland Division Orders is published for information :-

1. "In continuation of G.922 of 17th June, no action will be taken on 20th June, nor will the present perimeter be crossed until further definite orders are issued.

2. All units will be ready to undertake the moves laid down for "J" day at short notice.

3. Moves forecasted for "J" day plus 1 day and subsequent days are dependent on the Military situation on "J" day.

4. When the advance commences the policy as regards the use of gas shell and long range artillery bombardment is - In principle these means will only be employed against positions or places which have definitely been ascertained to be occupied by a hostile force, which, offering active resistance, or by an insurgent population.
No Gas shell will be used without Corps sanction.
No H.E. Bombardment without orders from D.H.Q.

5. ACKNOWLEDGE.

J. E. Smith

Captain,
Brigade Major,
2nd Highland Brigade.

21st June, 1919.

DISTRIBUTION.

1. Highland Division "G"
2. " " "Q"
3. 4th Gordon Hrs.
4. 5th " "
5. 51st " "
6. 53rd " "
7. 2nd Highland L.T.M.B.
8. 457th Field Coy., R.E.
9. No. 3 Company Train.
10. 2/3rd W. R. F. A.
11. Lowland Division
12. G. O. C.
13. Brigade Major.
14. Staff Captain.
15. Civil Administrator.
16. War Diary.
17. File.
18. Signal Officer.
19. Civil Staff Captain.

Appendix 9

War Diary.

(6)

(19)

S E C R E T

2nd Highland Brigade.
B.M.J.566/1.

1. Orders have been received to the effect that all preparations must be made to commence the move forward into Germany at 03-15 hours, zero, on the 24th June.

2. No troops will cross the perimeter until ordered by wire.

3. From receipt of these orders, an Officer will remain in the Office of each Unit. All Officers are to be warned that they are not to leave their Units to-day.

4. As soon as troops of the Lowland Division have passed the perimeter, the troops of 2nd Highland Brigade will be withdrawn and will concentrate, the 51st Gordon Highlanders in SOLINGEN, and the 5th Gordon Highlanders in WALD.

O.C. 51st Gordon Highlanders will issue instructions to ensure that the road from MUNGSTEN to SOLINGEN is not blocked for the 4th Gordon Highlanders moving out of SOLINGEN.

5. O.C. 4th Gordon Highlanders will be prepared to move at any time five hours after zero hour on receipt of orders from Brigade.

6. Contact aeroplanes, 7th Squadron, R.A.F. will fly yellow and red streamers from their tails, and will also be marked with black flaps attached to the rear edge of the lower plane, on each side of the body.

7. A C K N O W L E D G E.

J. E. Smith
Captain,
Brigade Major,
2nd Highland Brigade.

23rd June, 1919.

D I S T R I B U T I O N.

1. Lowland Division.
2. Highland Division "G"
3. " " "Q"
4. 4th Gordon Highlanders.
5. 5th " "
6. 51st " "
7. 53rd " "
8. 2nd Highland Bde. T.M.B.
9. 457th Field Coy., R.E.
10. No. 3 Company Train.
11. 2/3rd West Riding Field Amb.
12. Civil Administrator.
13. G. O. C.
14. Brigade Major.
15. Staff Captain.
16. Signal Officer.
17. Civil Staff Captain.
18. P. R. O.
19. War Diary.
20. File.

ADD TO PARA. 4. The perimeter posts at present held by 4th and 51st Gordon Highlanders will not be withdrawn till orders to that effect are received from Brigade.

Instructions will also be issued as to what is to be done with stores at the posts.

Appendix 10 War Diary

S E C R E T

2nd Highland Brigade,
B.M.J. 590/1.

1. In the event of peace being signed without any further advance taking place, orders may be expected for all troops to resume their normal dispositions, and the organization of areas and civil administration that existed prior to J - 3 day.

2. The first day of this move back to original locations will be known as A day. Units of this Brigade Group will move on C day, and will entrain at SOLINGEN.

3. The times of leaving and departing of trains and personnel are notified in administrative orders issued to units of Brigade Group.

4. RELIEFS. - Units of 2nd Highland Brigade will be relieved by the same units as were relieved on coming into this area.

A. Relief of Railway Guards at LADWIEN will be completed by noon on A day, arrangements to be made between O.C., 5th Gordons and Pioneer Battalion, Lowland Division.

B. Relief of Perimeter posts held by 5th Gordon Highlanders will be carried out by 09-00 hours on C day.

C. Relief of all other guards now furnished by units of this Brigade Group will be carried out on the evening of B day.

D. Posts held by 51st Bn. Gordon Highlanders will be relieved by the 51st Bn. H.L.I. before noon on C day. Detailed arrangements will be made between O.C. Battalions concerned.

E. The 2nd Highland Brigade Signal Section will be relieved by 1st Lowland Brigade Signal Section by noon on C day.

5. CIVIL ADMINISTRATION.

A. That portion of the Right sub-area now under the control of O.C. 5th Gordon Highlanders will be handed over to B.G.C., 2nd Lowland Brigade at 09-00 hours on B day.

B. The remaining portion of the Right sub-area will be handed over to B.G.C. 1st Lowland Brigade at mid-day C day.

6. Completion of all reliefs to be wired to Brigade Headquarters

7. On the return to DUREN, Units will take over all guards and duties as handed over on J-3 day with the following exceptions

(a) 5th Gordon Highlanders will find In-Lying Picquet.
(b) The guard on the Captured Vehicles and ammunition dump will no longer be found.

8. A C K N O W L E D G E.

J. E. Snell.

Captain,
Brigade Major,
2nd Highland Brigade.

25th June, 1919.

DISTRIBUTION.

1. Lowland Division.
2. 1st Lowland Brigade.
3. 2nd " "
4. Highland Division "G"
5. " " "Q"
6. 4th Gordon Hrs.
7. 5th " "
8. 51st " "
9. 53rd " "
10. 2nd Highland F.M.B.
11. 457th F. Coy. R.E.
12. No.5 Coy. Train.
13 2/2nd [illegible]
14 Civil Staff Capt.
15. Civil Administrator
16. [illegible]
17. Brigade Major,
18. Staff Captain.
19. Signal Officer.
20. War Diary.
21. File.

SECRET

ORIGINAL

WAR DIARY

of

HEADQUARTERS, 2nd HIGHLAND BRIGADE.

From 1st July, 1919.

To 31st July, 1919.

VOL. 31

A.B. Ritchie

Major General,
Commanding 2nd Highland Brigade.

ORIGINAL

Army Form C. 2118.

Instructions regarding War Diaries and Intelligence Summaries are contained in F. S. Regs., Part II. and the Staff Manual respectively. Title pages will be prepared in manuscript.

WAR DIARY
or
INTELLIGENCE SUMMARY.

2nd Highland Brigade Headquarters.

(Erase heading not required.)

Place	Date 1919.	Hour	Summary of Events and Information	Remarks and references to Appendices
SOLINGEN	July 1st.		Nothing to report.	
	2nd.		Brigade moved out of SOLINGEN area into DUREN area, entraining commenced 14-30 hours and finished 18-00 hours. Detraining at DUREN was completed at 24-00 hours. The Brigade took over all the billets they held before moving to SOLINGEN. Weather was very good for journey.	
DUREN	3rd.		One Company from the 4th Battalion Gordon Highlanders proceeded to the training area at HURTGEN to construct ranges.	
	4th.		Nothing to report.	
	5th.		One company from the 51st Gordon Highlanders moved to the training area at GEY.	
	6th.		Two companies from the 5th Battalion Gordon Highlanders proceeded to the training area at GROSSHAU AND KLEINHAU.	
	7th.		A party of 4 Officers and 16 Other Ranks from the Brigade proceeded to Paris to take part in the PARIS Victory March.	
			The 53rd Battalion Gordon Highlanders relieved the 5th Battalion Gordon Highlanders in the duties of finding the In-Lying Picquet.	App. 1.
	8th & 9th.		Preliminary heats run off for the events for the Brigade Sports.	
	10th.		Major General Sir. D. Campbell, commanding Highland Division, lectured to all troops of the Brigade stationed in the HURTGEN, GROSSHAU, GEY area.	
	11th.		2nd Highland Brigade Sports were held and were very sucessful. The day was observed as a general holiday throughout the Brigade.	
	12th, 13th, and 14th.		Nothing to report.	
	15th.		51st Battalion Gordon Highlanders relieved the 53rd Gordon Highlanders in the duties of finding the In-Lying Picquet.	App.2.
	16th, 17th, and 18th.		Nothing to report.	
	19th.		Observed as a general holiday throughout the British Empire on the coming of PEACE.	
	20th, to 24th,		Nothing to report.	
	25th.		Eliminating competition for Divisional Horse Show held on GERMANIA Sports Ground.	
	26th, and 27th.		Nothing to report.	
	28th.		The Rev. G. H. Heaslett lectured to the Brigade Group on VENERAL DISEASE.	
	29th.		The G.O.C. and staff attended the Divisional Horse Show held near NIDEGGEN.	

D. D. & L., London, E.C.
(A8304) Wt W1771/M2031 750,000 5/17 Sch. 52 Forms/C2118/14

ORIGINAL Army Form C. 2118.

WAR DIARY
or
INTELLIGENCE SUMMARY.
(Erase heading not required.)

2nd Highland Brigade Headquarters.

Instructions regarding War Diaries and Intelligence Summaries are contained in F. S. Regs., Part II. and the Staff Manual respectively. Title pages will be prepared in manuscript.

Place	Date	Hour	Summary of Events and Information	Remarks and references to Appendices
	1919.			
DUREN	July	30th.	The 5th Gordon Highlanders relieved the 4th Gordon Highlanders in the duties of finding the In-Lying Picquet.	App. 4.
		31st.	Nothing to report.	

A.B. Ritchie
Major General,
Commanding 2nd Highland Brigade.

D. D. & L., London, E.C. (A8204) Wt W1771/M2031 750,000 5/19 Sch. 58 Forms/C2118/14

App. I

2nd Highland Brigade.
B.M.J.667/7

S E C R E T

Reference DUREN DEFENCE SCHEME.

On Monday, July 7th, the 53rd Battalion Gordon Highlanders will relieve the 5th Battalion Gordon Highlanders in the duties of finding the In-Lying Picquet, The relief to be carried out by 18-00 hours.

All further details of the relief to be arranged by O.C. 53rd and 5th Gordon Highlanders.

From 18-00 hours June 7th, the responsibility of holding posts in accordance with Appendix 1, DUREN DEFENCE SCHEME, will be as follows :-

4th	Bn. Gordon Highlanders.	Posts	8, 9, & 11.
5th	" " "	"	2, 4, & 5.
51st	" " "	"	1, 3, & 7.
53rd	" " "	"	6.

The 4th, 5th, 51st. and 53rd Battalions Gordon Highlanders to acknowledge.

A.M.M. Carlisle
for Captain,
Brigade Major,
2nd Highland Brigade.

6th July, 1919.

COPIES TO :-

All recipients of previous orders re In-Lying Picquet.

R/662

WD

S E C R E T.

2nd. Highland Brigade.
B.M.J. 716/3

Reference DUREN DEFENCE SCHEME.

On Tuesday July 15th. the 51st. Bn. Gordon Highlanders will relieve the 53rd. Bn. Gordon Highlanders in the duties of finding the IN-LYING PICQUET.

The relief will be carried out by mid-day.

All further details of the relief to be arranged by O.C. 51st. and 53rd. Gordon Highlanders.

From mid-day July 15th. the responsibility of holding posts in accordance with Appendix 1, DUREN DEFENCE SCHEME? will be as follows.

4th. Bn. Gordon Highlanders.	Posts 8, 9, 11.
5th. Bn. Gordon Highlanders.	Posts 2, 4, 5.
51st. Bn. Gordon Highlanders.	Posts.1, 3, 6, 7.

The 4th., 5th., 51st., and 53rd., Battalions to acknowledge.

14th. July. 1919.

Captain,
Brigade Major,
2nd. Highland Brigade.

Copies to:-

All recipients of previous orders
re In-lying Picquet.

166 3

2nd. H.

SECRET.

B.M.J. 090/3.

Reference DUREN DEFENCE SCHEME.

On Wednesday July. 30th. 1919. the 5th. Bn. Gordon Highrs. will relieve the 4th. Bn. Gordon Highlanders in the duties of finding the INLYING PICQUET.

The relief will be carried out by mid-day.

All further details of the relief to be arranged by O.C. 4th. and 5th. Gordon Highlanders.

From mid-day July 30th. the responsibility for holding posts in accordance with Appendix 1, DUREN DEFENCE SCHEME will be as follows.

4th. Bn. Gordon Highlanders.	Posts. 8. 9. 11.
5th. Bn. Gordon Highlanders.	Posts. 2. 4. 5. & 6.
51st. Bn. Gordon Highlanders.	Posts. 1. 3. 7.

The 4th. 5th. and 51st. Bn. Gordon Highlanders will acknowledge receipt of this order.

[signature]

Captain,
Brigade Major,
2nd. Highland Brigade.

29th. July. 1919.

Copies to; -

All recipients of previous orders re INLYING PICQUET.

S E C R E T. O R I G I N A L.

W A R D I A R Y

of

HEADQUARTERS, 2nd. HIGHLAND BRIGADE.

FROM 1st. AUGUST 1919 to 31st. AUGUST 1919.

VOLUME NO. 32.

[signature] Capt for Lt Col for Brigadier-General,
Commanding 2nd. Highland Brigade.

S E C R E T. Headquarters, 2nd. Highland Brigade. O R I G I N A L.

Army Form C. 2118.

WAR DIARY
or
INTELLIGENCE SUMMARY.

(Erase heading not required.)

Instructions regarding War Diaries and Intelligence Summaries are contained in F. S. Regs., Part II. and the Staff Manual respectively. Title pages will be prepared in manuscript.

Place	Date	Hour	Summary of Events and Information	Remarks and references to Appendices
Duren.	1st		Nothing to report.	
Duren.	2nd.		Nothing to report.	
Duren.	3rd		Nothing to report.	
Duren.	4th		Nothing to report.	
Duren.	5th		55 horses proceeded to Cologne en route for England.	
Duren.	6th		53rd. Gordon Highlanders relieved 5th. Gordon Highlanders as Inlaying Picquet.	
Duren.	6th		Divisional Education School disbanded. All students returned to Brigade.	
Duren.	7th		Nothing to report.	
Duren.	8th		Brig-General J.W.Sandilands C.B., C.M.G., D.S.O., Cameron Highlanders assumed command of the 2nd. Highland Brigade vice Major-General A.B.Ritchie, C.B. , C.M.G.appointed to command of the Lancashire Division.	
Duren.	8th	13.44	4th. Gordon Highlanders and 457 Field Coy. R.E. left Duren by first train for Calais.	
Duren.	8th	18.35	2nd. Highland Brigade Headquarters, 5th. Gordon Highlanders and 2nd. Highland L.T.M. Battery left Duren by second train for Calais.	
Duren.	8th		G.O.C. 2nd. Highland Brigade and Brigade Major proceeded to Calais and Bologne respectively.	
Calais.	9th		G.O.C. 2nd. Highland Brigade and Brigade Major arrived at Calais and Bologne.	
Calais.	9th		G.O.C. 2nd. Highland Brigade inspected arrangements for detraining, billeting, feeding, and embarking troops at Calais.	
Calais.	9th		First and Second train arrived at Calais and personnel proceeded to nos. 5 & 8 Rest Camps for the night.	
Duren.	9th	13.44	51st. Gordon Highlanders and No.3 Coy. Train left Duren with No. 3 Train.	
Duren.	9th		All remaining horses proceeded to Cologne en route for England.	
Calais.	10th	08.15	G.O.C. 2nd. Highland Brigade and personnel of No.1 train ^embarked^ for Folkestone and entrained at Shorncliffe for Clipstone.	
Calais.	10th	11.00	Personnel of No. 2 train embarked for Folkestone and entrained at Shorncliffe for Clipstone.	
Calais.	10th		Personnel of No. 3 train arrived at Calais and proceeded to No. 5 Rest Camp.	
Calais.	11th	08.15	Personnel of No. 3 train embarked for Folkestone and entrained at Shorncliffe for Clipstone.	
Clipstone.	11th		Personnel of No. 1 train arrived at Clipstone Camp.and marched to billets.	
Clipstone	12th		Personnel of Nos. 2 & 3 trains arrived at Clipstone Camp and marched to billets.	
Clipstone.	12th		19792, Pte. J. O'Lone, 4th. Gordon Highlanders, att. 2nd. Highland Brigade H.Qs. accidentally drowned in Vicar's Water.	
Clipstone.	13th		G.O.C., 2nd. Highland Brigade inspected the lines of Units in this Brigade.	
Clipstone.	14th.		Nothing to report.	
Clipstone.	15th		G.O.C., 2nd. Highland Brigade lectured to all Officers in Brigade.	
Clipstone.	16th		5th. Bn. Gordon Highlanders took over Garrison Guards and Garrison Duties for the week from (reveille.	

D. D. & L., London, E.C. (A8504) Wt W1771/M2031 750,000 5/17 Sch. 52 Forms/C2118/14

S E C R E T.

Headquarters, 2nd. Highland Brigade.

WAR DIARY
or
INTELLIGENCE SUMMARY.

(*Erase heading not required.*)

O R I G I N A L.

Army Form C. 2118.

Instructions regarding War Diaries and Intelligence Summaries are contained in F. S. Regs., Part II. and the Staff Manual respectively. Title pages will be prepared in manuscript.

Place	Date	Hour	Summary of Events and Information	Remarks and references to Appendices
CONTD.				
Clipstone	17th		Nothing to report.	
Clipstone	18th		Units of the Brigade started to fire Annual General Musketry Course.	
Clipstone	19th		Nothing to report.	
Clipstone	20th		Nothing to report.	
Clipstone	21st		Nothing to report.	
Clipstone	22nd		Lt-Col. R.R.Forbes, D.S.O., 5th. Bn. Gordon Highlanders proceeded on 15 days leave.	
Clipstone	22nd		Major. J.T.Lawrence, D.S.O., M.C., D.C.M., 51st Bn. Gordon Highlanders proceeded on 15days leave	
Clipstone	22nd		25% of Brigade proceeded on 15 days leave.	
Clipstone	23rd		Nothing to report.	
Clipstone	24th		Nothing to report.	
Clipstone	25th		Captain I.E.Snell, Brigade Major, proceeded on leave for one month.	
Clipstone	26th		10 Other Ranks who joined the colours before 1st July 1916 dispatched for demobilization.	
Clipstone	26th	X	G.O.C., 2nd. Highland Brigade held conference of C.Os., Seconds-in-Command, and Adjutants at Brigade Headquarters.	
Clipstone	27th		Nothing to report.	
Clipstone	28th		Nothing to report.	
Clipstone	26th	X	Second 25% of Brigade proceeded on 15 days leave.(3rd. 25% September 4th.,4th.25% Sept 11th.)	
Clipstone	29th		Nothing to report.	
Clipstone	30th		Officer's Chargers arrived from Germany.	
Clipstone	31st		Nothing to report.	

J.A. Kimmon(?) Capt. for Lt-Col. Brigadier-General,
Commanding 2nd. Highland Brigade.

D. D. & L., London, E.C.
(A8204) Wt W1771/M2031 750,000 5/17 Sch. 52 Forms/C2118/14

SECRET DUPLICATE

WAR DIARY

of

HEADQUARTERS, 2nd HIGHLAND BRIGADE

From 1st September, 1919.
To 31st September, 1919.

VOLUME NO. 33.

[signature]

Brigadier General,
Commanding 2nd Highland Brigade.

SECRET Headquarters, 2nd Highland Brigade. **DUPLICATE** Army Form C. 2118.

WAR DIARY
or
INTELLIGENCE SUMMARY.
(Erase heading not required.)

Instructions regarding War Diaries and Intelligence Summaries are contained in F. S. Regs., Part II. and the Staff Manual respectively. Title pages will be prepared in manuscript.

Place	Date	Hour	Summary of Events and Information	Remarks and references to Appendices
Clipstone	1st to 7th		The Brigade, composed of 4th, 5th, and 51st Bns. Gordon Highlanders, were engaged in Musketry and Education and 50% of the men were on leave.	
"	7th to 14th		The same conditions were being experienced and in addition the Brigade undertaking the Camp and Garrison duties, with the result that very little training could be carried out.	
"	14th to 21st		By this time the majority of men had returned from leave, and training became better organized. Musketry was carried on. During this time orders were received that the 4th and 5th Bns. Gordon Highlanders would be reduced to cadre, the surplus personnel of these Battalions being posted to the 2nd Bn. London Regiment, London Scottish. The 2/14th London Regiment, London Scottish arrived in camp on the 21st under the command of Lt. Col. CANCH KAVANAGH.	
"	25th		Informationwas received forecasting the formation of the various Brigades in the Division. The 2nd Highland Brigade to consist of the 51st Bn. Gordon Highlanders, 8th Bn. Black Watch and surplus personnel of the 6th Bn. Black Watch, and 2/14 London Regiment and surplus personnel of the 4th and 5th Bns. Gordon Highlanders. Appendix 1.	
"	26th		Advance party of 8th Bn. Black Watch arrived in Camp. 11th Bn. Royal Scots Fusiliers was put under command of the G.O.C., 2nd Highland Brigade.	
"	27th		The Railway Strike commenced and orders were received by the Brigade to prepare to undertake strike duties on the Gt. Central Rly. between LEICESTER and NOTTINGHAM inclusive. Lt. Col. P.W. BROWN was put in command of the composite battalion of London Scottish and 4th and 5th Bns. Gordon Highlanders with Lt. Col. Forbes 2nd in command. Administrative instructions in the event of a move taking place were issued. Appendix 2. All ranks were confined to Barracks and Officers on leave were recalled. The G.O.C. returned from leave on the morning of the 27th.	
"	28th		Orders were received to prepare to move on the arrival of transport. Later in the day orders were received to hand over all maps and information to the London Reserve Brigade who would undertake duties previously allotted to this Brigade.	

D. D. & L., London, E.C.
(A8004) Wt. W1771/M2031 750,000 5/17 Sch. 52 Forms/C2118/14

SECRET Headquarters, 2nd Highland Brigade. **WAR DIARY** *or* **INTELLIGENCE SUMMARY.** DUPLICATE Army Form C. 2118.

Instructions regarding War Diaries and Intelligence Summaries are contained in F. S. Regs., Part II. and the Staff Manual respectively. Title pages will be prepared in manuscript.

(*Erase heading not required.*)

Place	Date	Hour	Summary of Events and Information	Remarks and references to Appendices
Clipstone	29th		Orders were received that this Brigade would be in reserve and would not move but that reconnaisance should be made in MANSFIELD so that the provision and petrol stores in that town could be protected if necessary.	J.S.S
"	30th		These reconnaissances at MANSFIELD were carried out. Men and Officers were still confined to Barracks. Certain commodities in the way of rations were cut down, but no serious hardships were felt.	J.S.S

J. S. Ewell [illegible]
for

Brigadier General,
Commanding 2nd Highland Brigade.

D. D. & L., London, E.C.
(A8004) Wt W1771/M2031 750,000 5/15 Sch. 52 Forms/C2118/14

HIGHLAND DIV.

~~formerly 62 DIV~~

1 HIGHLAND Bde

10 A & S H

1919 MAR – 1919 AUG

FROM. 32 DIV
97 Bde

Original

Confidential

War Diary Vol I

of

10th Argyll & Sutherland Highlanders

1st March 1919 to 31st March 1919

(Volume)

(6414) Wt. W3906/P1607 2,500,000 7/18 McA & W Ltd (E 3591) Forms W3091/4. Army Form W.3091.

Cover for Documents.

Nature of Enclosures.

Notes, or Letters written.

Army Form C. 2118.

WAR DIARY
or
INTELLIGENCE SUMMARY.

(Erase heading not required.)

Instructions regarding War Diaries and Intelligence Summaries are contained in F. S. Regs., Part II. and the Staff Manual respectively. Title pages will be prepared in manuscript.

10th Argyll and Sutherland [illegible]

Place	Date	Hour	Summary of Events and Information	Remarks and references to Appendices
MENDEN	1919 Mar. 6		Played a friendly match with the first fifth DEVONS and beat them by 2 goals to nil.	[illegible]
	11.		Played a friendly match with the West Riding Field Ambulance and won by 4 goals to nil.	[illegible]

(A7092) Wt W12859/M1293 75,0.0. 1/17. D. D. & L., Ltd. Forms/C.2118/14.

Instructions regarding War Diaries and Intelligence Summaries are contained in F. S. Regs., Part II. and the Staff Manual respectively. Title pages will be prepared in manuscript.

WAR DIARY
or
INTELLIGENCE SUMMARY.
(*Erase heading not required.*)

Army Form C. 2118.

10th Argyll & Sutherland Highlanders

Place	Date 1919	Hour	Summary of Events and Information	Remarks and references to Appendices
EMBKEN	March 12		Played a friendly match with the [illegible] (9th West Yorks) & won by 3 goals to one. Afterwards their [illegible] party gave us a most excellent entertainment.	W
	14		Moved to EMBKEN the [illegible] area D Company being accommodated in GINNEKEN a village about 2 kilos away.	
	21		C Coy moved into PISSENHEIM [illegible] from EMBKEN	
	28		The Commanding Officer attended a [illegible] by the Commander in Chief at which he [illegible] to senior officers throughout the Division on his return to take over the Command of the Home Forces.	
	29		The Battn has commenced [illegible] school and Training carried on.	
			Snow has [illegible]	
			The following officers [illegible] 9th A & S H:	
			A/Capt W E G MILLAR M.C	
			A/Capt C HETHERWICK M.C ([illegible] 1st B [illegible]).	
			A/Capt A S STEWART	
			Lt W A McL ROBB	198 O.R.
			Lt N M FINDLAY	
			Lt W C SMITH	
			2/Lt A. LISTER.	
			2/Lt E W. DAVIDSON.	
			2/Lt J B MACKAY.	
			Lt SOWTER.	

(A7092). Wt W12839/M1293 75 ,0:0. 1/17. D. D. & L., Ltd. Forms/C.2118/14.

Instructions regarding War Diaries and Intelligence Summaries are contained in F. S. Regs., Part II. and the Staff Manual respectively. Title pages will be prepared in manuscript.

WAR DIARY
or
INTELLIGENCE SUMMARY.
(Erase heading not required.) 10th Argyll & Sutherland Highlanders

Army Form C. 2118.

Place	Date 1919	Hour	Summary of Events and Information	Remarks and references to Appendices
EMBKEN	March 31		Lieut J. C F PENDER M.C. } 2nd Lieut T. R. HEGGIE } joined for duty.	[illegible]
			Lieutenant-General GODLEY Commanding the IV Corps visited Battalion Headquarters	[illegible]
			[signature] 10 A & S. H.	

(A7092). Wt W12839/M1293 75,000. 1/17. D. D. & L., Ltd. Forms/C.2118/14.

CONFIDENTIAL.

H 47.0.

W A R D I A R Y O F

10th Battalion ARGYLL AND SUTHERLAND HIGHLANDERS.

FROM 21st MAY, 1919.

T O 31st MAY, 1919.

****

BRITISH ARMY OF THE RHINE.

G E R M A N Y.

Instructions regarding War Diaries and Intelligence Summaries are contained in F. S. Regs., Part II. and the Staff Manual respectively. Title pages will be prepared in manuscript.

WAR DIARY
or
INTELLIGENCE SUMMARY.
(Erase heading not required.)

Army Form C. 2118.

10th Argyll & Sutherland Highrs

Place	Date	Hour	Summary of Events and Information	Remarks and references to Appendices
GLADBACH	May 21		2 Coys moved to Training Area at HAUSEN	[illegible]
	27		The Colour Party consisting of 4 officers & 30 ORs of 5th Bn A&SH proceeded home to Greenock	[illegible]
	31		The remainder of the Battn – moved to HAUSEN under Canvas	[illegible]

[illegible] Lt Col
Cm 10 A [illegible] [illegible]

(A7092). W1. W12839/M1293. 75,0.0. 1/17. D. D. & L., Ltd. Forms/C.2118/14.

48.0

9D

Confidential

War Diary

of

10th. Bn. Argyll & Sutherland Highlanders.

from 1 July 1919 to 31 July 1919

(Volume 7)

Confidential

VOLUME 7

Instructions regarding War Diaries and Intelligence Summaries are contained in F. S. Regs., Part II. and the Staff Manual respectively. Title pages will be prepared in manuscript.

WAR DIARY
or
INTELLIGENCE SUMMARY.
(Erase heading not required.)

Army Form C. 2118.

10th Argyll & Sutherland Highlanders

Place	Date	Hour	Summary of Events and Information	Remarks and references to Appendices
	1919			
HAUSEN	July 7		Batt: arrived HAUSEN on R. ROER	
			The following were selected to represent Bn. in the allies victory March in Paris on July 14 and proceeded.	
			No 201745 C.S.M. J. SIMPSON. M.M. (& bar)	
			200670 C.Q.M.S. W.R. JOHNSTONE M.M.	
			1714 Sergt J. ROBINSON M.S.M.	
			7357 L/Cpl J. McWILLIAMS M.M.	
	8		"C" Coy went on a Trip up the RHINE	
	11		PEACE HOLIDAY	
			At the [illegible] Highland Brigade sports all the open events were won by members of this Bn.	
			100 yds race won by Corp W. LOOKER	
			440 yds race won by Corp W. LOOKER	
			Relay Race won by { 2nd Lt. T. C. GOODMAN; S. Sergt T. G. CHAPMAN; Corp W. LOOKER; Pte R. H. BACON	
			Piping Contest won by Pipe Major J. WRIGHT M.S.M.	

A6945 Wt. W11422/M1160 350,000 12/16 D. D. & L. Forms/C./2118/14.

Volume 7.

(Continued)

Army Form C. 2118.

Instructions regarding War Diaries and Intelligence Summaries are contained in F. S. Regs., Part II. and the Staff Manual respectively. Title pages will be prepared in manuscript.

WAR DIARY
or
INTELLIGENCE SUMMARY.
(Erase heading not required.)

10th Argyll & Sutherland Highrs

Place	Date	Hour	Summary of Events and Information	Remarks and references to Appendices
HAUSEN	1919 July 11		After the Sports, Pipe Major Wright proceeded home for demobilization. He has served continuously with this Bn. since Oct. 1916	[illegible]
	14		General holiday.	[illegible]
	20		The Band was selected to attend the Peace Celebrations at ANTWERP and remained there for a week, playing at the Torchlight Procession and at a Ball given there.	[illegible]
	21		Bn. Sports. Weather so bad that they had to be completed following day.	[illegible]
	30		General FAYOLLE commanding the French Army of occupation on the RHINE came to Cologne. A Guard of Honour was drawn up in the DOM PLATZ from 5th Cameron Highlanders and the massed bands from 5th Bn. Camerons & 10th A. & S. Hrs were in attendance. They afterwards marched past.	[illegible]
			[illegible signature] Lt.Col. Cmdg. 10 A. & S. H.	

A6945 Wt. W11422/M1160 350,000 12/16 D. D. & L. Forms/C./2118/14.

Confidential

Original 49.0

10th (S.) Bn. Argyll & Sutherland Hdrs.

War Diary
for
August, 1919.

Callirck

Confidential

Army Form C. 2118.

Volume 8

WAR DIARY
or
INTELLIGENCE SUMMARY.
(Erase heading not required.)

10th Argyll & Sutherland Highrs

Instructions regarding War Diaries and Intelligence Summaries are contained in F. S. Regs., Part II. and the Staff Manual respectively. Title pages will be prepared in manuscript.

Place	Date	Hour	Summary of Events and Information	Remarks and references to Appendices
	1919			
HAUSEN.	Aug 2		Brigade Sports. News received that the Division is ordered home	MO
	5		200 men went for a trip up the Rhine.	MO
			The following are mentioned in Despatches	MO
			(in continuation of Peace Gazette)	
			Lt Col H.G. SOTHEBY DSO MVO	
			Capt A.B. WISHART	
			Capt J.D.S. YOUNG DSO MC	
			& Lt Col A.R.G. WILSON of the 1/5th Bn	
			S/6153 a/Sergt D McSPORRAN	
			201745 Cpl M. J. SIMPSON M.M.	
			201234 Pte N.G. ALEXANDER } of 1/5th Bn	
			40753 Pte J. McINTYRE M.M.	
	11		Battn entrained for NIEDERAU and billetted there for the night	MO
	12		Battn marched to DUREN and entrained at 7 P.M. for CALAIS.	MO
	13			

Page 7.

Instructions regarding War Diaries and Intelligence Summaries are contained in F. S. Regs., Part II. and the Staff Manual respectively. Title pages will be prepared in manuscript.

WAR DIARY
or
INTELLIGENCE SUMMARY. 10th Argyll & Sutherland Highlanders

(*Erase heading not required.*)

Army Form C. 2118.

Place	Date	Hour	Summary of Events and Information	Remarks and references to Appendices
	1919			
CALAIS	Aug 14	2. am	Arrived at CALAIS and camped in Rest Camp	M.D.
	14	11. am	Embarked for Dover with 5th Cameron Highlanders with Bands playing at the Ship Steamed out	M.D.
CATTERICK CAMP Yorkshire		2 P.M.	Entrained at Dover and reached CATTERICK CAMP Yorkshire at 7. am	M.D.
	15		on 15th Took over X Lines	M.D.
			The Battn. has at length returned as a Unit from Active Service after exactly 4 years and 3 months.	M.D.
			Battn. went on 15 days leave by Coys — One Coy going each week	

J. R. Sotheby Lt Col
10 A. & S. Hrs.

BEF

HIGHLAND DIV formerly
62 DIV

3 HIGHLAND Bde

1/4 SEAFORTHS

1919 MAR TO 1919 AUG

~~NO BOX~~

FROM 51 DIV— 154 BDE

Original

Confidential

War Diary

of

1/4th Bn. Seaforth Highlanders

Vol ~~XXVII~~ 54.

62 Div
3 Bde

From March 1st 1919

To March 31st 1919.

(6392) Wt. W6192/P875 1,500,000 4/18 McA & W Ltd (E 2815) Forms W3091/4.

Army Form W.3091.

Cover for Documents.

Nature of Enclosures.

Notes, or Letters written.

Instructions regarding War Diaries and Intelligence Summaries are contained in F. S. Regs., Part II. and the Staff Manual respectively. Title pages will be prepared in manuscript.

Volume 54

WAR DIARY
or
~~INTELLIGENCE SUMMARY~~. 1/4 Bn Seaforth Highrs.

(Erase heading not required.)

Army Form C. 2118.

Place	Date	Hour	Summary of Events and Information	Remarks and references to Appendices
In Germany EMBKEN.	1919. March 1		Dull day. There was no parade for Battn. The day was spent in cleaning up, being the first day in EMBKEN.	
"	2		There was no Church Parades for Battn.	
	3.		Good Day. H.Q. 1 & 2 Coys had baths. Coy. Commdrs held a Marching Order inspection of Coys.	
	4.		Wet Day. Parades under Coy. arrangements. A Party from Battn. attended a lecture in VLATTEM.	
	5.		Good Day Nos. 3 & 4 Coys had baths. The remainder of the day was devoted to cleaning up billets and preparing to move.	
	6.		Battn. moved on foot to ZULPICH via JUNTERSDORF, and entrained there for BUIR. The Battn detrained at BUIR at about 12:00 hrs. and marched to GOLZHEIM arriving there about 13:00 hrs. The Transport travelled by road to GOLZHEIM arriving there about half an hour previous to Bn.	
GOLZHEIM.	7		There was a muster Parade of all men who were transferred from 5th & 6th Bns; the remainder of Coys were at disposal of Coy. Commanders. The day was very cold.	

(A9175) Wt W2358/P363 600,000 12/17 D. D. & L. Sch. 52a. Forms/C2118/15.

Instructions regarding War Diaries and Intelligence Summaries are contained in F. S. Regs., Part II, and the Staff Manual respectively. Title pages will be prepared in manuscript.

WAR DIARY
or
~~INTELLIGENCE SUMMARY.~~ 1/4th Bn Seaforth Highrs.

(Erase heading not required.)

Army Form C. 2118.

Place	Date	Hour	Summary of Events and Information	Remarks and references to Appendices
Germany	1919 Mch.			
GOLZHEIM	8.		Good Day. Coys paraded for Drill etc. for one hour and then O.C. Coys held a Kit Inspection.	
	9.		There were no Church Parades for Battn.	
	10.		Usual routine of Drill etc. was carried out; and the construction of a Rifle Range was commenced.	
	11.		Cold Day. Nos. 3 & 4 Coys. paraded for Drill, & Physical Training etc. No 2 Coy was working on Rifle Range and No 1 Coy moved to new Billeting Area in ESCHWILER	
	12.		Good Day. Battn. parade was held.	
	13		Usual routine of Drill etc was carried out.	
	14.		Good Day The Battn carried out Route-march. Route - GOLZHEIM - ESCHWEILER - NORVENICH - BLATZHEIM - GOLZHEIM.	
	15.		Kit Inspection was held by Coy Commanders.	
	16		There were Church Parades for all denominations in the Battn.	
	17		Good Day, usual routine of parades. The Division (62nd) renamed "Highland Division"	

(A9175) Wt W2358/P360 600,000 12/17 D. D. & L. Sch. 52a. Forms/C2118/15.

Army Form C. 2118.

Instructions regarding War Diaries and Intelligence Summaries are contained in F. S. Regs., Part II, and the Staff Manual respectively. Title pages will be prepared in manuscript.

WAR DIARY
or
~~INTELLIGENCE SUMMARY~~.
(*Erase heading not required.*)

1/4 Bn Seaforth Highrs

Place	Date	Hour	Summary of Events and Information	Remarks and references to Appendices
In Germany GOLZHEIM.	1919 Mch. 18.		Usual Routine of Drill etc.	
	19		Good Day, Do. Do.	
	20.		Cold Day Do. Do.	
	21		Drill Day Battn. Route March was carried out.	
	22		Usual Routine of Drill etc.	
	23		Church Parades were held for all Denominations.	
	24		Usual Routine of Drill was carried out. No 3 Coy had baths in the afternoon.	
	25.		Usual Routine of Drill etc, No 4 Coy had baths in the afternoon	
	26		Wet Day and training accordingly was suitable to Wet Day. No 1 Coy had baths in the afternoon.	
	27		Companies were inspected on Coy Parade Grounds by B.G.C. who afterwards went round the Billeting Area.	
	28		A Party from Batt. went to Cologne to witness Football Match. Drill for remainder was carried out according to Programme of Training	
	29		Usual Routine of Drill etc, according to Programme was carried out. No 3 Coy had baths in the afternoon	

(A9175) Wt W2358/P360 600,000 12/17 D. D. & L. Sch. 52a. Forms/C2118/15.

Army Form C. 2118.

Instructions regarding War Diaries and Intelligence Summaries are contained in F. S. Regs., Part II. and the Staff Manual respectively. Title pages will be prepared in manuscript.

WAR DIARY
or
~~INTELLIGENCE SUMMARY.~~ 1/4 Bn Seaforth Highrs.

(Erase heading not required.)

Place	Date	Hour	Summary of Events and Information	Remarks and references to Appendices
In Germany GOLZHEIM	1919 March 30		Cold day with snow showers. There were Church Parades for all denominations. Remainder of men of No 3 Coy who did not have baths yesterday and all available men of No. 2. Coy had baths in the afternoon.	
	31.		Cold day & threatening to snow. Usual routine of Drill etc was carried out according to Programme of Training Battn. Baths were allotted to No 4. Coy in the afternoon.	

[illegible] Lt Col
Comdg 1/4th Seaforth Highrs

(A9175) Wt W2358/P360 600,000 12/17 D. D. & L. Sch. 52a. Forms/C2118/15.

Original

Confidential

War Diary

of

1/4th Bn. Seaforth Highlanders.

From 1st May 1919 to 31st May 1919

(6300) Wt. W6192/P875 1,500,000 4/18 McA & W Ltd (E 2815) Forms W3091/4.

Army Form W.3091.

Cover for Documents.

Nature of Enclosures.

Notes, or Letters written.

Instructions regarding War Diaries and Intelligence Summaries are contained in F. S. Regs., Part II. and the Staff Manual respectively. Title pages will be prepared in manuscript.

WAR DIARY
or
~~INTELLIGENCE SUMMARY.~~
(Erase heading not required.)

Army Form C. 2118.

Place	Date	Hour	Summary of Events and Information	Remarks and references to Appendices
	MAY 1919			
GOLZHEIM	1st.		Training carried out as per programme issued. No 1 Coy. fired on the range.	R.L.B.
	2.		No parades. Day devoted to re-organisation of Coys.	R.L.B.
	3		Parades as per training and sports programmes. No 2 Coy carried out a route march. No 1 Coy isolated at ESCHWEILER on account of infectious diseases.	R.L.B.
	4.		Church parades for all denominations except C of E.	R.L.B.
	5.		Usual routine drill No. 4 Coy firing on the range.	R.L.B.
	6.		Parades as per programme of training	R.L.B.
	7.		Usual drill and Education instruction. No 4 Coy carried out route march.	R.L.B.
	8.		Parades as per programme of training	R.L.B.
	9.		Parades as per programme issued. Advance party 7 officers 90 O.R's proceeded to take over new area NIDEGGEN proceeding by train from BUIR. Transport moved by road.	R.L.B.
	10.		Kit inspection for the battalion.	R.L.B.
	11.		Church parade for all denominations	R.L.B.

(A9175) Wt W2358/P360 600,000 12/17 D. D. & L. Sch. 52a. Forms/C2118/15.

Instructions regarding War Diaries and Intelligence Summaries are contained in F. S. Regs., Part II. and the Staff Manual respectively. Title pages will be prepared in manuscript.

WAR DIARY
or
INTELLIGENCE SUMMARY.
(Erase heading not required.)

Army Form C. 2118.

Place	Date	Hour	Summary of Events and Information	Remarks and references to Appendices
	MAY			
NIDEGGEN	12		Battalion moved to new area, with the exception of No 1 Coy remaining at ESCHWEILER entraining at BUIR and detraining NIDEGGEN; no 3 Coy being billetted at ZERKHALL, and the remainder at BRÜCK	R.L.B.
	13		Day devoted to re-organisation of Battn. Thorough inspection of billets carried out.	R.L.B.
	14		Parades as per programme issued. No 4 Coy. parade for medical inspection	R.L.B.
	15		Parades as per programmes issued.	R.L.B.
	16		—— do ——	R.L.B.
	17		Kit inspection for Battn. C.O's inspection of billets	R.L.B.
	18		Church parades for all denominations. C of E and Presbyterian combined	R.L.B.
	19		Parades as usual. Musketry and recreational training	R.L.B.
	20		Parades as per programme issued	R.L.B.
	21.		Companies carried out route marches independently. Fatigue party commenced work on construction of new rifle range.	R.L.B.
	~~22~~			
	22		Battalion had pleasure trip on the Rhine, proceeding by train NIDEGGEN — COLOGNE. No 1 Coy joined Battn party at BUIR, and proceeded with them, leaving them again at BUIR on return journey.	R.L.B.

(A9175) Wt W2358/P360 600,000 12/17 D. D. & L. Sch. 52a. Forms/C2118/15.

Army Form C. 2118.

Instructions regarding War Diaries and Intelligence Summaries are contained in F. S. Regs., Part II. and the Staff Manual respectively. Title pages will be prepared in manuscript.

WAR DIARY
or
INTELLIGENCE SUMMARY.
(Erase heading not required.)

Place	Date	Hour	Summary of Events and Information	Remarks and references to Appendices
	MAY			
NIDEGGEN	23		Parades as per programme of training	R.L.B.
	24		Kit and billet inspection for Battn. No 1 Coy joined Battn. from ESCHWEILER	R.L.B.
	25		Church parades for all denominations.	R.L.B.
	26		Parades as per programme of training.	R.L.B.
	27		Parades as per programme of training	R.L.B.
	28		Battalion parade under Commanding Officer. No 3 Coy removed from isolation	R.L.B.
	29		Parades as per programme issued.	R.L.B.
	30		Routine parades for all Coys. Divisional Commander inspected transport.	R.L.B.
	31		Kit and billet inspection for battalion	R.L.B.

[signature]
COLONEL,
COMDG. 4th BN. SEAFORTH HIGHRS

(A9175) Wt W2358/P360 600,000 12/17. D. D. & L. Sch. 52a. Forms/C2118/15.

Original.

Confidential.

War Diary

of

1/4th. Bn. Seaforth Highlanders

From 1st. June 1919. To 30th. June 1919.

(Volume III)

4th BATTn. SEAFORTH HIGHLANDERS.

Instructions regarding War Diaries and Intelligence Summaries are contained in F. S. Regs., Part II, and the Staff Manual respectively. Title pages will be prepared in manuscript.

WAR DIARY
or
~~INTELLIGENCE~~ SUMMARY.
(Erase heading not required.)

4th BATTn. SEAFORTH HIGHLANDERS

Army Form C. 2118.

Place	Date	Hour	Summary of Events and Information	Remarks and references to Appendices
	1919			
NIDEGGEN	June 1		Combined Presbyterian & C of E Church parade. Also parade for R.C's.	RLB
	2		Battn. formed up on Bn Parade ground for ceremonial drill and Commanding Officer's inspection.	RLB
	3		Ceremonial parade on Battn parade ground at 10.30 hrs. Remainder of day observed as General Holiday being King's birthday	RLB
	4		Recreational Training and Educational Training. No 3 Coy. musketry on range.	RLB
	5		Battalion parade for ceremonial drill at 10.30 hrs.	RLB
	6		Battalion parade on Bn parade ground for inspection.	RLB
	7		Inspection of all gas masks in battalion by Divisional Gas Officer.	RLB
	8		Church parades for all denominations.	RLB
	9		P & R.T. and Education Training No 1 Coy fired on Range.	RLB
	10		Training carried out as per Programme of Training.	RLB
	11		No 2 Coy fired on range. P & R.T. & Educational Training for remainder of Battalion.	RLB
	12		Training carried out as per Programme of Training. Lewis gunners firing on the range.	RLB

(A9175) Wt W2358/P360 600,000 12/17 D. D. & L. Sch. 52a. Forms/C2118/15.

Instructions regarding War Diaries and Intelligence Summaries are contained in F. S. Regs., Part II, and the Staff Manual respectively. Title pages will be prepared in manuscript.

WAR DIARY
or
~~INTELLIGENCE SUMMARY.~~
(Erase heading not required.)

Army Form C. 2118.

Place	Date	Hour	Summary of Events and Information	Remarks and references to Appendices
	1919 June 13		P&RT & Education Training for Nos 1. & 2 Coys. Advanced Guard Drill for Nos 3. & 4. Coys.	RCR
	14.		Kit & billet inspection for battalion	RCR
	15		Church parades for all denominations	RCR
	16		Parades as per Programme of Training	RCR
DUREN	17		Battn entrained at Nideggen to proceed to concentration point DUREN, and were billetted in DUREN BARRACKS for the night.	RCR
OHLIGS	18		Battn entrained at Duren en route to take over perimeter posts &c, in Lowland Division Area guarded by 5/6 Royal Scots, detraining at HILDEN and proceeding by road to OHLIGS.	RCR
	19.		Day spent in taking over posts by 2 platoons No 3. Coy. Remainder of battn at disposal of Coy Commanders.	RCR
	20.		No 2 Coy proceeded to HAAN to take over posts &c guarded by 11th Bn Royal Scots.	RCR
	21		Routine drill for Coys not on Guards &c.	RCR
	22		Combined Presbyterian & C of E Church Parade. R.C. Parade in R.C. Church OHLIGS.	RCR

(A9175) Wt W2358/P360 600,000 12/17 D. D. & L. Sch. 52a. Forms/C2118/15.

Army Form C. 2118.

Instructions regarding War Diaries and Intelligence Summaries are contained in F. S. Regs., Part II, and the Staff Manual respectively. Title pages will be prepared in manuscript.

WAR DIARY
or
~~INTELLIGENCE~~ SUMMARY.
(Erase heading not required.)

Place	Date	Hour	Summary of Events and Information	Remarks and references to Appendices
	1919 June 23		Parades under Coy arrangements	R.E.B.
	24		do	R.E.B.
	25		Lowland Division baths alloted to the Bn. for the day 0900-1200 hrs, 1300-16·30 hrs	R.E.B.
	26.		Parades under Coy arrangements	R.E.B.
	27		do.	R.E.B.
	28		Kit & billet inspection under Coy. arrangements. Baths allotted 0900 - 1230 hrs.	R.E.B.
	29		Church parades for all denominations. Football match in afternoon against	R.E.B.
			5/6 Royal Scots	R.E.B.
	30.		Parades under Coy arrangements Guards of No3 Coy relieved by 5/6 Royal Scots	R.E.B.

[signature illegible]
COLONEL
COMDG. 4th BN. SEAFORTH HIGHRS

(A9175) Wt W2358/P360 600,000 12/17 D. D. & L. Sch. 52a. Forms/C2118/15.

Confidential

War Diary

~ of ~

1/4th. Bn. Seaforth Highlanders.

From 1st. July. 1919. ~ To ~ 31st. July. 1919.

Original.

Volume IV

(6414) Wt. W3906/P1607 2,500,000 7/18 McA & W Ltd (E 3591) Forms W3091/4.

Army Form W.3091.

Cover for Documents.

Nature of Enclosures.

Notes, or Letters written.

7

4th BATTn. SEAFORTH HIGHLANDERS.

Instructions regarding War Diaries and Intelligence Summaries are contained in F. S. Regs., Part II. and the Staff Manual respectively. Title pages will be prepared in manuscript.

WAR DIARY
or
INTELLIGENCE SUMMARY.
(*Erase heading not required.*)

Army Form C. 2118.

4th BATTn. SEAFORTH HIGHLANDERS.

Place	Date	Hour	Summary of Events and Information	Remarks and references to Appendices
	1919			
OHLIGS	1st July		Battalion returned to old area in Nideggen, marching by road to HILDEN and thence by train to Duren. The night was spent in Duren Barracks.	R.E.B.
	2nd		Battalion proceeded from Duren Barracks by train to Nideggen, occupying billets as before previous number.	R.E.B.
NIDEGGEN	3.		No parades. Time spent in cleaning up of billets &c.	R.E.B.
	4		Time spent same as yesterday.	R.E.B.
	5.		Kit and billet inspections by Coy Commanders.	R.E.B.
	6.		Church Parade for Church of England party	R.E.B.
	7.		Parades under Company arrangements.	R.E.B.
	8		Official day for celebrating peace. Day observed as holiday in the Battalion. Football Match between Nos 3 + 4 Coys.	R.E.B.
	9.		Parades under Company arrangements	R.E.B.
	10.		Parades as per programme of Training	R.E.B.
	11.		Training carried on as usual. G.O.C. in C. paid a visit to the Bn.	R.E.B.
	12.		Kit and billet inspection by Coy. Commanders.	R.E.B.
	13.		Church Parade for all denominations	R.E.B.
	14.		Parades as per Programme of Training	R.E.B.
	15		Preliminary rounds of Bn Sports held on sports ground ZERKHALL under unfavourable weather conditions.	R.E.B.

A5834 Wt. W4973/M687 750,000 8/16 D. D. & L. Ltd. Forms/C.2118/13.

Instructions regarding War Diaries and Intelligence Summaries are contained in F. S. Regs., Part II. and the Staff Manual respectively. Title pages will be prepared in manuscript.

WAR DIARY
or
INTELLIGENCE SUMMARY.
(Erase heading not required.)

Army Form C. 2118.

Place	Date	Hour	Summary of Events and Information	Remarks and references to Appendices
	16 July		Battn sports on ground at ZERKHALL. There was a large attendance of spectators. Music being rendered by the band of the 3rd Kings Own Hussars.	
	17.		Parades as per Programme of Training.	
	18		Parades as per Programme of Training	
	19.		The Battn. less Nos. 1 + 4 Coys proceeded by train to Lendersdorf to take over Bde duties from 6th Black Watch. No 1 Coy proceeded to HERBESTHAL for duty on train guards. No 4 Coy proceeded by road to BOGHEIM to take over work on construction of rifle range.	
LENDERSDORF	20.		Divine service for all denominations. Cadre party for 9th Seaforth Hrs. Colours proceeded to U.K.	
	21.		Parades for Nos 2. + 3. Coys as per programme of Training	
	22		Battalion attended Lecture by Rev G.H. Heaslett	
	23.		Parades under Company arrangements	
	24		Parades under Coy arrangements	
	25.		Coys. at disposal of Coy Commanders. Football match against 3rd (H) T.M.B	
	26.		Kit + billet inspections	
	27		Divine service for all denominations.	
	28.		Parades as per Programe of Training	
	29		Battn carried out short route march	
	30.		Parades as per Programme of Training	
	31.		Parades as per Programme of Training	

S. Forbes Shand Capt.
COMDG. 4th SEAFORTH HIGHRS

Confidential.

War Diary

of

4th Bn. Seaforth Highlanders

from 1st August 1919 to 31st August 1919.

Original.

(6414) Wt. W3906/P1607 2,500,000 7/18 McA & W Ltd (E 3591) Forms W3091/4. Army Form W.3091.

Cover for Documents.

Nature of Enclosures.

Notes, or Letters written.

Instructions regarding War Diaries and Intelligence Summaries are contained in F. S. Regs., Part II, and the Staff Manual respectively. Title pages will be prepared in manuscript.

WAR DIARY
or
~~INTELLIGENCE SUMMARY.~~
(Erase heading not required.)

Army Form C. 2118.

4th Bn. Seaforth Highlanders.

Place	Date	Hour	Summary of Events and Information	Remarks and references to Appendices
LENDERSDORF.	Aug. 1st		Parades as per Programme of Training.	S.H.
	2		Parades as per Programme of Training. Football match V IV Corps Cyclist Battn.	S.H.
	3.		Church parades for all denominations.	S.H.
	5.		Parades under Company arrangements.	S.H.
	4.		No parades, day being observed as a Bank Holiday.	S.H.
	6.		Parades under Company arrangements.	S.H.
	7.		No Military Training. Brigade Sports being held in DUREN.	S.H.
	8.		Parades under Company arrangements.	S.H.
	9.		Kit Inspection and Medical Inspection for all O.R's.	S.H.
	10		Battalion preparations for move.	S.H.
	11		Battalion proceeded to U.K. embarking at Calais and Disembarking at Folkestone.	S.H.
BROCTON CAMP.	13		Battalion arrived at Brocton Camp, Staffordshire.	S.H.
	14		Time spent in thoroughly cleaning up kit and equipment.	S.H.
	15		Brigade Route March. Dress - Fighting Order.	S.H.
	16.		Kit inspections under company arrangements.	S.H.
	17.		Church Parades for all denominations.	S.H.

(A9175) Wt W2358/P360 600,000 12/17 D. D. & L. Sch. 52a. Forms/C2118/15.

Instructions regarding War Diaries and Intelligence Summaries are contained in F. S. Regs., Part II, and the Staff Manual respectively. Title pages will be prepared in manuscript.

WAR DIARY
or
~~INTELLIGENCE SUMMARY.~~
(Erase heading not required.)

Army Form C. 2118.

Place	Date	Hour	Summary of Events and Information	Remarks and references to Appendices
	Aug18		Parades under Company arrangements. Educational Training.	S.H.
	19		Parades as per Programme of Training.	S.H.
	20		Parades as per Programme of Training. Baths for H.Q. Coy	S.H.
	21		Battalion Route March.	S.H.
	22		Parades as per programme of training. Nos 2 & 3 Coys firing on the range.	S.H.
	23		Parades as per programme of training Nos 1 & 4 Coys firing on the range.	S.H.
	24		Church parades for all denominations.	S.H.
	26		Nos 1 & 4 Coys proceeded on leave. Parades for remainder as per programme of training.	S.H.
	25		Parades as per programme of training	S.H.
	27		Nos 2 & 3 Fired on the range.	S.H.
	28		Battalion took over duties as duty battalion for the 3rd (H) Brigade.	S.H.
	29		Parades under Company arrangements.	S.H.
	30		Parades under Company arrangements.	S.H.
	31		Church parades for all denominations.	S.H.
			S. Forbes Sharp. Lt-Col.	
			Commanding 4th Bn. Seaforth Highlanders.	

(A9475) Wt W2358/P360 600,000 12/17 D. D. & L. Sch. 52a. Forms/C2118/15.

~~51 DIV~~

~~153 Bde~~

HIGHLAND DIV
formerly 62.
3 HIGH. Bde

1/6 BN. R. HIGHLDRS
(BLACK WATCH)

1919 MAR TO 1919 AUG

~~Box 2728~~

FROM 51 DIV 153 Bde

Original

Confidential

War Diary

of

6th Bn Black Watch

Vol ~~XXVII~~ 56

From March 1st 1919

To March 31st 1919

(6392) Wt. W6192/P875 1,500,000 4/18 McA & W Ltd (E 2815) Forms W3091/4. Army Form W.3091.

Cover for Documents.

Nature of Enclosures.

Notes, or Letters written.

Instructions regarding War Diaries and Intelligence Summaries are contained in F. S. Regs., Part II. and the Staff Manual respectively. Title pages will be prepared in manuscript.

WAR DIARY
or
~~INTELLIGENCE SUMMARY.~~
(Erase heading not required.)

6 Bn The Black Watch (R.H).

Army Form C. 2118.

Place	Date 1919	Hour	Summary of Events and Information	Remarks and references to Appendices
MECHERNICH	March 1		Observed as a holiday	CMD
"	2.		Church parades	CMD
"	3		0900 – 1100 company training – 1100 hours Lecture. –	CMD
"	4		0900 – 1100 company training / 1100 – 1220 Specialist training	CMD
"	5		0900 – 1100 company training. 1100 – 1220 Specialist training.	CMD
"	6		0900 – 1100 company training 'D' Coy at disposal of company commander 1100 – 1220 specialist training	CMD
"	7.		company and specialist training. –	CMD
"	8.		Observed as a holiday.	CMD
"	9.		Church parades – A & B Coys proceed to HERBESTHAL and took over Supply guard from 5th D. of W. REGT.	CMD
"	10		company and specialist training. – Advance party moved to new area.	CMD
"	11.		companies at disposal of company commanders: – preparations for move to new area.	CMD
MERZENICH	12.		Battalion entrained at 0900 hours for MERZENICH – Detrained at 1200 hours at DÜREN; and marched to billets.	CMD
"	13.		Companies at disposal of company commanders.	CMD
"	14		1030 hours. B. G. C. inspected billets of Battalion – companies at disposal of company commanders	CMD
"	15		Observed as a holiday	CMD
"	16.		Church Parades	CMD
"	17.		0930 – 1230 hrs. Company training	CMD
"	18.		0930 – 1230 hours. Company training.	CMD

Instructions regarding War Diaries and Intelligence Summaries are contained in F. S. Regs., Part II. and the Staff Manual respectively. Title pages will be prepared in manuscript.

WAR DIARY
or
~~INTELLIGENCE SUMMARY~~. 6th Bn The Black Watch (R.H.)
(Erase heading not required.)

Army Form C. 2118.

Place	Date 1919 March	Hour	Summary of Events and Information	Remarks and references to Appendices
MERZENICH	19		0920 - 1230 hours. Company and specialist training.	CMD
	20.		Kit Inspection and company training	CMD
	21.		Battalion Ceremonial parade and company training	CMD
	22.		Observed as a holiday	CMD
	23.		Church Parades	CMD
	24.		Inspection of Companies by Commanding Officer	CMD
	25.		Inspection of Companies by Brigadier.	CMD
	26.		Company training. –	CMD
	27.		D and C companies Baths. A and B company training	CMD
	28		A and B coys. Baths. C and D company training	CMD
	29.		Observed as a holiday. Lecture at 1700 hours. Operation orders issued for C Company to move to HERBESTHAL	CMD
	30		Church Parades.	CMD
	31.		Company training.	CMD

[signature]
LIEUT. COLONEL,
Commanding 6th (Perthshire) BTTN. THE BLACK WATCH.

264152—Wt. W 5343/P 1707—1250M—9-18—W. & S. Ld.—(E 5808)—C 2118/17.

SECRET. ADDENDUM "A" Copy No. 11.

6th BATTALION The BLACK WATCH.

OPERATION ORDERS.

SATURDAY MARCH 29/19.

1. ADVANCE PARTY. O.C."C" Company will detail 6 N.C.Os. to report to Captain Hunter at HERBESTHAL and will learn their duties before the arrival of "C" Company.
They will proceed by the train leaving DUREN at 09.45 hours on Tuesday 1st April 1919.

2. MOVE.of "C" Company. On Wednesday 2nd April "C" Company will move by train to HERBESTHAL to take over the duties of supply Guards from "B" Company.
"C" Company will move as follows:
40 O.R. and a proportion of Officers by train leaving DUREN at 09.45 hours.
40 O.R. and a proportion of Officers by train leaving DUREN at 14.30 hours
Remainder of Company by train leaving DUREN at 14.30 hours.

3. DRESS. Full Marching Order Jerkins will be worn: Greatcoats in packs. Steel Helmets secured by straps on back of packs.

4. BLANKETS & EXTRA KIT. Blankets will be rolled in bundles of three labled and taken into the carriage with the men of each party. The second (old) kilts will be labelled under company arrangements and tied in bundles of five. Sacking for covering these bundles can be obtained from the Q.Master but it must be returned to him after use.
Each party will carry their own bundles on their respective trains

5. TRANSPORT. The Transport Officer will arrange the necessary transport to carry Officers kits blankets and extra kit of each party from MERZENICH to DUREN station.

6. COOKERS. "C" Company will take over the Cooker and Dixies now at HERBESTHAL but will take their other cooking utensils with the party proceeding by train leaving DUREN 13.30 hours on April 2nd.

7. MOVE OF "B" COMPANY. "B" Company will move from HERBESTHAL to DUREN by train as follows:
(a) 50 O.Rs. and a proportion of Officers by train leaving HERBESTHAL at 10.30 hours on Wednesday April 2nd.
(b) Remainder of "B" Company by train leaving HERBESTHAL at 16.30 hours on Thursday April 3rd.

8. DRESS. Full Marching Order. Jerkins to be worn Greatcoats will be in packs. Steel Helmets secured by straps on back of packs.

9. BLANKETS. Blankets will be rolled in bundles of three and carried on the train with the men.

10. TRANSPORT. Transport Officer will make the necessary arrangements for the transport to meet these trains on the respective dates and carry blankets and Officers Valises from DUREN Station to MERZENICH.

11. BILLETS. Men of "B" Company arriving from HERBESTHAL will be accommodated in billets in MERZENICH at present occupied by "C" Company.
The present "C" Coy. Officers' Mess will be taken over by "A" Coy's Officers.

12. MESSING. On thursday 3rd April "B" Company will take over "C" Coy. Dining Hall and details of "A" Company in MERZENICH will mess with them until the men of "B" Company at present in MERZENICH and the party of 50 O.Rs. of "B" Company arriving on the morning of Wednesday 2nd April will be attached to "D" Company for messing.
The Q.Master will arrange for the necessary redistribution of rations. O.C. "B" Company will render to to Q.M. as soon as possible a statement of the ration strength of his party arriving on Thursday 3rd April.

OPERATION ORDERS (Contd.)

13. Officers and men of "A" Company at present at HERBESTHAL will remain there for duty until further orders are issued to them.

14. Acknowledge.

Sd. E.D.NICOLL

Captain.

Adjutant 6th Bn.The Black Watch.

29/3/19.

Copy No. 1. File. Copy No.2 "A" Company. Copy No.3."B" Company.
: : 4 "C" Company. : : 5 "D" " : : 6 C.O.
: : 7 Q.M. 8 Adjt. : : 9. T.O.
: : 10.M.O. : :11/12 War Diary.

ADDENDUM "A"

SECRET. COPY No. 9.

6th. Battalion The Black Watch.

OPERATION ORDERS

1. MOVE: The Battalion will move to MERZENICH to:morrow by rail.

(A) ENTRAINING STATION: MECHERNICH.
(B) DETRAINING STATION: DUREN.

Battalion will march from DUREN to MERZENICH.

2. BLANKETS: All blankets will be rolled in bundles of 10 and labelled under Company arrangements. These blankets will be collected from Company Orderly Rooms by Motor Lorry at 07.30 hours.

Officers' valises and mess:boxes will be collected by Motor Lorry from Company Messes at 08.00 hours.

3. TRANSPORT will be at Entraining Station ready to commence loading at 08.00 hours.

4. FATIGUES: (a) O.C. "D" Company will detail a loading party of 1 Officer and 30 Pther Ranks to report to Transport Officer at Station at 08.00 hours prompt. This party will proceed to Station fully equipped ready to entrain after transport has been loaded.

(b). O.C. "C" Company will detail a party of 1 Officer and 30 Other Ranks to load tables etc. at Station. They will be at Station at 08.00 hours.

5. ENTRAINING OFFICER:

Lieutenant W.W. SPEID M.C. is detailed as Entraining Officer and will report at Station at 08.00 hours and have trucks and carriages allotted to Companies etc.

[signature] Captain
Adjutant 6th BLACK WATCH.

COPY No. 1 : File. COPY No. 2 : "C" Coy.
: : 3 : "D" Coy. : : 4 : T.O.
: : 5 : Q.M. : : 6 : Adjt.
: : 7 : C.O. : : 8 : M.O.
: : 9/10 : War Diary.

SECRET. **6th. Battalion The Black Watch (R.H.)**

ADDENDUM to OPERATION ORDERS

of to:day's date.

Para. 4. "C" Company Cooker will also be taken.

1. DRESS: Full Marching Order: Greatcoats will be worn: Leather jerkins in packs: Steel Helmets secured by straps on back of packs.

Water bottles will be filled before leaving.

2. DETACHED: Other Ranks of "A" Company not proceeding with Company. will be attached to "C" Company for rations pay discipline and accomodation from to:morrow.

Other Ranks of "B" Company will be similarly attached to "D" Company from to:morrow.

8/3/19.

(Sgd.) R.D.NICOLL Captain
Adjutant 6th. BLACK WATCH.

APPENDIX B.

6th BATTALION THE BLACK WATCH.

	OFFICERS:	OTHER RANKS.
Strength of Battalion on 4th March	32	478
: : : : 11th :	30	456
: : : : 18th :	34	562
: : : : 25th :	30	630
: : : : 28th :	45	630

Above are the actual numbers of Officers and Other Ranks with the Battalion.

APPENDIX C.

6th Battalion The Black Watch (R.H)

OFFICERS and OTHER RANKS JOINED during month of MARCH ~~191~~ 1919.

OFFICERS.

Lieut.	W.BAIRD	18/3/19.
Lieut.	A.D.McDIARMID	13/3/19.
Lieut.	F.W.WHITEHEAD	do.
Lieut.	A.C.SKINNER	do.
Lieut.	D.A.GRANT	12/3/19.
Lieut.	W.D.G.REID	do.
2/Lieut.	H.L.BIRRELL	do.
2/Lieut.	J.McAUSLAN	do.
2/Lieut.	T.McLURE	do.
Lieut.	D.B.McLAREN	20/3/19.
2/Lieut.	W.O.FRASER	25/3/19.
2/Lieut.	J.S.MATHEWSON	do.
2/Lieut.	G.S.WALKER	do.
Lieut.	P.W.DANE	do.
Capt.	G.A.BUTLER	do.
2/Lieut.	J.HERALD	do.
Lieut.	H.HARRISON	do.
2/Lieut.	H.B.HARLEY	do.
Lieut.	A.LEITCH	do.
Lieut.	G.G.WEIR	do.
Lieut.	W.G.ROBERTSON	do.
2/Lieut.	C.K.COLLINS	26/3/19.
Lieut.	H.M.THOMSON	27/3/19.
2/Lieut.	C.MacDONALD	28/3/19.
2/Lieut.	H.Mair	25/3/19.

OTHER RANKS.

Number		Date
183	:	13/3/19
57	:	14/3/19
6	:	26/3/19.
246.		

APPENDIX D.

6th Battalion The BLACK WATCH .

OFFICERS and OTHER RANKS AWARDED DECORATIONS during MONTH.

Lieutenant Colonel F.R.TARLETON D.S.O. LEGION D'HONNEUR CROIX DE CHEVALIER

APPENDIX E.

6th Battalion The BLACK WATCH.

List of Officers.

Lieut.Colonel	F.R.Tarleton	D.S.O.	Commanding Officer.
Major	H.G.S.MacKay	M.C.	2nd in Command.
Lieut.	H.W.H.Renton	M.C.	Assistant Adjutant.
Lieut. & Q.M.	J.C.Wilson	M.C.	Quartermaster.
Lieut.	J.C.A.Hewatt		Intelligence Officer.
2/Lieut.	J.Lindsay		Transport Officer.
2/Lieut.	J.B.Cable	M.C.	Sports Officer.
Lieut.	P.Low		Lewis Gun Officer.

"A" Company.

Lieut.	A.D.McDiarmid.		
Lieut.	A.C.Skinner		Leave 21/3/19 to 4/4/19.
2/Lieut.	F.W.F.Whitehead		
Lieut.	S.E.Masson		
2/Lieut.	F.H.Johnson	M.C.	
2/Lieut.	G.R.D.Hodge	M.C.	
2/Lieut.	A.P.A.Robertson		
2/Lieut.	J.Herald.		
2/Lieut.	J.S.Mathewson		
Lieut.	H.M.Thomson.		

"B" Company.

Captain	P.C.Hunter		
Lieut.	L.M.Fulton	M.C.	Leave 28/3/19 to 11/4/19.
Lieut.	N.M.Jones		
Lieut.	D.B.McLaren		
Lieut.	J.Carstairs.		
Lieut.	W.Baird	M.M.	
Lieut.	A.Leitch		
2/Lieut.	D.McCowan		
2/Lieut.	G.S.Walker		
2/Lieut.	H.Mair.		

"C" Company.

Captain	J.E.M.Richard		
Lieut.	D.Grant		
Lieut.	W.D.G.Reid	M.M.	Course 26/3/19.
Lieut.	G.S.Weir		
2/Lieut.	R.Craik		
2/Lieut.	J.M.Walker	D.S.O.	Leave 28/3/19 to 11/4/19.
2/Lieut.	H.L.Birrell		
2/Lieut.	M.T.McArthur.	M.C.D.C.M.	Leave 21/3/19 to 4/4/19.
2/Lieut.	W.O.Fraser		
2/Lieut.	C.K.Collins.		
2/Lieut.	C.MacDonald.		

"D" Company.

Captain	F.S.McNicoll		
Captain	G.A.Butler		
Lieut.	W.W.Speid	M.C.	
Lieut.	W.F.Brodie.		
Lieut.	H.Harrison		
2/Lieut.	T.McLure.		
2/Lieut.	J.Smart.		Demob.Train Guard 6/3/19.
2/Lieut.	P.W.Dane		
2/Lieut.	H.B.Harley.		
Lieut.	W.G.Robertson.		
2/Lieut.	J.McAuslan.		

ATTACHED.

Captain	E.C.Cobb U.S.A.M.C.
Captain	G.A.Mills C.F.

DETACHED.

Captain	R.G.A.Dickson	187th T.M.B. 19/3/19.
2/Lieut.	J.C.McKenzie	Traffic Control 5/3/19.

6th BATTALION THE BLACK WATCH.

LIST OF APPENDICES:

OPERATION ORDERS.	A.
STRENGTH OF BATTALION DURING MONTH.	B.
LIST OF OFFICERS AND OTHER RANKS JOINED DURING MONTH.	C.
LIST OF OFFICERS AND OTHER RANKS AWARDED DECORATIONS DURING MONTH.	D.
LIST OF OFFICERS AS AT 31/3/1919.	E.

==

Original

Confidential

War Diary

of

6th Bn. The Black Watch

From 1st May 1919 to 31st May 1919.

(6392) Wt. W6192/P875 1,500,000 4/18 McA & W Ltd (E 2815) Forms W3091/4.

Army Form W.3091.

Cover for Documents.

Nature of Enclosures.

Notes, or Letters written.

SECRET.

W A R D I A R Y.

of

6th (Perthshire) BATTALION The BLACK WATCH. (R.H.)

From 1st MAY to 31st MAY 1919.

ooooOoooo

VOLUME 58.

Instructions regarding War Diaries and Intelligence Summaries are contained in F. S. Regs., Part II. and the Staff Manual respectively. Title pages will be prepared in manuscript.

Army Form C. 2118.

WAR DIARY
or
INTELLIGENCE SUMMARY.
(*Erase heading not required.*)

MAY 1919

Place	Date	Hour	Summary of Events and Information	Remarks and references to Appendices
MERZENICH	1		Company Training, Adjutants parade 14 00 hrs. ~~[illegible]~~	[illegible]
	2		Company Training, adjutants parade at 1400 hrs.	[illegible]
	3		Company Training ~~adjutants~~	[illegible]
	4		Divine Service at 10.30 hours	[illegible]
	5		Company Training, adjutants parade 1400 hrs	[illegible]
	6		Company Training	[illegible]
	7		Company Training. Lecture 14 30 hrs by Rev. Canon Mayrick on "Amusements of the Ancient Romans". Conference at 10.30 hrs Coy Commanders	[illegible]
	8		Company Training Adjutants parade 14 00 hours Football match v [illegible] Batt	[illegible]
	9		Company Training, adjutants parade 14 00 hours	[illegible]
	10		Company Training.	[illegible]
	11		Divine Service at 10 30 hours.	[illegible]
	12		Company Training adjutants parade 14 00 hours. Lecture 14 30 hours by the Bishop of [illegible] on "Imperialism, ancient & modern"	[illegible]
	13		Company Training, Adjutants parade 14 00 hours. Riding School 17 00 hrs ~~[illegible]~~	[illegible]
	14		Company Training Baths allotted B Coy. One platoon of D Coy to HERBESTHAL to relieve A Coy there.	[illegible]
	15		Company Training Adjutants parade 14 00 hours ~~[illegible]~~	[illegible]
	16		Company Training. Lecture 14 30 hours by Major Healy [illegible]. "The British Empire, its wide world geographical situation"	[illegible]
	17		Company Training. Adjutants parade 14 00 hours. Company Commanders Conference at 11 00 hours	[illegible]
	18		Divine Service 10 30 hours	[illegible]
	19		Company Training. Tactical Scheme for Officers of A & B Coys under the Commanding Officer	[illegible]
	[illegible]		One platoon of D Coy to HERBESTHAL to relieve one platoon of B Coy	[illegible]

D. D. & L., London, E.C.
(A8004) Wt. W1771/Mz 31 750,000 5/17 Sch. 52 Forms/C2118/14

Instructions regarding War Diaries and Intelligence Summaries are contained in F. S. Regs., Part II. and the Staff Manual respectively. Title pages will be prepared in manuscript.

Army Form C. 2118.

WAR DIARY
or
INTELLIGENCE SUMMARY.

MAY (*Erase heading not required.*) 1919

Place	Date	Hour	Summary of Events and Information	Remarks and references to Appendices
MERZENICH	20th		Company Training adjutant's parade 14.00 hours, [illegible] one platoon of 'D' Coy to HERBESTHAL to relieve platoon of 'C' Coy.	
	21		Company Training Baths allotted 'A' Coy. H.Qrs & one platoon of 'D' Coy to HERBESTHAL to relieve 'C' Coy	
	22.		Company Training, adjutant's parade 14.00 hours.	
	23.		Company Training adjutant's parade 14.00 hours	
	24.		Company Training. Inspection of Transport by the Divisional General. (Major General Sir David Campbell KCB)	
	25		Divine Service at 10.30 hours. Company Commanders conference at 11.00 hrs.	
	26.		Company Training adjutant's parade 14.00 hrs.	
	27.		Company Training adjutant's parade 14.00 hours.	
	28.		Company Training Baths allotted to 'B' Coy.	
	29		Company Training adjutant's parade 14.00 hrs. [illegible]	
	30.		Battalion proceeded by route march to LINDORSDORF.	
	31.		Companies employed on improving billets. Company commanders conference at 11.00 hrs	

D. D. & L., London, E.C. (A8004) Wt. W1771/M2731 750,000 5/17 Sch. 52 Forms/C2118/14

SECRET. COPY NO.......

6th BATTALION THE BLACK WATCH.

OPERATION ORDERS. MONDAY 12th MAY 1919.

1. MOVE of "D" COMPANY (on WEDNESDAY 14th inst.)

   O.C. "D" Company will detail one Platoon to proceed by train to HERBESTHAL to take over the duties of Checkers from "A" Company. Platoon will proceed by train leaving DUREN at 09.45 hours.

2. DRESS. Full Marching Order.

3. BLANKETS & EXTRA KIT: Blankets will be rolled in bundles of three, labelled and taken into the carriage with the men of the party. The second (old) Kilt will be labelled under Company arrangements and tied in bundles by Sections.
   Sacking for covering these bundles can be obtained from the Quarter-Master, but must be returned to him after use.

4. TRANSPORT: The Transport Officer will arrange the necessary transport to carry Officers Kit, blankets and extra kit of the men from [illegible] to DUREN Station.

5. REDISTRIBUTION of RATIONS: O.C."D" Company will render to the Quartermaster by 1800 hours on Tuesday a statement of the Ration Strength of the Party leaving on WEDNESDAY.

6. MOVE of "A" COMPANY: "A" Company will move from HERBESTHAL to DUREN by train leaving HERBESTHAL at 16.30 hours on WEDNESDAY 14th inst

7. DRESS: Full Marching Order.

8. BLANKETS: Blankets will be rolled in bundles of three, labelled, and carried on the train with the men.

9. TRANSPORT: Transport Officer will make the necessary arrangements for transport to meet the above train on the date specified and carry Offic kit and blankets from DUREN Station to [illegible].

10. BILLETS: O.C. "A" Company will arrange billets for this party.

11. REDISTRIBUTION of RATIONS: O.C."A" Company will render to the Quartermaster by 18.00 hours on Tuesday a statement of the ration strength of the party arriving from HERBESTHAL .

12. COOKING UTENSILS: "A" Company will bring back all dixies, holdall and knives belonging to the Company which are at HERBESTHAL.

[signature]

Lieutenant.
A/Adjutant 6th Black Watch.

COPIES TO:-
C.O.
O.C."A" Coy, O.C."C" Coy, O.C."D" Coy, T.O, Q.M, War Diary, File.

SECRET. COPY NO.........7

6th BATTALION, The BLACK WATCH.

OPERATION ORDERS.

1. **MOVE of "D" COMPANY:-** On MONDAY, 19th MAY, "D" Company will commence to move by train to HERBESTHAL to take over the duties of Supply Guards from "C" Company.
"D" Company will move as follows:-
1 Platoon by train leaving DUREN at 09.45 hours on the 19th inst
1 : : : : : : 09.45 : : : 20th :
1 Platoon and Company Headquarters by train leaving DUREN at 09.45 hours on the 21st inst

2. **DRESS:-** Full Marching Order.

3. **BLANKETS and EXTRA KITS:-** Blankets will be rolled in bundles of three, labelled and taken into the carriage with the men of the party. The second (old) kit will be tied in bundles by Sections and labelled under Company arrangements. Sacking for covering these bundles can be obtained from the Quarter-Master, but must be returned to him after use.

4. **TRANSPORT:-** The Transport Officer will arrange the necessary transport to carry Officers' kits, blankets and extra kit of the men from MERZENICH to DUREN Station.

5. **DISTRIBUTION of RATIONS:-** O.C. "D" Company will render to the Quarter-Master by 09.00 hours daily a statement of ration strength of the parties.

6. **COOKER:-** "D" Company will take over the Cooker and Dixies now at HERBESTHAL.

7. **MOVE of "C" COMPANY:-** "C" Company will move from HERBESTHAL to DUREN as follows:-
1 Platoon byv train leaving HERBESTHAL at 16.50 hours on 19th ins
1 : : : : : : 16.50 hours on 20th ins
1 : and Company Headquarters by train leaving HERBESTHAL at 16.50 hours on 21st ins

8. **DRESS:-** Full Marching Order.

9. **BLANKETS:-** Blankets will be tied in bundles of three, labelled and carried in the train with the men.

10. **TRANSPORT:-** The Transport Officer will arrange for the necessary transport to meet the above trains on the dates specified and carry Officers' kits/ & blankets from DUREN Station to MERZENICH.

11. **BILLETS:-** Men of "C" Company will be accomodated in the billets presently occupied by "D" Company.

12. **RATIONS:-** O.C. "C" Company will render a statement daily by 09.00 hou to the Quarter-Master showing strength of the parties arriving from HERBESTHAL.

13. **MESSING:-** The parties arriving on the 19th and 20th inst. will be attached to "D" Company for messing.

14. ACKNOWLEDGE.

18th MAY, 1919.

[signature] Lieut.,
A/Adjutant, 6th BLACK WATCH.

Copy No. 1 to "C" Coy. Copy No. 2 to "D" Coy. Copy No. 3 to Q.M.
: : 4 : T.O. : : 5 : C.O. : : 6 : File.
Copies No. 7 and 8 to War Diary.

SECRET. **1/6th Black Watch Warning Order No.8.**

Copy No. 11...

27th MAY 1919.

Map Reference 1.L. 1/100,000
2.N. 1/100,000.

Following is in continuation of Warning Order for action in event of a move forward issued 22/5/19.

1. The Greater part of 1st line Transport will move to [illegible] Area by train; remainder will march brigaded under Capt. R.G.A. DICKSON The Black Watch on J.- 2 day.
STARTING TIME, 9 am.
STARTING POINT, Junction of [illegible] and Main DUREN, COLOGNE Road. 1st Stage [illegible], 2nd Stage OPLADEN, 3rd Stage HILDEN.
(Detail of transport going by train will be issued later)

2. On J.- 3 day, Lieut. [illegible] with 1 N.C.O. per Coy. (less B.& D.Coys) will proceed to HILDEN and take over accommodation from 5th Scottish Rifles. 1 Officer and 2 N.C.Os. to be detailed by O.C. "B" Company will proceed to LANGENFELD and take over accommodation from 4th Royal Scots.

3. On J.- 2 day Battalion will march to DUREN Station.
DRESS. Marching Order.
STARTING POINT. Road Junction at N.E. Corner of Cemetary S.W. of [illegible]
STARTING TIME. to be detailed later.
ORDER of MARCH. Headquarters, Colour Party, "C", "A", "B",
ROUTE. Railway Crossing 600 yards N.W. of "D" of [illegible]--S.W. of Railway to Tram Line through DUREN--thence under railway bridge to Station.
100 yards distance between Companies.

4. COLOUR PARTY will consist of Lieut. [illegible] M.C. a Subaltern to be detailed by O.C. "A" Coy. and three N.C.Os. to be detailed by O.C. Headquarter Company.

5. Battalion will entrain at DUREN Station. Headquarters Coy. "A" "B" "C" Coys. for HILDEN. "D" Company, with Lewis Gun Limbers and Cooker, will take over the duties at LANGENFELD until relieved by Troops of the 1st Brigade from OPLADEN or Machine Gunners and will detrain when the train reaches that Station.

6. Completion of relief of Units and posts will be reported by O.C. Companies to Battalion Headquarters at HILDEN.

7. Maps are issued as follows:-

4.	2.N.	1/100,000	Per Company.
4.	1.L.	1/100,000	
1.	Sheet [illegible]	1/250,000.	

8. ACKNOWLEDGE.

Sd. D.A. GRANT
Lieut.
A/Adjutant 6th Black Watch.

COPIES TO:- No.1. C.O. 2.-6 O.C.Coys. 7. Q.M.&T.O. 9 Lt. [illegible] 10.11 War Diary. 12. FILE.

SECRET.

COPY No. 11......

6th Battalion The Black Watch.

OPERATION ORDERS.

29th MAY 1919.

Map reference:- Sheet, 1.L Germany 1/100,000.

1. MOVE. The Battalion will move to LINDERSDORF by route march tomorrow.
DRESS. Marching Order.
STARTING POINT. Road Junction at S.W. corner of cemetery S.W. of MERZENICH.
STARTING TIME. 10.00 hours.
ORDER of MARCH. Headquarters, Colour Party, A.C.& B. Companies
ROUTE. Point 500 N.E.of "L" in DISTELRATH - Point 200 N.W. of "R" in DISTELRATH.Point 438 - Point 163 KRANTHAN - LINDERSDORF.
100 yards distance between Companies.

2. COLOUR PARTY. will consist of a subaltern to be detailed by O.C. "A"Coy. and one to be detailed by O.C."D" Coy.and three N.C.Os. to be detailed by O.C.Headquarter Company.

3. TRANSPORT. The transport will move independently.
STARTING TIME. 10-15 ~~09.00~~ hours.
STARTING POINT. Road Junction at S.W. corner of Cemetery S.W. of MERZENICH.
ROUTE. DISTELRATH-DUREN-KRANTHAN-LINDERSDORF.

4. BAGGAGE. Blankets,spare kilts and tunics,rolled in bundles by sections will be stacked at Company Offices by 07.30 hours.
Officers'valises,mess boxes,and Company Stores will be stacked at 08.45 hours. at Coy Offices

5. STORES. All wash basins,tools,fire buckets,ablution benches,tables, forms,meat safes will be returned immediately to Q.M.Stores.

6. RATIONS. Dinner will be cooked on the march.Remainder of the unexpired part of the day's rations will be carried on the man.

7. LOADING PARTY. Company in waiting will detail one platoon (minimum strength 20 O.Rs.) to report to Q.M.Stores at 08.00 hours tomorrow.

8. DUTIES. All duties found by this Battalion will remain until further orders.

9. LEWIS GUNS. A.No.1 Lewis Gunner of each Company will accompany the Company Lewis Gun Limbers.

10. ACKNOWLEDGE.

Sd. D.A.GRANT. Lieut.
A/Adjutant 6th Black Watch.

Copy No.1. to C.O. Copy No.2.to 6 Coy. Copy 7 to T.O. Copy No.8.to Q.M.
No.9 to Brigade. No. 10.to 11. War Diary. No. 12 File.

SECRET. 8th Battalion The Black Watch. COPY NO.......

29/5/19.

WARNING ORDER No. 3.

Following is in continuation of Warning Order No.2.for action in the event of a move forward issued 27th May 1919.

1. The following transport will proceed by rail:-
No.1.Train Two Baggage Waggons.
No.2. 9. Lewis Gun Wagons,four cookers,2 watercarts,1 maltose cart,1 mess cart,eleven,riders,7 pack mules 3 spare Animals,blankets,rations,surplus kits.
Personnel for transport and stores to be at station three hours before scheduled time of departure.
Horses will be watered before entraining.
Ropes will be provided for tying up the horses in the trucks.
Horses will be unharnessed,harness stacked in the middle of each truck and two men must travel in each truck.

2. Company on duty will detail an entraining Officer to report to Brigade Representative at the entraining station half an hour before the specified time for transport to arrive.He will be in possession of a statement showing:-

No. of Officers
: : Other Ranks.
: : Animals.
: ; 2.Wheeled Vehicles.
: : 4. : :

to be entrained.

3. Ammunition will be issued before entraining,up to 120 rounds per man.
This may be drawn from the reserve at the Quartermaster's Stores.

4. ACKNOWLEDGE.

Sd. D.A.GRANT. Lieut.
A/Adjutant 8th Black Watch.

COPIES TO:-
No.1.C.O. No.2.-6 Coys. No.7.to T.O. No.8.Q.M. No.9.10.War Diary. 11 File.

APPENDIX B.

6th BATTALION THE BLACK WATCH.

	OFFICERS.	OTHER RANKS.
Strength of Battalion on 2nd MAY.	38	452.
" " " " 9th "	30	524.
" " " " 16th "	33	544.
" " " " 23rd "	33	513.
" " " " 30th "	29	539.

Above are the actual numbers of Officers and Other Ranks with the Battalion.

APPENDIX C.

6th BATTALION The BLACK WATCH.

OFFICERS and OTHER RANKS JOINED during month of MAY, 1919.

OFFICERS.

N I L .

OTHER RANKS.

2	:	1/5/19.
9	:	2/5/19.
5	:	8/5/19.
3	:	9/5/19.
3	:	18/5/19.
2	:	23/5/19.
2	:	27/5/19.
1	:	31/5/19.
27.		

6th Battalion The Black Watch.

List of Officers

Rank	Name	Decoration	Remarks
Lieut.Colonel.	W.GREEN	D.S.O.	Commanding Officer.
Lieut.Colonel.	F.R.TARLETON	D.S.O.	Leave 4/5/19.
Captain	P.B.HEPBURN	M.C.	O.C."C" Coy. Leave.
:	F.S.McNICOLL		Leave 8/5/19.
Lieut.	L.M.FULTON	M.C.	O.C."B" Company.
:	P.LOW		Lewis Gun Officer.
:	W.F.BRODIE.		O.C."D"Company.
:	J.CARSTAIRS		
:	G.A.BUTLER		Signalling Officer(Course)
:	W.W.SPEID	M.C.	
:	N.M.JONES		
:	A.D.McDIARMID		Course 3/5/19.
:	D.A.GRANT.		Acting Adjutant.
:	W.D.G.GRANT.		
:	W.BAIRD	M.M.	
:	A.LEITCH.		
:	G.G.WEIR		Hospital 6/5/19.
:	H.M.THOMSON		Bde.P.R.O. 31/3/19z
:	S.E.MASSON		
:	D.KINNOCH		
:	H.W.H.RENTON	M.C.	Intelligence Officer.
: & Q.M.	J.C.WILSON	M.C.	Quartermaster.
2/Lieut.	J.LINDSAY		Transport Officer.
:	F.W.F.WHITEHEAD		
:	G.R.D.HODGE	M.C.	
:	F.H.JOHNSON	M.C.	
:	J.M.WALKER	D.S.O.	
:	J.C.McKENZIE		Attd.Traffic Control 5/3/19.
:	J.SMART		
:	M.T.McARTHUR	M.C.D.C.M.	
:	D.McCOWAN		Attd.Demob.Train Guard.7/5/19.
:	J.B.CABLE	M.C.	
:	R.CRAIK		Leave 15/5/19.
:	J.McAUSLAN		
:	H.L.BIRRELL		Hospital 28/4/19.
:	J.HERALD.		
:	J.S.MATHEWSON		
:	G.S.WALKER		
:	H.MAIR		
:	C.K.COLLINS		
:	H.B.HARLEY		Assist.Education Officer.
:	R.J.PRESCOTT		
:	J.McGLADDERY.		

ATTACHED.

Rank	Name	Corps	Remarks
Captain	W.M. KERR	R.A.M.C.	Medical Officer.
: (Rev)	D.CONACHER	C.F.	Chaplain.

6th BATTALION THE BLACK WATCH.

LIST OF APPENDICES.

Original.

Confidential.

War Diary

of

6th. Bn. The Black Watch. (R.H.)

From 1st. June 1919 to 30th. June 1919.

(Volume 59)

SECRET.

W A R D I A R Y.

of

6th (Perthshire) BATTALION The BLACK WATCH. (R.H.)

From 1st JUNE to 30th JUNE 1919.

VOLUME 59.

Instructions regarding War Diaries and Intelligence Summaries are contained in F. S. Regs., Part II. and the Staff Manual respectively. Title pages will be prepared in manuscript.

WAR DIARY

or

~~INTELLIGENCE SUMMARY.~~ 6th Bn. The Black Watch.

(Erase heading not required.)

Army Form C. 2118.

Place	Date 1919 JUNE	Hour	Summary of Events and Information	Remarks and references to Appendices
LENDERSDORF	1		Divine Service at 10.30 hours	HWR
"	2		Practice Ceremonial Parade for Kings Birthday	HWR
"	3		Kings Birthday Ceremonial Parade at 10.00 hours. Remainder of day observed as a holiday	HWR
"	4		Company training	HWR
"	5		Company training. Adjutants Parade at 14.00 hours. C Company proceeded to BOGHEIM to work on Rifle range under construction	HWR
"	6		Company training. Adjutants Parade at 14.00 hours	HWR
"	7		Company training. Conference of Company Commanders and Specialist Officers at 11.00 hours	HWR
"	8		Divine Service at 10.30 hours	HWR
"	9		Company training. Adjutants Parade at 14.00 hours	HWR
"	10		Company training.	HWR
"	11		Company training.	HWR
"	12		Company training. One platoon of B Coy proceeded to MALMEDY for guard duties	HWR
"	13		Company training.	HWR
"	14		Company training.	HWR
"	15		Divine Service at 10.30 hours	HWR
"	16		Company training.	HWR
"	17		Company training. C Company returned to LENDERSDORF from BOGHEIM	HWR

264152—Wt. W 5343/P 1707—1250M—9-18—W. & S. Ld.—(E 5808)—C 2118/17.

Instructions regarding War Diaries and Intelligence Summaries are contained in F. S. Regs., Part II. and the Staff Manual respectively. Title pages will be prepared in manuscript.

WAR DIARY
or
~~INTELLIGENCE SUMMARY.~~ 6th B. The Black Watch.

(*Erase heading not required.*)

Army Form C. 2118.

Place	Date 1919 JUNE	Hour	Summary of Events and Information	Remarks and references to Appendices
LENDERSDORF	18		Battalion, less detachment at HERBESTHAL, entrained at DUREN for HILDEN. The platoon of B Coy. from MALMEDY rejoined the battalion at DUREN before the entraining. The battalion went into billets in HILDEN	HWR
HILDEN.	19		D Coy rejoined battalion from HERBESTHAL, arriving in busses. Conference for Company Commanders & Specialist Officers at 18.00 hours	HWR
"	20		Company training	
"	21		Battalion Inspection Parade at 10.00 hours. B Coy. took over examining posts at DICKHAUS and KEMPERDICK from 8th Battalion, The Black Watch	HWR
"	22		Divine Service at 10.30 hours	HWR
"	23		Company Training	HWR
"	24		Company Training	HWR HWR
"	25		Company Training	
"	26		Company Training	HWR
"	27		Company Training	HWR
"	28		Company Training	HWR
"	29		Divine Service at 10.00 hours	HWR
"	30.		Company Training. B Coy. relieved at examining posts at DICKHAUSE and KEMPERDICK by 4th Battalion, Royal Scots Fusiliers	HWR.

[signature]

LIEUT. COLONEL,
Commanding 6th (Perthshire) BATTN. THE BLACK WATCH.

D. D. & L., London, E.C.
(A8004) Wt W1771/M2031 750,000 5/17 Sch. 52 Forms/C2118/14

APPENDIX "A"

6th Battalion The Black Watch.

SECRET.

Copy No....5....

WARNING ORDER. 10/6/19.

1. "B" Coy. (less one platoon) will take over detachment duties at MONTJOIE and one Platoon "B" Coy. (approximate strength 1 officer 2 N.C.Os. & 30 Other Ranks) will take over the detachment duties at MELMEDY on the 12th inst.

2. Company Cooks, Lewis Gun Limber and Company Commander's charger will proceed to MONTJOIE by road. An officer will accompany this party.

3. An Officer and one N.C.O. will proceed to MONTJOIE and one N.C.O. to MALMEDY today to make arrangements for the relief.

4. Details of time and train arrangements will be notified later.

5. ACKNOWLEDGE.

Dalgrain
Lieut.
A/Adjutant 6th Black Watch.

Copies to:- No.1.C.O. No.2.O.C."B"Coy. No.3.Q.M. No.4.T.O. Nos.5 &6 No.7. File.

APPENDIX "A".

SECRET. 6th Battalion The Black Watch. Copy No.......

WARNING ORDER NO.1.

Action in the event of a Move Forward.

1. J.Day is the day of termination of the Armistice.

2. On J -2 days the 3rd Highland Brigade moves by train to BENRATH Area in relief of the Lowland Division.

3. On J -2 days the Battalion, less "D" Coy. will march to DUREN Station where it will entrain for HILDEN.
DRESS:-Marching Order.
STARTING POINT:- "A" Company Mess House.
STARTING TIME:- To be detailed later.
ORDER OF MARCH:- Headquarters, "A" Coy. Colour Party, "B" and "C".
ROUTE:- KRAUTHSN - DUREN to Railway Station.
100 yards distance between Companies.

4. COLOUR PARTY. H.W.H.RENTON M.C. A subaltern to be detailed by O.C. "A" Company, 3 N.C.Os. to be detailed by O.C.H.Q.Coy.

5. TRANSPORT:- will march to DUREN Station by same route as Battalion.
STARTING TIME:-will be detailed later.
It will arrive at Station 3 hours before the starting time of train.
Horses will be watered before entraining.
Transport Officer is responsible that ropes are available for tying up horses in the trucks.
Horses will be unharnessed, harness stacked in the centre of each truck. Two men willtravel in each truck.

6. RATIONS. The unexpired portion of the days rations will be carried on the man. One days rations will be carried on the train.

7. Lieut. J. Carstairs will act as Battalion entraining Officer, he will report at Battalion H.Q. for instructions at 6 pm. on J.-3 days.

8. On J -3 days Lieut. Harley with 1 N.C.O. per Company (less "D" Coy.) will proceed by train to HILDEN and take over accommodation and list of duties from 8th Bn. Scottish Rifles.

9. Companies will return all wash basins, latrine buckets, and fire buckets to Q.M. Stores by 4.30 hours on J.-3 days.
All heavy Luggage, spare kilts, jackets, and blankets in excess of 1 per man and all Officers' baggage in excess of 1 package per officer and all rifles and equipment of men on leave, will be stacked at Q.M. Stores by 7 pm, on J-3 days.
Remaining blankets per man and Officers valises and mens kits will be stacked at Q.M.Stores by 1½ hours after Reveille on J-2 day.

10. Company in waiting will find 2 platoons on J-3 days and 2 platoons on J,-2 days for work at Q.M. Stores.

11. O.C. Companies will render a state showing entraining strength by 7 pm, on J-3 day.

12. "D" Company will remain at HERBESTHAL until relieved. Men of "D" Company in LANDERSDORF will be attached to "C" Company.

13. Completion of relief and taking over of posts will be reported to Battalion Headquarters.

14. Maps of New Area have been issued.

15. ACKNOWLEDGE.

Sd. D.A.GRANT. Lieut.
A/Adjutant 6th Bn. The Black Watch.

Copy to:- No.1.C.O. No.2. to 7, Coys. 8.T.O. 9, Q.M. 10 &11 War Diary. No.12. File.

APPENDIX "A".

SECRET. 6th Battalion The Black Watch. Copy.No........

ADDENDUM To WARNING ORDER No.1.

Para.8. After 8th Scottish Rifles add "and 4th Royal Scots."

Sd. D.A.GRANT.Lieut.
A/Adjutant 6th Black Watch

SECRET. ADDENDUM to WARNING ORDER No.1. Copy No......

Para. 9. For Men's Kits read MESS KITS.

"D" Company will be releived on J.-1 day by a Company detailed b 2nd Midland Divsion.

Further Orders will be issued as regards move to join Battalion.

The detachment at Malmedy will be releived on a date to be notified lat

Detachment of "C" Company at Golf Course will rejoin on J.- 3 day.

Sd. D.A.GRANT. Lieut.
A/Adjutant 6th Black Watch.

16/6/19.

SECRET. 6th Bn. The Black Watch. Copy No.............

ADDENDUM TO WARNING ORDER NO.1.

STARTING TIME. 14.45 hours.

DRESS:- Marching Order(kilt aprons will be worn)
(Company Commanders will be mounted)

TRANSPORT:-

Starting Time:- 13.15 hours.
Starting Point:- "A" Company Mess House.
Order of March:- "B" Company - Transport

Mess kit will be stacked at Q.M.Stores not later than 13.00 hours.

The following table shows the train arrangements:-

		LOADS.	DEP.	Arr.HILDEN.
No1.Personnel	(2 Coaches	17.30 hrs.	18.00 hrs.	20.23 hrs.
~~No.1.Omnibus~~	(& 38 Covers.			
No.1. Omnibus	(1Coach 30 Covers & 17 Flats.	16.00 hrs.	18.56 hrs.	22.28 hrs.

17/6/19.

Sd. D.A.GRANT.Lieut.
A/Adjutant 6th Black Watch.

Copies to:- No.1.C.O. No.2-7 Coys. No.8.T.O.No.9.Q.M. No.10.Lt.Carstairs
: 11 & 12 War Diary No.13.File.

APPENDIX "A".

SECRET. Copy No......6

6th Battalion The Black Watch.

OPERATION ORDERS.

WEDNESDAY 4th JUNE 1919

1. MOVE of "C" COMPANY on Thursday 5th inst.

   "C" Company will proceed by route march to BOGHEIM tomorrow, when it will be employed in construction of ranges.

2. DRESS: Marching Order.
   Starting time : 10.00 hours.
   Starting Point : Company Parade Ground.
   ROUTE: FISCHICH (point 158) KUFFERATH, DERRHEIM, and BOGHEIM.

3. Company Cooker will accompany the Company in the march.

4. All valises, blankets, spare kits and palliasses, (full) delf, will be stacked at Company Headquarters by 09.00 hours tomorrow.
   It will be conveyed to BOGHEIM by motor lorry.
   All kit of men on leave will be handed over to Quartermaster by 09.00 hours.

5. On arrival at BOGHEIM the Company will pitch its own Camp.
   Tents will be delivered under arrangements to be made by Division.

6. Rations for 6th inst will be carried by lorry.

7. Acknowledge.

[signature] Lieut.
A/Adjutant 6th Black Watch.

Copy No.1 to C.O. Copy No.2 to O.C."C"Coy. Copy No.3 to [illegible]
" " 4 " Q.M. " " 5 " File. " " 6 & 7 War Diary.

APPENDIX "A"

SECRET. Copy.No......

ADDENDUM to WARNING ORDERS No.1

Only war equipment will be taken forward in the first instance.

All surplus kits stores palliases beds blankets in excess of 1 per man tents etc will be stored in dumps.

Number of tents left in the stores will be reported to this office by 18.00 hours on J=3 day.

Cook:houses latrines and other structures that cannot be collected will be handed over to the Burgomaster.
Lists of such stores will be made out in quadruplicate and handed in to Orderly Room by 18.00 hours on J=3 day.

O.C."C"Company will detail one Section as Guard over dump at BOGHEIM and the Platoon less one Section as Guard over the stores at LENDERSDORF.

Four days rations will be left with the Guards.

O.C.Companies before leaving will obtain from the owners of the billets occupied by their Companies the usual certificate that no damage has been done.

Battalion will entrain as under :

No.3 Train Personnel (less "B" & "D" Company and Transport.)

No.1 Omnibus Train. "B"Company Transport (blankets rations and surplus kit will be loaded on this train.)

"B"Company will proceed to the station with the Transport and load No.1 Omnibus train.

(Sgd) D.A.GRANT
Lieut.
A/Adjutant 6th BLACK WATCH

18/8/19.

APPENDIX "A"

12

SECRET. 6th Battalion The BLACK WATCH. COPY NO......

ADDENDUM to WARNING ORDER No.1.

For No.1 Personnel Train read " No.3.Personnel"

For No.1. Omnibus : : "No.2. Omnibus".

Lieut.
A/Adjutant 6th Black Watch.

Copies to:- No.1. C.O.No.2.-6 Coys. No.7.M.O.No.8.T.O.No.9.Q.M.No.10. Lt. Carstairs. No.11.& 12.War Diary. No.13.File.

APPENDIX "A"

SECRET. COPY No. 10....

6th Battalion The BLACK WATCH.

23/6/ 19.

WARNING ORDER No.1.

1. Troops will be prepared to move forward by 05.15 hours 24th inst.

2. From receipt of this order an Officer will be on duty at each Coy. Headquarters.
The Subaltern of the Day will sleep in the Orderly Room. No Officer will leave the Battalion Area.

3. On receipt of order occupy posts.
"D" Company will place Guards as under:-
One Platoon to Post Office and Telephone Exchange at 107 Kaiser Wilhelm Strasse.
One Platoon to Gas works and Electric Sub-Station at KIRCHHOFSTRASSE
One Platoon Water works at HULSON.
"A" Company will be responsible for guarding HULSON STATION and the Railway from HILDEN to OLHIGG by constant patrols.

4. As soon as all Lowland Division Troops have passed through the posts held by "B" Company the Company will concentrate at MEIDE and hold itself in readiness to move at short notice.

Sd. D.A.GRANT.
Lieut.A/Adjt.
6th Black Watch.

Copies to:- No.1.C.O.Nos. 2.to 6.Coys.No.7.Q.M.No.8.T.O.Nos.9 & 10.War Diary.
No.11.File.

APPENDIX "A".

13.

SECRET. 6th BATTALION The BLACK WATCH. Copy No.. ....

WARNING ORDER No.2.

Action in event of MOVE backward.

1. "A" day is ZERO day.

2. On "A" day perimeter posts will be relieved by Troops of the 3rd Lowland Brigades.
Completion of reliefs to be reported to this office by wire.

3. On "B" day Battalion will march to HILDEN Station where it will entrain for DUREN.
DRESS. Marching Order (Kilt aprons will be worn.)
Companies will march independently to the Station by 13.30 hours.
On arrival at DUREN the Battalion will march to billets at LENDERSDORF.
ORDER of MARCH. "H.Q." "A" "B" "C" and "D".

4. COLOUR PARTY. Lieut.H.W.H.RENTON M.C. a Subaltern to be detailed by O.C."D" Company, and 3 N.C.O's to be detailed by O.C."H.Q." Company.

5. TRANSPORT. (Less two baggage wagons, 2 Lewis gun wagons and the tip cart which will proceed by road.) will march to HILDEN Station and ~~xx~~ entrain for DUREN.
It will arrive at station three hours before starting time of the train.
Horses will be watered before entraining.
Transport Officer is responsible that ropes are available for tying up horses in the truck.
Transport proceeding by road will march independently to billets in OPLADEN where it will be concentrated under command of O.C. 528 Coy. R.A.S.C.
Guides will meet Transport at Road Junction ½ mile North of N in OPLADEN (sheet GERMANY 2 K 1/100000)
STARTING TIME. 12.00 hours.
ROUTE. Hagel; Kreuz, Richrath, Immigrath, Landenfeld, and Opladen.

6. RATIONS. The unexpended portion of the days rations will be carried on the men. Two days rations will be carried on the personnel train.

7. Lieut.J.CARSTAIRS will act as Battalion Entraining Officer. He will report to Orderly Room at 10.00 hours on "A" day for instructions.

8. Lieut.J.M.WALKER D.S.O. and one N.C.O. per Company will proceed by train to DUREN on "A" day and arrange for billets at LENDERSDORF.

9. Companies will return to Q.M.Stores by 16.30 hours on "A" day all basins, latrine buckets etc.
Officers valises, blankets, will be stacked at Q.M.Stores 1½ hours after reveille on "B" day.
Mess kits will be stacked at Q.M.Stores by 12.30 hours.

10. O.C.Companies will render to Orderly Room by 18.00 hours on "A" day state showing entraining strength.

11. Company in waiting will find one platoon on "A" day and one platoon on "B" day for work at Q.M.Stores.

WARNING ORDER NO.2 (Continued)

12. The following table shows the train arrangements:

TRAIN.	UNITS.	LOADS.	DEPARTS.
No.1 Personnel.	H.Q.3rd. H.Bde. 6th. Black Watch. 3rd. H.T.M.B.	1400 hours.	1430 hours.
No.1 OMNIBUS.	1 Coy. 8th. Black Watch. Transport Bde. H.Q. Transport 6th. Black Watch. Transport T.M.B. 4 Cookers 8th. Black Watch. Surplus Kit(Rations) of Bde. H.Q. 6th. B.W. and 3rd. H.T.M.B.	1500 hours.	1800 hours.

Journey to DUREN takes about 3 Hours.

13. Acknowledge.

Sd. D.A.Grant. Lieut. A/Adjutant.
6th. Black Watch.

26/6/19.

Copies to:
(1) C.O. (2.6.) Coys. (7) T.O. (8) Q.M. (9) Lt. Carstairs. (10)3rd. High.Bde.
(11) M.O. (12) R.S.M. (13 &14) War Diary.(15) File.

APPENDIX "A"

SECRET. 6th Battalion The Black Watch. COPY NO......7

AMENDMENT to WARNING ORDER No.2. 29/6/19.

Map Reference Sheet:- Germany 2 K. 1/100.000.

Para.3. Delete "Companies will march independently to the Station by 13.30 hours" and substitute:-
" Battalion will march to the Station.
Starting Point. Cross Roads 220^x N.W.of "H".HAGEL (Map squar (8.B.)).
Order of March. H.Q. "A", COLOUR PARTY, "B", "C", "D". Coys.
Starting Time. 13.10 hours."

Sd. D.A.GRANT. Lieut.A/Adjt.
6th Black Watch.

SECRET. 6th Battalion The Black Watch. COPY NO.....10..

June 30th will be "A" Day.

ACKNOWLEDGE.

Sd. D.A.GRANT. Lieut,A/Adjt.
6th Black Watch.

Copies to:- All Companies T.O. Q.M. M.O. Lts. Carstairs,Johnstone,Renton,
Signal Officer.

APPENDIX."B"

6th Battalion The Black Watch.

STRENGTH of BATTALION ON:-	OFFICERS.	OTHER RANKS.
2/6/19.	30.	577.
9/6/19.	28.	584.
16/6/19.	28.	587.
23/6/19.	26.	669.
30/6/19.	26.	649.

APPENDIX "C".

6th Battalion The BLACK WATCH.

OFFICERS & OTHER RANKS JOINED DURING MONTH OF JUNE 1919.

OFFICERS.

N I L .

OTHER RANKS.

4.	2/6/19.
11.	12/6/19.
2.	16/6/19.
3.	20/6/19.
1.	27/6/19.
21.	

APPENDIX. "D".

6th Battalion The BLACK WATCH.

OFFICERS & OTHER RANKS AWARDED DECORATIONS during MONTH.

Lieut. W.MACINTYRE ,(Demobilized)	MILITARY CROSS.
No. 265030 R.Q.M.S. J.HOOD. (Demobilized)	MERITORIOUS SERVICE MEDAL.

6th Battalion The Black Watch.

List of Officers.

Lieut.Colonel	W.GREEN D.S.O.	Commanding Officer.
Lieut.Colonel	F.R.TARLETON D.S.O.	Leave 4/5/19.
Lieut.	D.A.GRANT	A/Adjutant.
Lieut.	H.W.H.RENTON M.C.	Assist.Adjutant.
Lieut.& Q.M.	J.C.WILSON M.C.	Quartermaster.
Lieut.	P.LOW.	Lewis Gun Officer.
Lieut.	G.A.BUTLER	Signalling Officer.
2/Lieut.	H.B.HARLEY	Assist.Educational Officer.
2/Lieut.	J.LINDSAY	Transport Officer.
	"A" Company.	
Lieut.	A.D.McDIARMID	Company Commander.
Lieut.	S.E.MASSON	
Lieut.	F.H.JOHNSON M.C.	
2/Lieut.	G.R.D.HODGE M.C.	
2/Lieut.	F.W.F.WHITEHEAD.	
	"B" Company.	
Lieut.	L.M.FULTON M.C.	Company Commander.
Lieut.	N.M.JONES	
Lieut.	D.KINNOCH.	
Lieut.	J.CARSTAIRS	P.R.I.
Lieut.	A.LEITCH	
2/Lieut.	D.McCOWAN	Train Guard Cologne.
Lieut.	W.BAIRD M.M.	Leave 11/6/19 to 25/6/19.
	"C" Company.	
Captain	P.B.HEPBURN M.C.	Company Commander.
Lieut.	W.D.G.REID M.M.	
Lieut.	J.M.WALKER D.S.O.	
2/Lieut.	R.CRAIK	
2/Lieut.	M.T.McARTHUR M.C. D.C.M.	
	"D" Company.	
Lieut.	W.W.SPEID M.C.	Company Commander.
Lieut.	J.B.CABLE M.C.	
2/Lieut.	J.McAUSLAN	
2/Lieut.	J.McGLADDERY.	
2/Lieut.	G.S.WALKER.	

DETACHED.

Lieut.	H.M.THOMSON	"A" Coy.	Attcd.3rd Highland Bde.P.R.O.
Lieut.	G.G.WEIR	"C" :	Hospital 6/5/19.
Lieut.	W.F.BRODIE	"D" :	Attd.Bde.P.R.O.
2/Lieut.	H.L.BIRRELL	"C" :	Hospital.
2/Lieut.	J.HERALD	"A" :	Attcd. R.A.O.C. Cologne.
2/Lieut.	R.J.PRESCOTT	"B" :	Attcd. T.M.B. 27/6/19.
2/Lieut.	C.K.COLLINS.	"C" :	Attcd. D.D.O.S.(H,)Div. 18/5/19

ATTACHED.

Captain (Rev.)	D.COMACHER C.F.	
Captain	T.KENWORTHY M.C.	R.A.M.C.

LIST OF APPENDICES.

OPERATION ORDERS	"A".
STRENGTH OF BATTALION DURING MONTH.	"B".
LIST OF OFFICERS & OTHER RANKS JOINED DURING MONTH	"C".
LIST OF DECORATIONS AWARDED DURING MONTH.	"D".
LIST of OFFICERS.	"E".

Confidential

War Diary

of

6th Bn. Black Watch (R. H.)

From 1st July 1919 ~ To ~ 31st July 1919.

Original.

Volume 10

50

(6414) Wt. W3906/P1607 2,500,000 7/18 McA & W Ltd (E 3591) Forms W3091/4.

Army Form W.3091.

Cover for Documents.

Nature of Enclosures.

Notes, or Letters written.

SECRET.

W A R D I A R Y.

of

6th (Perthshire) BATTALION The BLACK WATCH (R.H.)

From 1st JULY 1919 to 31st JULY 1919.

VOLUME 60.

Instructions regarding War Diaries and Intelligence Summaries are contained in F. S. Regs., Part II. and the Staff Manual respectively. Title pages will be prepared in manuscript.

WAR DIARY
or
~~INTELLIGENCE SUMMARY.~~ WB
(Erase heading not required.)

Army Form C. 2118.

Place	Date	Hour	Summary of Events and Information	Remarks and references to Appendices
HILDEN	1.7.19		Battalion entrained at HILDEN for DUREN. Marched from DUREN to Billets at LENDERSDORF.	WB
LENDERSDORF	2-7-19		Coy Training.	WB
- Do - Do -	3-7-19		Company Training. D Coy proceeded to ~~HER~~ HERBESTHAL on Detachment, C Coy to BOGHIEM to construct Rifle Range.	WB
- Do - Do -	4.7.19		Company Training.	WB
- Do - Do -	5.7.19		Company Training.	WB
- Do - Do -	6.7.19		Divine Service at 11-30 hours	WB
- Do - Do -	7.7.19		Coy Training and Education. Lt. Col. Green D.S.O., Lieut H W Renton M.C. Lieut J Gable MC and party of 7 (Seven) O. R.s with Colours proceeded to PARIS to represent Battalion in Victory March of 14 7 19	WB
- Do - Do -	8.7.19		Holiday to celebrate Peace. Divine Service at 10.00. Gymkhana in afternoon. Concert by Batt. Concert Party in Evening	WB
Do - Do	9.7.19		Company Training	WB
- Do - Do -	10.7.19		Company Training and Education.	WB
- Do - Do -	11.7.19		Company Training.	WB
- Do - Do -	12.7.19		Company Training. "Croix De Guerre" pinned on Colours by GENERAL BERDOULAT [illegible] PARIS	WB
- Do - Do -	13.7.19		Divine Service 11.00 hours.	WB
Do - Do -	14.7.19		Coy Training and Education Lecture to Batt at 14.00 on War Saving Certificates	WB
Do - Do -	15.7.19		Coy Training.	WB
- Do - Do -	16.7.19		Company Training	WB
- Do - Do -	17.7.19		Company Training and Education	WB

D. D. & L., London, E.C.
(A5004) Wt W1771/M2031 750,000 5/17 Sch. 52 Forms/C2118/14

Army Form C. 2118.

Instructions regarding War Diaries and Intelligence Summaries are contained in F. S. Regs., Part II. and the Staff Manual respectively. Title pages will be prepared in manuscript.

WAR DIARY
or
~~INTELLIGENCE SUMMARY.~~ WB

(Erase heading not required.)

Place	Date	Hour	Summary of Events and Information	Remarks and references to Appendices
LENDERSDORF	18.7.19		Company Training. Party representing Batt. at Paris Victory March rejoins Battalion	WB
-Do- -Do-	19.7.19		Battalion proceeded to new Billets at BRUCK relieving 11 Batt Seaforth Highlanders. A.B. Colour Party & H.Q. Coys entrained LENDERSDORF 10.00. C Coy joined train at MAUBACH. "D" Coy entrained HERBESTHAL 16-30 hours	WB
BRUCK	20.7.19		Divine Service 10.30 hours	WB
-Do- -Do-	21.7.19		Company Training and Education	WB
-Do- -Do-	22.7.19		Company Training and Education Coy Commanders and Specialist Officers Conference. 6th Black Watch win first prize in Brigade 1st Line Transport Competition.	WB
-Do- -Do-	23.7.19		Company Training	WB
-Do- -Do-	24.7.19		Company Training and Education	WB
-Do- -Do-	25.7.19		Company Training and Education	WB
-Do- -Do-	26.7.19		Company Training and Education "D" Coy inspected by Commanding Officer at 09-30 hours	WB
-Do- -Do-	27.7.19		Divine Service at 10-30 hours	WB
-Do- -Do-	28.7.19		Company Training and Education	WB
-Do- -Do-	29.7.19		Company Training and Education	WB
-Do- -Do-	30.7.19		Company Training and Education	WB
-Do- -Do-	31.7.19		Company Training and Education	WB
				WB

[signature]
LIEUT. COLONEL,
Commanding 6th (Perthshire) BTN. THE BLACK WATCH.

D. D. & L., London, E.C.
(A8004) Wt W1771/M2031 750,000 5/17 Sch. 52 Forms/C2118/14

SECRET. 6th. Battalion The Black Watch. Copy No. 12...

WARNING ORDER.

Map Reference 1L Germany 1/100,000.

The Battalion will be prepared to move to BRUCK NIDEGGEN on Saturday 19th inst. to take over billets of 1/4th Seaforth Highlanders as under:

"A"	Company	Black Watch.	No.1	Company	Seaforth Highlanders.
"B"	do.	do.	No.2	do.	do.
"C"	do.	do.	No.3	do.	do.
"B"	do.	do.	No.4	do.	do.
"H.Q."	do.	do.	"H.Q."	do.	do.

ADVANCE PARTY. 2/Lt.J.C.McArthur M.C. D.C.M. and 1 N.C.O. per Company will proceed by 0820 train from LENDERSDORF tomorrow FRIDAY 18th.

1. "A" "B" and "H.Q." Companies.

A. MOVE. Companies will move by march route from Lendersdorf.
DRESS. Marching order.
STARTING POINT. "A" Company Officers Mess.
STARTING TIME. Notified later.
ORDER of MARCH. "H.Q." Colour Party. "A" and "B" Company.
ROUTE. NIEDEREAU. KREUZAU. UDINGEN. GOICH. NIDEGGON. BRUCK.

B. COLOUR PARTY. ~~2/Lieut. M.T.McARTHUR M.C.D.C.M.~~ LIEUT W BAIRD M.M. and one Subaltern to be detailed by O.C. "A" Company. and 3 N.C.O's to be detailed by O.C. "B" Company.

C. TRANSPORT, will move independently.
STARTING TIME. Notified later.
STARTING POINT. Bridge 800x W. of K in KROUSHN.
ROUTE. NIDEREAU. KREAZAU. DROVE.BOICH. NIDEGGON. BRUCK.

D. STORES. Beds, Wash basins, Latrine, buckets Tables, etc. to be at Q.M. Stores by 16.30 hours Friday 18th.

E. BAGGAGE. Spare kilts and tunics to be rolled in bundles by Sections to be stacked at Q.M.Stores by 18.00 hours FRiday 18th. Blankets, Officers valises, Mess boxes will be stacked at Q.M.Stores one hour after reveille Saturday 19th.

F. RATIONS. Dinner will be cooked on the march. Unexpended portion of the days rations will be carried on the man.

G. LOADING PARTY. Company in waiting will detail one Platoon minimum strength 30 other ranks to report to Q.M.Stores at 08.00 hours Saturday 19th. They will parade in marching order and carry unexpended portion of the days rations.

2. "C" Company.

H. MOVE. Company will move by march route from BOGHEIM to BRUCK.
DRESS. Marching Order.
STARTING TIME. 09.00 hours.
ROUTE. UNT MAUBACH, LEVENSBACH, NIDEGGON.

I. RATIONS. As in para 1 sub:para F.

J. BAGGAGE. One Motor Lorry will be allotted for conveyance of baggage.

2.

WARNING ORDER continued.

3. "D" Company.

k. MOVE. Company will proceed by train HERBESTHAL to NIDEGGON.
TRAIN ARRANGEMENTS. Time of departure to be notified later.

W Baird
Lieut.

17/7/19. A/Adjutant 6th Bn. The BLACK WATCH

Copies No: No.1 C.O. No.2 "A" Coy. No.3 "B" Coy. No.4 "C" Coy.
No.5 "D" Coy. No.6 "H.Q." Coy. No.7 M.O. No.8 Q.M.
No.9 T.O. No.11 & 12 War Diary No.12 File.

SECRET. COPY No...11.....

6th BATTALION, The BLACK WATCH.

ADDENDUM to WARNING ORDER of 17/7/19.

Para. 1. Sub-para. "A":	Starting Time	-	09.00 hours.
	Order of March	-	100 yards between Compani
	Route	-	For UDINGEN, read DROVE.
Sub-para. "C".	Transport	-	First Line will move in rear of Battalion.
	Starting Time	-	09.00 hours.
Sub-para. "F"	Rations	-	Meal will be served at DROVE. Messing Officer will make necessary arrangements for cooking, & conveyance of Rations.
Para. 2. "C" Company. Sub-para. "I"	Rations	-	Company arrangements.

(Sgd.) H.W. RENTON, Lieut,,
A/Adjutant 6th BLACK WATCH.

18th JULY, 1919.

SECRET. COPY No. 11

6th BATTALION, The BLACK WATCH.

FURTHER ADDENDUM of WARNING ORDER of 17/7/19.

1. Sub-para. "A" MOVE: "A", "B" and "H.Q." Companies will entrain at LENDERSDORF for NIDEGGEN.
STARTING TIME - 09.00 hours.
STARTING POINT - "A" Company Officers' Mess.

2. Sub-para. "C" TRANSPORT will move by road.
STARTING TIME - 08.00 hours.
STARTING POINT - Same.
ROUTE - Same.

3. Sub-para "F" RATIONS - Cooks will prepare dinners while on the move.

4. ENTRAINING OFFICER - Lieut. S.E. MASSON will report at LENDERSDORF Station at 09.00 hours.

5. REVEILLE - 05.30 hours. BREAKFAST: - 07.00 hours.

18th JULY, 1919.

(Sgd.) H.W. RENTON, Lieut.,
A/Adjutant, 6th BLACK WATCH.

APPENDIX "A"

SECRET. 6th Battalion The BLACK WATCH. Copy No......

OPERATION ORDERS No.1.

Wednesday 2nd July 1919.

1. MOVE of "C"Company. "C"Company will march to Camp at BOGHEIM.

2. STARTING TIME. 10.45 hours.

3. POINT. Company Parade Ground.

4. DRESS. Marching Order.

5. TRANSPORT. Company Cooker, 1 Watercart, and Lewis Gun Limber will move with the Company.
Two Limbers will be provided to carry Officers valises and kits.

(Sgd) H.W.RENTON Lieut.
A/Adjutant 6th Black Watch.

Copies to :- No.1 C.O. No.2 "C"Coy. No.3 "Q.M." No.4 T.O. No.5 File.
No.6 & 7 War Diary.

APPENDIX "A".

SECRET. 6th Battalion The Black Watch. Copy No.. ....

OPERATION ORDERS No.2

1. "D" Company will proceed to HERBESTHAL to:morrow and take over duties.

2. Company will march to DUREN station where it will entrain on train leaving DUREN at 09.02 hours.

3. STARTING POINT. Company Billets.

4. STARTING TIME. 07.00 hours.

5. DRESS. Marching Order.

6. TRANSPORT. 4 Limbers will be available to take kit to Station, All kit to be loaded by 07.00 hours.

7. Company Cooker and Lewis Gun Limber and 2 mukes will entrain at DUREN at 08.00 hours.
They will leave LENDERSDORF at 06.30 hours.

8. O.C."D" Company will arrange for necessary loading party.

9. Reveille for "D" Company 05.30 hours, Breakfast at 06.15 hours to be xx prepared by "A" Company.

10. Unexpended portion of days rations will be carried on the men, following days rations will be carried on the train.

11. Completion of relief will be reported to Battalion Headquarters by wire.

2/7/19.

(Sgd) H.W.RENTON. Lieut.
A/Adjutant 6th Black Watch.

Copies to :- No.1 C.O. No.2 "D" Coy. No.3 "A" Coy. No.4 Q.M. No.5 T.O. No.6 & 7 War Diary, No.8 FILE.

APPENDIX "B".

6th Battalion The BLACK WATCH.

STRENGTH OF BATTALION ON:-		OFFICERS.	OTHER RANKS.
	2/7/19.	29.	703.
	9/7/19.	25.	681.
	16/7/19.	23.	656.
	23/7/19.	24.	676.
	30/7/19.	25.	692.

Above are the actual number of OFFICERS & OTHER RANKS with the Battalion.

APPENDIX. "C"

6th Battalion The BLACK WATCH.

OFFICERS AND OTHER RANKS JOINED DURING MONTH OF JULY 1919.

OFFICERS.

NIL.

OTHER RANKS.

1.	16/7/19.
1.	24/7/19.
1.	26/7/19.
3.	

6th BATTALION The BLACK WATCH (R.H.).

LIST of OFFICERS.

Lieut.Colonel.	W.GREEN	D.S.O.	Commanding.
Lieut.	H.W.H.RENTON	M.C.	Adjutant.
Lieut.	W.BAIRD	M.M.	A/Adjutant.
Lieut.	J.C.WILSON	M.C.	Q.M.
Lieut.	P.LOW		Lewis Gun Officer.
Lieut.	H.B.HARLEY		Educ.Officer (Leave 3/8/19)
2/Lieut.	J.LINDSAY		Transport Officer.

"A" Company.

Capt.	G.A.BUTLER		Coy.Commander.
Lieut.	S.E.MASSON		
:	F.H.JOHNSON	M.C.	
2/Lieut.	G.R.D.HODGE	M.C.	
:	F.W.F.WHITEHEAD		~~Leave 20/7/19.~~

"B" Company.

Capt.	L.M.FULTON	M.C.	Coy.Commander.
Lieut.	N.M.JONES		
:	D.KINNOCH		Leave 7/8/19.
:	J.CARSTAIRS		P.R.I.
:	A.LEITCH		

"C" Company.

Capt.	P.B.HEPBURN	M.C.	Company Commander.
Lieut.	W.D.G.REID	M.M.	
:	J.M.WALKER	D.S.O.	Leave 14/8/19.
2/Lieut.	R.CRAIK		
:	M.T.McARTHUR	M.C. D.C.M.	
Lieut.	G.G.WEIR		Attd. "A" Coy.

"D" Company.

Capt.	D.A.GRANT		Coy.Commander.
Lieut.	W.F.BRODIE		
:	J.B.CABLE	M.C.	
2/Lt.	J.McAUSLAN		
:	J.McGLADDERY		
:	G.S.WALKER.		

DETACHED.

Rank	Name	Honours	Coy	Remarks
Lieut.Colonel.	F.R.TARLETON	D.S.O.	(H.Q.)	Extended Leave (4/5/19)
Lieut.	A.D.McDIARMID		("A")	Actg. Civil Staff Capt. NIDEGGEN 20/7/19
Lieut.	W.W.SPEID	M.C.	("D")	Hospital - 16/7/19.
:	H.M.THOMSON		("A")	Attd. 2nd H.Bde. P.R.O.
2/Lt.	D.McGOWAN		("B")	Demob.Train Guard-7/5/19.
:	J.HERALD		("A")	R.A.O.C.(Attached)
Lieut.	C.K.COLLINS		("C")	R.A.O.C (do.)
2/Lt.	R.J.PRESCOTT		("B")	Attd. T.M.B.-27/5/19.

ATTACHED.

Captain	T.KENWORTHY	M.C.	R.A.M.C.
" (Rev.)	D. CONACHER		C.F.
Lieut.	T.E.PEART	M.C.	Attcd.as Educ.Instructor.

LIST of APPENDICES.

OPERATION ORDERS	"A"
STRENGTH of BATTALION DURING MONTH	"B"
LIST OF OFFICERS & OTHER RANKS JOINED DURING MONTH.	"C"
LIST OF OFFICERS	"D".

Confidential

War Diary

of

6th. Bn. The Black Watch.

from 1st August 1919 to 31st August 1919.

Original.

(6414) Wt. W3906/P1607 2,500,000 7/18 McA & W Ltd (E 3591) Forms W3091/4.

Army Form W.3091.

Cover for Documents.

Nature of Enclosures.

Notes, or Letters written.

SECRET.

W A R D I A R Y.

of

6th. (Perthshire) BATTALION The BLACK WATCH (R.H.)

=*

From 1st. August 1919 to 31st August 1919.

VOLUME 61.

=*=*=*=*=*=*=*=*=*=*

Instructions regarding War Diaries and Intelligence Summaries are contained in F. S. Regs., Part II. and the Staff Manual respectively. Title pages will be prepared in manuscript.

WAR DIARY
or
~~INTELLIGENCE SUMMARY~~.

(*Erase heading not required.*)

Army Form C. 2118.

Place	Date	Hour	Summary of Events and Information	Remarks and references to Appendices
NIDEGGAN.	1/8/19		BATTALION SPORTS.	WB
:	2/8/19		Do. Do.	WB
:	3/8/19		DIVINE SERVICE 10.30 hours. COY. COMDRS. & SPECIALIST OFFICERS' CONFERENCE at 11.45 hours.	WB
:	4/8/19		COMPANY TRAINING.	WB
:	5/8/19		COMPANY TRAINING. "A" Coy. FIELD FIRING.	WB
:	6/8/19		COMPANY TRAINING.	WB
:	7/8/19		COMPANY TRAINING.	WB
:	8/8/19		COMPANY TRAINING.	WB
DUREN.	9/8/19		BATTALION ENTRAINED NIDEGGAN for DUREN. MARCHED to BARRACKS, DUREN.	WB
	10/8/19		MARCHED to DUREN STN. ENTRAINED for CALAIS, leaving DUREN 13.30 hours.	WB
CALAIS.	11/8/19		CONTINUED JOURNEY in TRAIN. ARRIVED CALAIS 18.00 hours. MARCHED to REST CAMP for NIGHT.	WB
:	12/8/19		EMBARKED for ENGLAND. H.Q.Coy. at 10.00 hours. A.B.C.D. at 11.15 hours. ARRIVED FOLKSTONE. MARCHED TO SHORNCLIFFE STN. ENTRAINED for BROCTON at (H.Q.Coy.at 15.45 & A.B.C.D. at 18.30 hours). H.Q.Coy. ARRIVED at 23.45 hours	WB
BROCTON.	13/8/19		MARCHED to CAMP. A.B.C.D. Coys. ARRIVED 03.30. MARCHED to CAMP, ARRIVING 04.30 hours.	WB
:	14/8/19		COY. PARADES. COY. COMMDRS. & SPECIALIST OFFICERS CONFERENCE 12.00 hours.	WB
:	15/8/19		BRIGADE ROUTE MARCH.	WB
:	16/8/19		COY. TRAINING.	WB
:	17/8/19		DIVINE SERVICE at 10.30 hours.	WB
:	18/8/19		COY. TRAINING.	WB
:	19/8/19		COY. TRAINING.	WB
:	20/8/19		COY. TRAINING.	WB
:	21/8/19		COY. TRAINING.	WB
:	22/8/19		COY. TRAINING.	WB
:	23/8/19		COY. TRAINING & INSPECTION of BARRACKS.	WB
:	24/8/19		DIVINE SERVICE at 10.30 hours.	WB
:	25/8/19		COY. TRAINING. A. & D. COYS. PROCEEDED on 15 DAYS LEAVE.	WB
:	26/8/19		COY. TRAINING. EDUCATION.	WB
:	27/8/19		BATTALION ROUTE MARCH.	WB
:	28/8/19		COY. TRAINING. B. & C. COYS. MUSKETRY at RANGE.	WB
:	29/8/19		COY. TRAINING.	WB
:	30/8/19		BATTALION PARADE. INSPECTION of BARRACKS.	WB
:	31/8/19		DIVINE SERVICE at 10.00 HOURS.	WB

D. D. & L. London, E.C.
(A8004) Wt W1771/M2031 750,000 5/17 Sch. 52 Forms/C2118/14

APPENDIX "A".

S E C R E T. Copy No......

6th BATTALION THE BLACK WATCH, (R.H.)

WARNING ORDER No.1.

1. Battalion will be prepared to move to DUREN on FRIDAY 8th and to entrain there on SATURDAY 9th inst.

(Sgd.) H.W.RENTON. Lieut.
A/Adjutant 6th BLACK WATCH.

Copies to:- No.1 C.O. No.2 "A" Coy. No.3 "B" Coy. No.4 "C" Coy. No.5 "D" Coy. No.6 "H.Q." Coy. No.7 Q.M. No.8 T.O. No.9 M.O. Nos.10 & 11 War Diary No.12 File.

APPENDIX "A".

SECRET.

6th BATTALION The BLACK WATCH.

Copy No....

OPERATION ORDERS No.3

1. Battalion will move by train to DUREN where they will be accomodated in Barracks tomorrow.
DRESS:- Full Marching Order.

2. TRAINS:- "B" and "C" Companies and COLOUR PARTY will leave NIDEGGAN by first train at 10.20 hours.
Headquarters, "A" and "D" Companies will proceed by second train at 12.45 hours.
Companies will be at station 45 minutes before time of departure of train.

3. COLOUR PARTY: Lieut.W.BAIRD M.M. and Lieut.P.LOW and 3 N.C.Os. from Headquarters Company.

4. KITS. Officers' Kits, Mess Boxes and Blankets will be at Quartermaster's Stores at 08.00 hours. All packages to be clearly marked with nmme of Company and Unit.
One Platoon of "D" Company to parade at Orderly Room at 09.00 hours, in full marching order, and will be employed in loading Motor Wagons.

5. TENTS. All Tents will be struck and returned to Quartermaster"s Stores by 09.00 hours.

6. O.C.Companies will report, personally, to Commanding Officer, that the billets occupied by their Companies are perfectly clean.

7. BILLETING PARTY. 1 N.C.O. from each Company will proceed by the 06.30 train to DUREN and report to Lieut.McGREGOR at the Barracks there.

(Sgd.) H.W.RENTONN Lieut.
Adjutant 6th Bn.The BLACK WATCH.

Copies to:- No.1 C.O. No.2 to 6. Coys. No.7 Q.M. No.8 T.O.
No.9 M.O. No.10 & 11 War Diary. No.12 File.

APPENDIX "A".

SECRET. 6th BATTALION The BLACK WATCH. Copy No...

OPERATION ORDER NO.4.

9/8/19.

1. The Battalion will entrain tomorrow at DUREN station.
2. Battalion will parade at a time to be notified later and march to Station by shortest route. Interval of 100 yards between Companies.
ORDER of MARCH: Headquarters, "C" "D" "A" and "B" Companies.
COLOUR PARTY: consisting of Lieut.P.LOW, Lieut.W.BAIRD M.M. and 3 N.C.Os. from H.Q.Coy. will march in the centre of Headquarter Company.
3. DRESS. Full Marching Order. Blanket to be rolled and carried on top of Pack.

4. ENTRAINING OFFICER: Lieutenant T.McGREGOR.

5. LOADING PARTY. One Officer and one Platoon (minimum 30 ~~men)~~ from "A" Company will load stores on train at a time to be notified later.

6. RATIONS: Unexpended portion of days rations to be carried. Two days rations on train.
7. HALTES REPAS: have been arranged at HUY:CHARLEROI:CHISLEENGHEN:MERRIS

8. BILLETS. O.C. Companies to report personally to Commanding Officer that Billets occupied by their Companies are clean.

9. ACKNOWLEDGE.

Sd. H.W.RENTON. Lieut.
Adjutant 6th Bn. The BLACK WATCH.

9/8/19.

COPIES TO: No.1 C.O. Nos.2 to 6 Coys. No.7 T.O. No.8 Q.M. No.9 M.O. Nos.10 and 11 War Diary.No.12 File.

APPENDIX "B".

6th BATTALION The BLACK WATCH.

STRENGTH of BATTALION ON:-		Officers.	Other Ranks.
	2/8/19.	24	709
	9/8/19.	25	759
	16/8/19.	29	795
	23/8/19.	32	815
	30/8/19.	14	345

Above are the actual number of Officers and Other Ranks with the Battalion.

APPENDIX "C".

6th BATTALION The BLACK WATCH.

OFFICERS AND OTHER RANKS JOINED DURING MONTH of AUGUST, 1919.

OFFICERS.

NIL.

OTHER RANKS.

1	5/8/19.
1	7/8/19.
1	8/8/19.
1	14/8/19.
1	15/8/19.
2	18/8/19.
1	24/8/19.
8.	

APPENDIX "D".

6th BATTALION The BLACK WATCH.

OTHER RANKS AWARDED DECORATIONS during MONTH.

No.265642 Sergeant J.A.G.KERR. now demobilized. MILITARY MEDAL.

APPENDIX "E".

6th BATTALION The BLACK WATCH.

LIST of OFFICERS.

Lieut.Colonel	W.GREEN	D.S.O.	Commanding.
Captain	P.B.HEPBURN	M.C.	2nd in Command Leave 8/9/19.
Lieut.	H.W.H.RENTON	M.C.	Adjutant.
Lieut.	W.BAIRD.	M.M.	A/Adjutant.
Lieut.	J.C.WILSON	M.C.	Quartermaster.
Lieut.	P.LOW		Lewis Gun Officer. Leave 8/9/19.
Lieut.	T.McGREGOR.		Signalling Officer.
Lieut.	H.B.HARLEY		Educational Officer.
2/Lieut.	J.LINDSAY		Transport Officer.

"A" Company.

Captain	G.A.BUTLER		Company Commander Leave 8/9/19.
Lieut.	S.E.MASSON		Do.
Lieut.	F.H.JOHNSON	M.C.	Do.
2/Lt.	G.R.D.HODGE	M.C.	Do.
2/Lt.	F.W.F.WHITEHEAD		
2/Lt.	G.S.WALKER		Leave 8/9/19.

"B" Company.

Lieut.	A.D.McDIARMID		Company Commander.
Lieut.	N.M.JONES		
Lieut.	D.KINNOCH		
Lieut.	J.CARSTAIRS		Leave 8/9/19.
Lieut.	A.LEITCH		
Lieut.	G.G.WEIR		Leave 8/9/19.

"C" Company.

Lieut.	W.D.G.REID	M.M.	Company Commander.
Lieut.	J.M.WALKER	D.S.O.	
2/Lt.	R.CRAIK.		
2/Lt.	M.T.McARTHUR	M.C.D.C.M.	Leave 8/9/19.

"D" Company.

Captain	D.A.GRANT		Company Commander.
Lieut.	W.F.BRODIE		Leave 8/9/19.
Lieut.	J.B.CABLE	M.C.	Do.
Lieut.	L.M.FULTON	M.C.	Do.
Lieut.	W.W.SPEID	M.C.	Do. 13/9/19.
2/Lt.	J.McAUSLAN		Do. 8/9/19.
2/Lt.	J.McGLADDERY		Do. Do.

DETACHED.

Major (T.Lieut.Col.)	F.R.TARLETON	D.S.O.	Extended leave 4/5/19.
2/Lieut.	D.McCOWAN	"B"	Train Guard. 7/5/19.
2/Lieut.	J.HERALD	"A"	R.A.S.C.COLOGNE.
2/Lieut.	C.K.COLLINS	"C"	Do. Do.
2/Lt.	R.J.PRESCOTT	"B"	T.M.B. 27/5/19.

ATTACHED.

Captain (Rev.)	D.CONNACHER	C.F.	Leave 8/9/19.

LIST of APPENDICES.

B.E.F.

HIGHLAND DIV formerly
62 DIV

1 HIGHLAND BDE H.Q.

1919 MAY to 1919 AUG

NO BOX

CONFIDENTIAL.

WAR DIARY OF

1st HIGHLAND BRIGADE HEADQUARTERS,

FROM 1st MAY, 1919.

TO 31st MAY, 1919.

BRITISH ARMY OF THE RHINE.

GERMANY.

Army Form C. 2118.

Instructions regarding War Diaries and Intelligence Summaries are contained in F. S. Regs., Part II. and the Staff Manual respectively. Title pages will be prepared in manuscript.

WAR DIARY
or
INTELLIGENCE SUMMARY.
(*Erase heading not required.*)

Place	Date	Hour	Summary of Events and Information	Remarks and references to Appendices
	1.5.19		B. G. C visited Rifle Range in course of construction near BLENS	[illegible]
	2.5.19		Nil	[illegible]
	3.5.19		Nil	[illegible]
	4.5.19		Nil	[illegible]
	5.5.19		Nil	[illegible]
	6.5.19		Nil	[illegible]
	7.5.19		B. G. C visited Divisional Hd Qts at KREUZAU	[illegible]
	8.5.19		Capt a/Lieut. Col Hume-Gore 52nd Gordons left 1st Highland Bde to report as 2nd in C to 53rd Gordon Highlrs	[illegible]
	9.5.19		Nil	[illegible]
	10.5.19		B. G. C. visited all Units in the Brigade Group.	[illegible]
	11.5.19		B. G. C with Major Gordon attended Church Service of 52nd Gordons at Fussenich	[illegible]
	12.5.19		Major Bissett. D.S.O., M.C. returned to Bde from leave to U.K. and resumed duties of Brigade Major	[illegible]
	13.5.19 to 18.5.19		Nil	[illegible]
	19.5.19		Major Bisset D.S.O. M.C. left 1st Highland Bde to report as G.S.O. II. IX. Corps.	[illegible]
			Capt. A.G. Dunsterville took over duties as BDE MAJOR	
			B.G.C. attended Conference Highland Divisional Headquarters.	

(A9175) Wt W2355/P360 600,000 12/17 D. D. & L. Sch. 52a. Forms/C2118/15.

Army Form C. 2118.

Instructions regarding War Diaries and Intelligence Summaries are contained in F. S. Regs., Part II. and the Staff Manual respectively. Title pages will be prepared in manuscript.

WAR DIARY
or
INTELLIGENCE SUMMARY.
(Erase heading not required.)

Place	Date	Hour	Summary of Events and Information	Remarks and references to Appendices
	20.5.19.		Conference Bde Headquarters of Battalion Commanders.	A.W.
			B.G.C. attended Conference at Division Headquarters.	
	21.5.19		Nil.	A.W.
	22.5.19		Warning order received from Division Headquarters re action to be taken in event of Armistice being broken off. A/Staff Capt visited new area to be occupied by 1st Highland Brigade in event of Armistice being broken off. ~~[illegible]~~ i.e. OPLADEN area.	A.W.
	23.5.19.		Conference with Batt Commanders at Bde Headquarters.	
			B.G.C. visited Div. Headquarters and 5th Cameron Hdrs.	
			5th Batt Cameron Hdrs moved from FUSSENICH to Camp at HAUSEN.	A.W.
	24.5.19		B.G.C. inspected guard mounting 52nd Gordon Hdrs. FUSSENICH	A.W.
	25.5.19		NIL	A.W.
	26.5.19		B.G.C. visited all units in Brigade	A.W.
	27.5.19.		B.G.C. visited 52 Bn Gordon Highlanders FUSSENICH	A.W.
	28.5.19		Staff Capt, a/Civil Staff Capt, with billeting officers of Bns. visited new area to be taken over by 1st Highland Bde in event of armistice being broken off. ie. OPLADEN, LEICHLINGEN area.	A.W.
	29.5.19.		NIL	A.W.

(A9475) Wt W2356/P360 600,000 12/17 D. D. & L. Sch. 52a. Forms/C2118/15.

Instructions regarding War Diaries and Intelligence Summaries are contained in F. S. Regs., Part II. and the Staff Manual respectively. Title pages will be prepared in manuscript.

WAR DIARY
or
INTELLIGENCE SUMMARY.
(Erase heading not required.)

Army Form. C. 2118.

Place	Date	Hour	Summary of Events and Information	Remarks and references to Appendices
	30-5-19		B.G.C. visited 526. Coy. R.A.S.C.	[illegible]
BLENS	31		1st Highland Bde Hd Qrs + 1st Highland T.M.B moved to the Brigade training Area at Blens. 10th Argyll & Sutherland Highlanders marched to Camp near HAUSEN. Capt Dunstaville proceeded on leave to U.K. pending joining his Regiment. Capt G. H. Gordon M.C. assumes duties of Brigade Major - pending appt of new B. Major. Capt Brodie reported from 4th Gordons to take up duties as Staff Capt vice Capt Harland M.C. appointed D.A.A.G. Lowland Division.	[illegible]

Geo H Gordon Capt
1st HIGHLAND BRIGADE

(A9175) Wt W2358/P360 600,000 12/17 D. D. & L. Sch. 52a. Forms/C2118/15.

CONFIDENTIAL.

WAR DIARY

OF

1st HIGHLAND BRIGADE HEADQRS.

FROM 1st JUNE, 1919

TO 30th JUNE, 1919.

- Volume 6 -

Instructions regarding War Diaries and Intelligence Summaries are contained in F. S. Regs., Part II. and the Staff Manual respectively. Title pages will be prepared in manuscript.

WAR DIARY
or
INTELLIGENCE SUMMARY.
(*Erase heading not required.*)

Army Form C. 2118.

Place	Date	Hour	Summary of Events and Information	Remarks and references to Appendices
GERMANY BLENS	June 1st		Nil	GWG
	2nd		Brig Genl visited 5th Camerons & 10th Argyll & Sutherland Highlrs and watched training.	GWG
	3rd		Brig-Genl inspected The 5th Cameron Highlrs & Transport at 8.30 A.M. and afterwards addressed the troops.	GWG
	4th		Brig-Genl inspected The 10th Argyll & Sutherland Highlanders & Transport at 8.30am at ~~[illegible]~~ HAUSEN, and afterwards addressed the troops. Capt HARLAND proceeded to Lowland Division as D.A.A.G.	GWG
	5th		Nil.	
	6th		General Sir William Robertson inspected near HAUSEN, 5th Camerons & 10th A & S. Highlrs and afterwards their respective Camps.	GWG
	7th		Nil	GWG
	8th		Nil	GWG
	9th		A General Holiday granted to the troops.	GWG
	10th		Sir David Campbell the Divisional Commander visited the 10th A & S Highlrs & saw them training.	GWG
	11th		Brig Genl & Staff Capt went to Sports of 4th Gordons in DUREN	GWG
	12th		Nil	GWG
	13th		Nil	GWG
	14th		52nd Gordons moved from Billets in FÜSSENICH to Camp near BLENS. 53rd Gordons Games at MERODE	GWG

(A9175) Wt W2358/P360 600,000 12/17 D. D. & L. Sch. 85a. Forms/C2118/15.

Instructions regarding War Diaries and Intelligence Summaries are contained in F. S. Regs., Part II. and the Staff Manual respectively. Title pages will be prepared in manuscript.

WAR DIARY
or
INTELLIGENCE SUMMARY.
(Erase heading not required.)

Army Form C. 2118.

Place	Date	Hour	Summary of Events and Information	Remarks and references to Appendices
BLENS.	June			
GERMANY.	15th		Brig. Genl. Brigade Major & Staff Capt. attended Church Service of 10th A&S. Highlrs near HAUSEN.	GWG
			Brig-Genl. G. S. G. Craufurd C.B. CMG. CIE. DSO. visited Brig: Genl. 1st Highland Bde at BLENS.	GWG
	16th		Nil	GWG
	17th		Orders issued re move of Brigade to OPLADEN AREA	GWG
	18th		Brigade moved by train and march route to DUREN AREA. Bde HdQrs opened	
			at 1 P.M. at OPLADEN.	GWG
	19th		The whole Brigade concentrated in OPLADEN AREA	GWG
OPLADEN GERMANY	20th		~~Capt~~ Brig. Genl. visited all regimental and other guards in Bde. Area Opladen	JRP
	21st		Brig. Genl. called at IV. Corps. Staff Capt. visited units	JRP
	22nd		Nil	JRP
	23rd		Brig. Genl. and Civil Staff Capt. went round sub-area	JRP
	24th		Brig. Genl. presided at G.C.M. SOLINGEN.	JRP
	25th		Brig. Genl. visited 10th A.&S.H. at LEICHLINGEN.	JRP
	26th		Brig. Genl. visited G.O.C. II Corps. H.A. WIESDORF — G.O.C. IV Corps and Brig. Genl. visited	
			10th A.&S.H. at LEICHLINGEN, and 5th Cameron Hrs. at OPLADEN.	JRP
	27th		Nil	JRP

(A9475) Wt W2350/P360 600,000 12/17 D. D. & L. Sch. 52a. Forms/C2118/15.

Army Form C. 2118.

WAR DIARY
or
INTELLIGENCE SUMMARY:
(Erase heading not required.)

Instructions regarding War Diaries and Intelligence Summaries are contained in F. S. Regs., Part II. and the Staff Manual respectively. Title pages will be prepared in manuscript.

Place	Date	Hour	Summary of Events and Information	Remarks and references to Appendices
OPLADEN GERMANY	June 28		Nil.	WP
	29		Brig Genl. & Staff Capt. went round Perimeter line	WP
	30.		A day – Brigade entrained OPLADEN for DUREN Area – staging there night 30 June/1 July	WP
			Brigade office closed OPLADEN 1200 hours & opened BLENS 1400 hours	WP

A K Robertson
Lieut. Colonel,
for Brigadier General,
Commdg. 1st Highland Bde.

War Diary

3 MH/1354

1ST HIGHLAND BRIGADE MOVEMENT ORDER NO. 1.

1. To-day being J-3 day, the moves already ordered will be carried out.

2. The Brigade Intellegence Officer (Lt. S. S. Cameron) with the Billetting Officers of 5th Cameron Highlanders and 10th Argyll and Sutherland Highlanders will proceed to the OPLADEN Area to-morrow 18th instant.

3. The Staff Captain will supervise the entraining at HEIMBACH, HAUSEN and BLENS on 18th instant and will accompany the train to DUREN, he will be at Duren Barracks on the night of the 18th and proceed to OPLADEN by the Omnibus Train on the 19th instant. An entraining state showing number of Officers and men, should be handed to Staff Captain by Units entraining respectively HEIMBACH, HAUSEN, BLENS.

4. The Brigadier General Commanding and A/Brigade Major will proceed to OPLADEN on J-1 day (19th. instant).

5. Brigade Headquarters will close at BLENS at 0700 hours on J-1 day, and open at 1200 hours at OPLADEN.

6. On J-1 day O.C. Units will hand Staff Captain at DUREN STATION entraining state showing separately:-

Officers
Men
L.D. Horses.
H.D. "
Mules.
Pack animals.
Vehicles (axles).

7. Transport proceeding by road of 52nd. Gordon Highlanders, 5th. Cameron Highlanders, 10th. Argyll and Sutherland Highlanders, 1st. Highland Trench Mortar Battery and Brigade Headquarters will pas starting point (BLENS STATION) at 0800 hours and proceed by route march to Concentrate at GLADBACH, route NIDEGGEN, THUM, FROITZHEIM, VETTWEISS. Transport Officer of 52nd. Gordon Highlanders will be in command of Brigade Colum. Transport Officer 10th. Argyll and Sutherland Highlanders will proceed to GLADBACH in advance to reconnoitre suitable place for parking Transport. Special attention will be paid to keeping all roads clear. Transport Officers will hand Officer in charge of Brigade Column state showing strength men, horses, and vehicles.

8. OC. Brigade Column will notify O.C. No. 2 Coy. Train, FROITZHEIM, of arrival of column at GLADBACH.

9. ACKNOWLEDGE.

G. Gordon
Captain.
Brigade Major.
1st. Highland Brigade.

17th. June, 1919.

Issued through Signals at................
To all recipients of 1st. Highland Brigade Warning Order No.1.

War Diary

AMENDMENT TO WARNING ORDER NO. 1, DATED 27/5/19, and AMENDMENT THERETO DATED 5/6/1919.

Sunday, June 15th. 1919.

1. Para 4 of Amendment dated 5/6/19 line 3. After 10th. Argyll and Sutherland Highlanders add "and 52nd. Battalion Gordon Highlanders less 2 Companies".

2. Para 4 of Amendment dated 5/6/19 last section commencing "5th. Battalion Cameron Highlanders and 150 all ranks" is cancelled and the following is substituted:-

"Brigade Headquarters, 1st. Highland Trench Mortar Battery, 52nd. Gordon Highlanders, 10th. Argyll and Sutherland Highlanders and 150 all ranks, 2/1st. (W.R.) Field Ambulance will move by train from HAUSEN.

On arrival at KREUZAU, 2/1st. (W.R.) Field Ambulance will proceed by march route to STOCKHEIM, and 52nd. Gordon Highlanders to NIDERAU, Brigade Headquarters, 1st. Highland Trench Mortar Battery and 10th. Argyll and Sutherland Highlanders will proceed by train to DUREN to BARRACKS.

5th. Battalion Cameron Highlanders will proceed by march route from HAUSEN to BOICH, - THUM - DROVE area.

3. Para 6 of Warning Order dated 27/5/19 is cancelled and the following substituted:-

"Units will move light. Dumps of surplus stores will be formed by 52nd. Gordon Highlanders at BLENS, by 5th. Cameron Highlanders and 10th. Argyll and Sutherland Highlanders at HAUSEN.

52nd. Gordon Highlanders will take charge of Brigade Headquarters and 1st. Highland Trench Mortar Battery Baggage and will move it to their store atBLENS on J-3 day.

Each Battalion will leave an Officer and one platoon in charge of Brigade Dumps.

[signature]

Captain.
Staff Captain.
1st. Highland Brigade.

Copies to all recipients of Warning Order No. 1.

War Diary

SECRET.

1st. Highland Brigade.

AMENDMENT TO WARNING ORDER No. 1 dated 27/5/1919.

Thursday 5th. June, 1919.

Para 4 is cancelled and the following is substituted:-

4. Moves as under will take place on J-2 day. Brigade Headquarters, 1st. Highland Trench Mortar Battery, and 10th. Argyll and Sutherland Highlanders will move by train consisting of 40 covered trucks from BLENS to DUREN BARRACKS.

Timing of Train as under.

HEIMBACH	1100 hours.
DUREN	1300 "

Stops at HAUSEN and KREUZAU of 20 minutes duration each.

Officer Commanding, 10th. Battalion Argyll and Sutherland Highlanders will detail an entraining Officer to take over train at HEIMBACH and allot accomodation.

Personnel and baggage may travel on this train only. No animals or vehicles.

5th. Battalion Cameron Highlanders and ~~180~~ 150 all ranks of 2/1st. Field Ambulance will move by same train from HAUSEN to KREUZAU. From KREUZAU, 5th. Battalion Cameron Highlanders will proceed by march route to NIEDERAU - DROVE - BOICH - THUM area, and 2/1st. Field Ambulance to STOCKHEIM.

6. Throughout para for "GLADBACH" read "HAUSEN".

ADD Tents, Heavy Baggage and stores to be dumped of Brigade Headquarters and 1st. Highland Trench Mortar Battery will be taken to HAUSEN and stored at dump at 5th. Battalion Cameron Highlanders.

REFERENCE ADMINISTRATIVE INSTRUCTIONS.

5. LORRIES.

2nd. line. For "entraining station" read "DUREN Station"

(cont'd)..

AMENDMENT 1st. HIGHLAND BRIGADE ENTRAINING INSTRUCTIONS.

Para 2. Add.

Entraining and detraining Officer for 2nd. and 3rd. personnel Train and for 2nd. Omnibus Train will be detailed by Officer Commanding, 10th. Battalion Argyll and Sutherland Highlanders.

Para 4. (a) (b) (c) (d) is cancelled and the following is substituted:-

4. The following Transport, personnel and animals will proceed by 2nd. Omnibus Train on J-1 day.

			Animals.	
(a) 10th. A.& S.H.	Axles.	Men.	L.D.	H.D.
4 limbered G.S. Wagons, L.G.	8	12)		
S.A.A. limber	2	2)		
Cookers.	6	9)	10.	14.
Watercart.	2	4)		
Baggage wagons	4	6)		
Officers Charges		10	10	
(b) 1st. Highland Brigade Headquarters.				
1 G.S.	2	3	4	
1 mess cart.	1	2	1	
1 limbered G.S. wagon	2	3	2	
Officers Charges.		4	4	
(c) 52nd. Gordon Highlanders.				
1 limbered G.S. wagon S.A.A.)	2	2		
2 G.S. wagons (baggage))	4	4		
1 limbered G.S. wagon (L.G.))	2	3	15	4
2 Cookers.)	4	6	(includes chargers)	
1 Watercart.)	1	2		
(d) 5th. Cameron Highrs.				
limbered G.S. wagons L.G.)	8	12		
" " " S.A.A.)	2	2		
Cookers)	6	9	15	9
Watercart.)	2	4		
Baggage wagons.)	4	6		
Officers Charges.		10.	10.	

ACKNOWLEDGE.

[signature]
Captain.
Staff Captain.
1st. Highland Brigade.

Copies to:-

1 G.O.C.
2 Brigade Major.
3 Staff Captain.
4 Highland Division "A".
5 2nd. Highland Brigade.
6 3rd. Highland Brigade.
7-13 List "A".
14 Brigade Agricultural Officer.
15 Signal Officer.
16. Civil Staff Captain.
17 P.R.O.
18 B.R.M.S.
19-20 War Diary.
21 Brigade Supply Officer.
22 File.

War Diary

1st. Highland Brigade.
B.M.H./1361.

SECRET.

1. CIVIL ADMINISTRATIVE.

(1) Commanding Officers or Seconds in Command when not below the rank of Field Officer, will hold summary civil Courts on the following days:-

52nd. Gordon Highlanders Mondays at BERGNEUKIRCHEN.
5th. Cameron Highlanders Wednesdays at OPLADEN.
10th. Arg. and Suth. Highrs. Fridays at LEICHLINGEN.

The same methods will hold good as obtained in the old Area before the move to the training Area.

(2) If other troops are already carrying out the above duties, they will continue to do so pending other orders on the subject.

2. MILITARY PRECAUTIONS. with a view to suppressing Civil disturbances.

(1) Every Commanding Officer is responsible for preparing and keeping up to date a 'Defence Scheme' or 'Plan' for the employment of troops in which the action to be taken by all troops under his command in case of Civil disturbances is clearly laid down. Commanding Officers will invariably keep a reserve of troops in his own hand.

Existing schemes will be taken over and when necessary revised. If other troops are still in their Areas, Commanding Officers will take over the local command if senior and make such amendments to the existing Defence Scheme as may be required in consultation with the Officer formerly in Command. If junior, will obtain instructions from the Officer Commanding. In any case, schemes will be submitted by Commanding Officers as soon as possible to Brigade Headquarters and the name and Unit of the local Commander given.

3. Brigade Headquarters will be informed at once of any civil unrest or disturbances.

James [signature]

Captain.
a/ Brigade Major.
1st Highland Brigade.

19th June, 1919.

Copy to:-
1. G.O.C.
2. Brigade Major.
3. Staff Captain.
4. Civil Staff Captain.
5. P.R.O.
6. 52nd Gordon Highlanders.
7. 5th Cameron Highlanders.
8. 10th Argyll and Suth. Highrs.
9. 1st Highland T.M. Battery.
10. 526th Company R.A.S.C.
11. 460th Field Company R.E.
12. 2/1st Field Ambulance.

War Diary

ADDENDUM
TO
1ST HIGHLAND BRIGADE
WARNING ORDER NO. 1 OF 27 - 5 - 19.

1. Transport proceeding by Rail entraining DUREN J-1 day will march to respective staging area and will spend night J-2 - J-1 day there, viz.,:-

Brigade Headquarters 1st Highland Trench Mortar Battery 10th Argyll & Sutherland Highlanders	DUREN BARRACKS.
5th Cameron Highlanders	THUM - BOICH area.
52nd Gordon Highlanders	NIEDERAU.
2/1st (W.R) Field Ambulance	STOCKHEIM.

Moves will be made under unit arrangements.

2. On J-1 day Transport will move with Battalions from staging area to DUREN Station unless further orders are issued.

C.W. Gordon
Captain.
Brigade Major.
1st Highland Brigade.

17th June, 1919.

War Diary

SECRET **MEMO. TO UNITS OF BRIGADE GROUP**

1. The following instructions are issued for information in the first instance, but will be applied should the necessity arise in the event of the Brigade being ordered forward of the new Area -

2. The policy as regards the action of the outpost troops on the Perimeter from J-3 day to J-1 day inclusive will be as follows:-

There will be no change in present procedure, and existing instructions as regards circulation will be carried out.

It may be anticipated that there will be a greater number of individual attempts to evade circulation regulations.

Outpost troops will be warned accordingly and where it is found necessary re-inforced.

3. The policy as regards action by aeroplanes during the advance will be as follows:-

In the first instance, and until the enemy discloses an intention to resist our advance, aeroplanes will not take any offensive action with machine guns against enemy personnel on the ground, but will confine themselves to reconnaissance and forwarding reports.

If aeroplanes are fired at from the ground from places which are definitely known to be occupied by <u>our</u> troops they will take the necessary action to ensure their own safety by returning the fire. There will in no case be any bombing from aeroplanes without previous orders from General Headquarters.

4. During the advance Red Very Lights (1") will be used by the Infantry as a signal to indicate that their advance is being resisted by the enemy.

5. (a) In the event of active hostile resistance to our advance, and fighting ensuing, prisoners and documents will be passed back in the usual way to Brigade Headquarters

(b) Important prisoners should be passed back as quickly as possible and documents which are sent back with the escort should be tied in separate bundles according to the unit from which they were obtained.

6. (a) The Signal Service of formations will take over such lines as are required for military use.

(b) Local commanders will take steps to occupy and guard important postal, telegraphic and telephone offices.

(c) Until the Security Section G.S. (I) has arranged for supervision and control, all civilian signal traffic through occupied offices must be stopped by means other than the destruction of lines and instruments. German personnel and especially Postmasters, will be forced to remain at their offices ready to work communications, but German personnel are not to be permitted to touch any signal apparatus in occupied offices except in the presence of a representative of the Signal Service.

(d) The above orders forbidding the destruction of lines and instruments will still apply in the case of a temporary withdrawal from an occupied office, but in this case instruments should be removed, the lines being left uncut.

(e) If the enemy offers organised resistance to our advance, and fighting ensues or becomes imminent, a new situation will have arisen, and Local Commanders will then use their discretion as to severing communications in order to prevent tactical information being conveyed from our lines to the enemy.

7. (a) The railways of primary importance in the British zone are as follows:-

(a) HERBESTHAL - DUREN - COLOGNE - OPLADEN - GRAVRATH - HAGEN - SCHWERTE, and thence to PADERBORN:

(i) by the line UNNA - SOEST - LIPPSTADT.

(ii) by the line ARNSBERG - BRILON - BUREN.

(b) COLOGNE - SIEGBURG - EITORF - SIEGEN - PLETTENBERG - HAGEN.

(Over

(CONTINUED)

7. (b) The essential measures to be taken by advancing troops in the first instance to secure complete control over these railways are as follows:-

To occupy stations and important junctions to prevent any destruction of material or the escape of personnel; to put up the notices of which copies will be provided; to occupy the head railway offices of the various German systems; to compel German personnel to remain at their posts, more especially the head managers and sub-managers of the systems; to stop all movements of trains until control of the general management has been taken over by the Sous-Commission of the C.I.C.F.C. (see Paras. c. and d. below).

(c) As soon as the railway Sous-Commission has been established at ELBERFELD all railway movements will be controlled by that body, and no stopping or altering of trains will be made without reference to it through the Liaison Traffic Officer there.

(d) Once the Sous-Commission has taken over, commanders will ensure that :-

(i) No railway working is interfered with and no railway officials are molested or interfered with in their work. In the first instance these railway officials will have no passes, but the Sous-Commission at ELBERFELD will provide them as soon as practicable.

(ii) No railway telephones or telegraphs are interfered with; they are vital to the continued working of the railway.

(iii) No railway buildings or premises are commandeered or occupied without reference to the Railway Liaison Officer concerned.

8. The Sous-Commission C.I.C.F.C. is in charge of all railways in the present occupied area, and the above instructions chiefly refer to the railways in the present unoccupied area in the event of an advance.

9. A C K N O W L E D G E.

Captain.
Brigade Major.
1st Highland Brigade.

18th June, 1919.

Copy to all Recipients of Warning Order No. 1.

SECRET. War Diary

1st Highland Brigade. Copy......20......

Order No. 2.

(Reference GERMANY 1.100,000 - 2.K.Map)

1.(a) In the event of an advance, the protection of railways is of primary importance. The Brigade is responsible for a portion of the COLOGNE-OPLADEN - WOHWINKEL railway as follows:-

5th Cameron Highlanders from MANFORT (1½ Miles N. of DUNNWALD, square 12D) inclusive to OPLADEN Station inclusive.
52nd Gordon Highlanders from OPLADEN Station exclusive to Bridge over River WUPPER inclusive.
10th Argyll & Sutherland Highlanders from Bridge over River WUPPER exclusive to ZIEGWEBERSBERG (about ½ mile N. of LEICHLINGEN) inclusive.
The 2nd Brigade, with whom touch will be maintained will guard the railway N. from ZIEGWEBERSBERG.

(b) The measures for the defence of the railway will include guards at all Bridges and at OPLADEN Station. Destruction of material will be prevented. Arrangements will also be made for active patrolling of the railway.

(c) Reconnaissances will be carried out on arrival in the Area. Commanding Officers will forward to Brigade Headquarters the proposed guard and patrolling details which will be put into force from J Day onwards.

2. All important electric power stations, water works and telegraphic offices in the Brigade Area will be guarded. A list of localities to be guarded will be issued as soon as possible but necessary action will be taken on arrival by Commanding Officers without waiting for orders. A list of guards posted will be forwarded to Brigade Headquarters as soon as possible after posting.

3 (a) An inlying picquet of one Company will be detailed by Officers Commanding 5th Cameron Highlanders and 10th Argyll & Sutherland Highlanders and of two platoons by Officer Commanding, 52nd Gordon Highlanders. Populated localities will be patrolled frequently by dayand night. Any organised acts of hostility by the inhabitants will be prevented.

(b) All Units will arrange for alarm posts on arrival. If billets are scattere it may be necessary to have platoon or even section alarm posts. Battalion and Company alarm posts will be reported to Brigade Headquarters as soon as possible after arrival. After Units have been dismissed to their billets they will again be fallen in on their alarm posts, the objects of which will be explained to every man. Subsequently, practice will be given from time to time in rapidly turning out both by day and by night on the alarm posts in fighting order.

4 (a) All ranks will be reminded that they are in a hostile country and in the new area most of the inhabitants will be unfavourably disposed towards us in secret whatever their outward bearing may be. The country will be full of enemy agents. All ranks will be careful to say nothing in the presence of the inhabitants which may be of assistance to the enemy in any operations that may take place. The greatest secrecy regarding all movements of troops will be maintained.

(b) Officers will carry pistols when ever they are out of their billets and keep them at hand in billets.

(c) Officers will not walk about alone. An Officer not accompanied by another will have have a runner with him.

[signature]
Captain.
Brigade Major.
1st Highland Brigade.

18th June 1919.

Copy to all recipients of Warning Order No. 1.

War Diary

ADDENDUM to amendment to 1st. Highland Brigade Warning Order No.1 dated 27/5/19, and Amendment thereto dated 5/6/19. Para 3.

---

1. The following Officers will be in charge of their respective Battalion Dumps.

52nd. Gordon Highrs.	2/Lieut. J.G.McLeod.
5th. Cameron Highrs.	2/Lieut. J. Stirling.
10th. A.&.S.Highrs.	Lieut. W.B.Goodwin.

and the last mentioned Officer will be O.C. the three detachments.

2. Each detachment will be left with 10 boxes S.A.A. which will on no account be used for training purposes. All S.A.A. will be kept separate from other stores.

3. Brigade Headquarters reserve of S.A.A. will be kept in small house by BLENS Bridge - at present used as Brigade Headquarters Q.M. Ration Store, and Lieut. W.B. Goodwin will hold the key and inspect S.A.A. periodically.

4. The key of the Rifle Range Target shed will also be handed to O.C. Detachments.

Captain.
Brigade Major.
1st. Highland Brigade.

17th. June, 1919.

Copies to all recipients of 1st. Highland Brigade Warning Order No. 1. and Amendment to ditto.

Workbury

B.M.H./1369.

1ST HIGHLAND BRIGADE.

1. Reference Brigade Order No. 2, dated 18th instant, Para 1 (a) will be amended to read as follows :-

5th Cameron Highlanders,	No alteration.
52nd Gordon Highlanders,	From OPLADEN Station exclusive to the level crossing 1000 yards N. of the bridge over the river WUPPER inclusive.
10th Arg. & Suth'd. Hdrs.	From level crossing 1000 yards N. of the bridge over river WUPPER exclusive to KIEGWEBERSBERG inclusive.

2. ACKNOWLEDGE.

James R. Park

Captain.
A/Brigade Major.
1st Highland Brigade.

21st June, 1919.

To :- All recipients of Brigade Order No. 2.

War Diary

SECRET.

1st. Highland Brigade.
B.H.H./1370.

The code for notifying 'J' day, should the latter fall on or after the 20th. June 1919, will be as follows :-

20th. June, ... A.

21st. June, ... B.

22nd. June, ... C.

etc. etc.

ACKNOWLEDGE.

[signature]
Captain.
A/Brigade Major.
1st. Highland Brigade.

21st. June, 1919.

Issued to all recipients of 1st. Highland Brigade Warning Order No. 2.

War Diary

1st Highland Brigade.

B.M.H./ 1361.

SECRET.

1. CIVIL ADMINISTRATIVE.

(1) Commanding Officers or Seconds in Command when not below the rank of Field Officer, will hold summary civil Courts on the following days:-

52nd. Gordon Highlanders Mondays at BERGENKIRCHEN.
5th. Cameron Highlanders Wednesdays at OPLADEN.
10th. Arg. and Suth. Highrs. Fridays at LEICHLINGEN.

The same methods will hold good as obtained in the old Area before the move to the training Area.

(2) If other troops are already carrying out the above duties, they will continue to do so pending other orders on the subject.

2. MILITARY PRECAUTIONS. with a view to suppressing Civil disturbances.

(1) Every Commanding Officer is responsible for preparing and keeping up to date a 'Defence Scheme' or 'Plan' for the employment of troops in which the action to be taken by all troops under his command in case of Civil disturbances is clearly laid down. Commanding Officers will invariably keep a reserve of troops in his own hand.

Existing schemes will be taken over and when necessary revised. If other troops are still in their Areas, Commanding Officers will take over the local command if senior and make such amendments to the existing Defence Scheme as may be required in consultation with the Officer formerly in Command. If junior, will obtain instructions from the Officer Commanding. In any case, schemes will be submitted by Commanding Officers as soon as possible to Brigade Headquarters and the name and Unit of the local Commander given.

3. Brigade Headquarters will be informed at once of any civil unrest or disturbances.

James [illegible]
Captain.
a/ Brigade Major.
1st Highland Brigade.

19th June, 1919.

Copy to:-

1. G.O.C.
2. Brigade Major.
3. Staff Captain.
4. Civil Staff Captain.
5. P.R.O.
6. 52nd Gordon Highlanders.
7. 5th Cameron Highlanders.
8. 10th Argyll and Suth. Highrs.
9. 1st Highland T.M. Battery.
10. 526th Company R.A.S.C.
11. 460th Field Company R.E.
12. 2/1st Field Ambulance.

War Diary

1st Highland Brigade Warning Order No. 2.

To be read in conjunction with 1st Highland Brigade Warning Order dated 22nd June 1919.

1. In the event of peace being signed without any further advance taking place alltroops will resume their normal dispositions and the organisation of Areas and Civil Administration that existed prior to J-3 day.

2. A wire will be sent giving date of "A" day on which day 1st Highland Brigade moves. Moves and reliefs will be carried out in accordance with Administrative Instructiond to be issued later.
Units must be prepared to carry out moves at short notice.

3. On arrival in DUREN Area guards will be found by Battalions as on J-3 day.

4. All guards taken over from H.A. II Corps, will remain on duty until relieved.
Guards etc., additional to those found by H.A., II Corps including understudies for Civil Staff Captain, Police etc. will rejoin Units without awaiting relief.

5. No relief or movement will be made until date of "A" day is notified to Units.

6. Transport which advanced by road will return by road. Remainder will proceed by Omnibus Train.

7. 1st Highland Brigade less 5th Cameron Highlanders will stage on night A/B day in DUREN BARRACKS.
5th Cameron Highlanders will stage on night A/B day in DROVE - THUM - BOICH area.

8. On B day Units will proceed as on J-2 day, viz.,
5th Cameron Highlanders by route march, remainder of Brigade Group by train to BLENS - HAUSEN and HEIMBACH.

9. ACKNOWLEDGE.

Captain,
Staff Captain,
1st Highland Brigade.

24th June, 1919.

Copies to :-
1. G.O.C.
2. Brigade Major.
3. Staff Captain.
4-10. List "A".
11. Signal Officer.
12. Civil Staff Captain.
13. P.R.O.
14. Lieut. Cameron.
16-17. War Diary.
18. Highland Division "A".
19. File.

****

Headquarters

1st Highland Brigade.

War Diary for

July, 1919.

CONFIDENTIAL.

Instructions regarding War Diaries and Intelligence Summaries are contained in F. S. Regs., Part II. and the Staff Manual respectively. Title pages will be prepared in manuscript.

WAR DIARY
or
~~INTELLIGENCE SUMMARY~~.
(*Erase heading not required.*)

Army Form C. 2118.

Place	Date	Hour	Summary of Events and Information	Remarks and references to Appendices
	July			
Blens	1		Units of Brigade arrived in Blens-Hausen Training Area	W.C.
	2		Brig. Gen. J. Campbell, C.B., C.M.G., D.S.O. proceeded on leave to U.K.	
			Lt Col. A. B. Robertson, C.M.G., D.S.O. took command of Brigade	W.C.
	3.	09.30	Brigade Ceremonial Parade held at Hausen	
			Capt. B. C. Brodie, M.C. - Staff Captn proceeded to U.K. on leave	
			Capt. J. P. Park took over duties of Staff Captn	W.C.
	4		Capt & Bt Major E. B. Costin, D.S.O., joined 1st Highland Bde from U.K. (Cadre 90th Inf Bde) and	
			took over duties of Brigade Major vice Capt. G. H. Gordon, M.C.	W.C.
	5		Nil	W.C.
	6	10.00	Brigade Commander attended Open Air Church Parade at Hausen	W.C.

(A9475) Wt W2358/P360 600,000 12/17 D. D. & L. **Sch. 52a.** Forms/C2118/15.

Army Form C. 2118.

Instructions regarding War Diaries and Intelligence Summaries are contained in F. S. Regs., Part II. and the Staff Manual respectively. Title pages will be prepared in manuscript.

WAR DIARY
or
~~INTELLIGENCE SUMMARY.~~
(Erase heading not required.)

Place	Date	Hour	Summary of Events and Information	Remarks and references to Appendices
Blens	7		Capt. G. H. Gordon, D.C. took over duties of Civil Staff Captain	
			1 Off & 12 O.R. proceed to Paris to take part in Victory March	W.B.C.
	8			
	9	}	Nil	W.B.C.
	10			
	11		General Holiday for British Army of the Rhine to celebrate Peace	W.B.C.
	12	}	Nil	W.B.C.
	13			
Hausen	14	0930	Bde Commander attended Bde. Ceremonial Parade at Hausen	W.B.C.
	15		Nil	W.B.C.
	16		G.O.C. returned from leave in U.K. Capt. G. H. Gordon – Civil Staff Captn – proceeded on leave to U.K.	W.B.C.
	17	}	Nil	W.B.C.
	18			

(A9475) Wt W2358/P360 600,000 12/17 D. D. & L. Sch. 52a. Forms/C2118/15.

Instructions regarding War Diaries and Intelligence Summaries are contained in F. S. Regs., Part II. and the Staff Manual respectively. Title pages will be prepared in manuscript.

WAR DIARY

or

~~INTELLIGENCE SUMMARY.~~

(Erase heading not required.)

Army Form C. 2118.

Place	Date	Hour	Summary of Events and Information	Remarks and references to Appendices
Blens	19		General Holiday in view of Peace Celebrations in U.K.	[initials]
	20/28		Nil	[initials]
	29		G.O.C. inspected Camerons at Hausen. Div Horse Show held at Hausen	[initials]
	30		French General Fayolle inspected 5th Camerons at Cologne, who were forming his guard of Honour.	[initials]
	31		Capt. Park appointed Bde. Demobilization Officer	[initials]

2nd August, 1919

J. McCampbell [signature]
Brigadier General,
Commanding 1st Highland Brigade

(A9475) Wt W2358/P360 600,000 12/17 D. D. & L. Sch. 52a. Forms/C2118/15.

CONFIDENTIAL. **Volume 32.**

WAR DIARY

of

1st Highland Brigade

1st August — 31st August

1919.

Instructions regarding War Diaries and Intelligence Summaries are contained in F. S. Regs., Part II, and the Staff Manual respectively. Title pages will be prepared in manuscript.

WAR DIARY
or
~~INTELLIGENCE SUMMARY.~~

(*Erase heading not required.*)

Army Form C. 2118.

August, 1919

Place	Date	Hour	Summary of Events and Information	Remarks and references to Appendices
BLENS	1		Nothing to report.	GBE.
"	2	14.00	Brigade Games held at HAUSEN. Brigade Championship Cups presented to 5th Bn	
			Camerons by Major General Sir David Campbell, K.C.B.	
"	3		Official news received that Division is shortly moving home	
		09.00	Bde. Church Parade held at HAUSEN.	
"	4		A large percentage of 1st Highland Brigade proceeded on Rhine Trips.	
"	5/7		Nil	
"	8		Mob. stores proceeded to England via Antwerp (Appendix 1)	GBE.
"	9/10		Arrangements made for move of Brigade H.Q. on morning of 11th (Schedule 1, App. 2.)	
BLENS / DUREN.	11		Brigade H.Q. closed at BLENS at 1400 hours and opened DUREN 1400 hours in	
			27 HOLTZSTRASSE, D.	
	12/		Proceeded en route to Calais at 18.30 hours, via, CHARLEROI, TOURNAI and	
	/13		ARMENTEIRS. arriving CALAIS 01.00 14th (Appendix 3)	
"	14.		Brigade H.Q. embarked Calais 1030 hours arriving DOVER 1300 hours	
			Entrained DOVER 1530 hours	
"	15		Arrived Catterick Camp, Yorkshire, 0630.	

Instructions regarding War Diaries and Intelligence Summaries are contained in F. S. Regs., Part II, and the Staff Manual respectively. Title pages will be prepared in manuscript.

WAR DIARY or ~~INTELLIGENCE SUMMARY.~~

(Erase heading not required.)

August 1919

Army Form C. 2118.

Place	Date	Hour	Summary of Events and Information	Remarks and references to Appendices
Blens	1		Nothing to Report	
"	2	14.00	Brigade Games held at Hausen. Brigade Championship Cup	
"			presented to 5th Camerons by Major General Sir David Campbell K.C.B.	
"	3		Official news received that Division is shortly moving Home.	
"	"	0900	Bde Church Parade held at Hausen	
"	4		A large percentage of 1st Highland Bde proceeded on Rhine Trip	
"	5/7		NIL	
"	8		Mob. Stores proceeded to England via Antwerp (Appendix 1)	[illegible]
"	9/10		Arrangements made for move of Bde H.Qs on morning of 11th {Schedule 1 Appendix 2}	
BLENS/DUREN	11		Brigade H.Qs closed at Blens 14.00 hrs opened Duren 14.00 hrs in	
			37 Holtz Strasse	
	12		Proceeded en route to Calais at 17.30 hours, via Charleroi, Tournai	
	13		and ARMENTIERS arriving CALAIS 06 00 hrs 14th (Appendix 3)	
	14		Bde H.Qrs embarked Calais 10.30 hrs arriving DOVER 13.00 hrs	
			Entrained DOVER 15.30 hrs	
"	15		Arrived CATTERICK CAMP YORKS. 0630 hrs	

(A9175) Wt W2358/P360 600,000 12/17 D. D. & L. Sch. 52a. Forms/C2118/15

Instructions regarding War Diaries and Intelligence Summaries are contained in F. S. Regs., Part II, and the Staff Manual respectively. Title pages will be prepared in manuscript.

WAR DIARY
or
~~INTELLIGENCE SUMMARY.~~
(Erase heading not required.)

Army Form C. 2118.

August, 1919

Place	Date	Hour	Summary of Events and Information	Remarks and references to Appendices
CATTERICK	16		Brigade H.Q. opened at 0900 hours	
	17/21		Nil	
	22		25% of Brigade proceeded on 15 days leave	
	23/27		Nil	
	28		Brig. Gen. J. Campbell, C.B., C.M.G., D.S.O. proceeded on leave	
			25% of Brigade proceeded on 15 days leave	
			Lt. Col. A.B. Robertson, C.M.G., D.S.O. assumed Command of 1st Highland Bde vice.	
			Brig. Gen. J. Campbell, C.B., C.M.G., D.S.O.	
	29/31		Nil	
			15th Sept., 1919	
			E. B. Costin Major for Lieut Colonel, Commanding 1st Highland Brigade	

(A9475) Wt W2358/P360 600,000 12/17 D. D. & L. Sch. 52a. Forms/C2118/15

Instructions regarding War Diaries and Intelligence Summaries are contained in F. S. Regs., Part II. and the Staff Manual respectively. Title pages will be prepared in manuscript.

WAR DIARY AUGUST 1919.
or
~~INTELLIGENCE SUMMARY.~~
(*Erase heading not required.*)

Army Form C. 2118.

Place	Date	Hour	Summary of Events and Information	Remarks and references to Appendices
CATTERICK	16		Brigade H.Q. opened at 0900 hrs.	
	17/21		NIL	
	22		25% of Brigade proceeded on 15 days leave	
	23/27		NIL	
	28		Brig. Gen J. Campbell C.B. C.M.G. D.S.O. proceeded on leave	
			25% of Brigade proceeded on 15 days leave	
			Lt Col. B.B. Robertson C.M.G. D.S.O. assumed command of 1st Hld Bde vice	[illegible initials]
			Brig. Gen J. Campbell C.B. C.M.G. D.S.O.	
	29/31		NIL	

13th Sept., 1919

E.B. Costin Major
for Lieut. Colonel,
Commanding 1st Highland Brigade

(A9175) Wt W2358/P360 600,000 12/17 D. D. & L. Sch. 52a. Forms/C2118/15

(Appendix I)

ORDERS BY CAMP COMMANDANT,
1st HIGHLAND BRIGADE.
7th August, 1919.

Guns, vehicles, stores and equipment for entrainment for ANTWERP, will parade at BLENS at 0730 on 8th August, 1919 under Lieut. LISTER, 1st Highland Trench Mortar Battery, and proceed to Sugar Factory, Paradies Strasse, DUREN, where they will report to C.R.E. and be parked for the night of 8/9th August, 1919.

The mules will proceed to animal collecting camp, DUREN under orders to be issued later, and mule drivers will be issued with necessary rations. Two days forage will be carried for mules.

Horses, all classes, belonging to Brigade Headquarters Signal Section, and 1st Highland Trench Mortar Battery, will be paraded at BLENS at 11.00 hours under Lieut. McEwing, 10th Argyll and Sutherland Highlanders, and proceed to animal collecting Camp, DUREN arriving there between 14.00 and 15.00 hours on 8th instant. This party will march to COLOGNE on 9th inst under a Senior Officer, to be detailed by Division.

Conducting party will consist of 1 man to 3 horses. Two days forage to be taken for horses.

All ranks to take unexpired portion of day's rations, and four days rations.

James R. Park

Captain,
for Staff Captain,
1st Highland Brigade.

7th August, 1919.

TRAIN CIRCULAR H/SC/1A.
EQUIPMENT TRAINS.

Trains No. 1, 2, 3 and 4 have entrained to-day.

Train No.	Serial No.	UNITS.	Strength All ranks	Entraining Station.	Depart	Date 1919	Destination.	Arrive.	Date 1919.
5.	M.B.17	62nd M. G. Battalion	125	Duren	10.29	9/8	Antwerp	20.34	9/8
6.	M.B.18	52nd Btn Gordon Hdrs.	36						
	M.B.19	5th Btn Cameron Hdrs.	36						
	M.B.20	10th Bn. Arg. & Suth'd. Hdrs.	36	Duren	14.48	9/8	Antwerp	21.00	10/8
	M.B.21	1st Brigade H.Q.	11						
	M.B.22	1st Brigade Sig. Section							
7.	M.B.23	2/1st Field Ambulance	50						
	M.B.24	No. 2 Coy. Train	51	Duren	18.00	9/8	Antwerp	03.32	10/8
	M.B.25	H.Q. & No.1 Sect. Sig. Co.	28						
	M.B.26	H.Q., R.E.	1						
8.	M.B.27	H.Q., Divl. Train	3						
	M.B.28	No1 Coy. Train	107	Duren	21.46	9/8	Antwerp	07.40	10/8
	M.B.29	Divl. H.Q.	9						
9	M.B.30	"A" Bty. 310th Bde., R.F.A.	40						
	M.B.31	"B" Bty -do-	40	Duren	16.20	10/8	Antwerp	20.34	10/8
	M.B.32	"C" Bty -do-	40						
	M.B.33	H.Q., -do-	4						
10.	M.B.34	"D" Bty. 310th Bde., R.F.A.	40						
	M.B.35	"A" Bty. 312th -do-	40	Duren	14.48	10/8	Antwerp	01.00 ~~[illegible]~~	11
	M.B.36	"B" Bty. 312th -do-	40						
	M.B.37	H.Q., 312th -do-	4						
11.	M.B.38	"C" Bty. 312th Bde. R.F.A.	40						
	M.B.39	"D" Bty. 312th -do-	40	Duren	18.00	10/8	Antwerp	0352	11/8
	M.B.40 c	Part of 1 Sect. D.A.C.	50						
12.									

SCHEDULE 1.

(Appendix 2)

Column.	1	2	3	4	5	6	7
Serial letter.	Depart.	Time.	Date.	Unit.	Detrain.	Time of arrival.	REMARKS.
A.	HAUSEN.	11.20.	10/8.	5th Camerons.	DUREN.	12.25.	Stage night 10/11th DUREN BARRACKS
B.	HAUSEN.	14.50	10/8.	5th Camerons.	DUREN.	15.55.	Stage night 10/11th DUREN BARRACKS. 1st T.M.B. will travel on this train.
C.	BLENS.	18.30.	10/8.	52nd Gordons.	DUREN.	19.37.	Stage night 10/11th DUREN BARRACKS.
D.	BLENS.	21.58.	10/8.	52nd Gordons.	DUREN.	22.50.	Stage night 10/11th DUREN BARRACKS.
E.	HAUSEN.	05.33.	11/8.	10th Argylls.	LENDERSDORF.	06.39.	Stage night 11/12th at NIDERAU.
F.	HAUSEN.	06.39.	11/8	10th Argylls.	LENDERSDORF.	08.12.	Stage night 11/12th at NIDERAU. 1st Bde. H.Q. will travel on this train and will detrain DUREN, staging night 11/12th at Bde. H.Q. 27, HOLZ STRASSE.

War Diary

(Appendix 3)

ADMINISTRATIVE INSTRUCTIONS H/S.C./A.2.

1. TRAINS.

Trains HAUSEN - BLENS - LENDERSDORF - DUREN - will proceed on 10th and 11th instant as shown in Schedule 1 attached.

2. BILLETS.

Battalions will send billeting parties forward to-day to arrange billets.

Units in Duren will immediately report arrival and departure to Town Commandant, DUREN.

3. SUPPLIES.

Rations will be delivered as under :-

(A) 10th instant.

Rations will be delivered direct to HAUSEN STATION at 10.00 hours, to 5th Cameron Highlanders and 1st Highland T.M.B. Units will send representatives to meet lorry and 5th Cameron Highlanders will furnish loading party of 1 section.

460th Field Coy. Royal Engineers rations will be delivered at STOCKHEIM. Representative will meet lorry at 09.30 hours at STOCKHEIM CHURCH to take over rations.

Rations will be issued to 52nd Gordon Highlanders at DUREN BARRACKS 10th instant at 10.00 hours.

Other Units of Brigade Group will receive rations as usual.

(B). 11th instant.

Rations will be delivered to 5th Cameron Highlanders, 1st Highland T.M.B. and Brigade Headquarters at DUREN BARRACKS at 09.30 hours. Representative of Brigade Headquarters will meet rations at above time and place.

Rations will be issued to 10th Argyll & Sutherland Highrs. at NIDERAU. Guide will meet lorry on DUREN - KREUZAU road at the last house in NIDERAU at the northern end of the village (i.e. the end nearest DUREN.)

Units will draw on day of entraining 2 days rations for the journey at R.S.O. office, DUREN STATION two hours before entraining. Quarter Master or R.Q.M.S. should attend personally.

In addition the unconsumed portion of the current days rations will be taken.

4. TRANSPORT.

(A) Baggage.

The following lorries have been asked for on 10th instant and will report at hours stated below.

5th Cameron Highlanders.	3 lorries.	at 08.15 hrs.
52nd Gordon Highlanders.	3 "	08.15 "
460th Field Coy. R. E.	1 "	09.00 "

All stores and kit required to go on personnel trains will be loaded on above lorries.

Two journeys can be made if required.

3 lorries for 10th Argyll and Sutherland Highlanders, and 1 for Brigade Headquarters have been asked for, 11th instant.

(cont'd).

(B) Tents.

Additional lorries have been asked for to transport tents of 5th Cameron Highlanders and 52nd Gordon Highlanders to IV Corps Troops Ordnance.

Half of all tents of 5th Cameron Highlanders, 52nd Gordon Highland, and 1st Highland T.M.B. will be struck by 08.00 hours and the remainder by 14.00 hours on 10th instant.

Lorries have been asked for to transport tents of 10th Argyll and Sutherland Highlanders on 11th instant.

All lorries mentioned in (A) and (B) above will make a double trip if required, and an N.C.O. should be sent with lorries with orders to this effect.

5. LOADING PARTIES.

Units will make own arrangements for loading and unloading parties to travel with lorries.

Loading parties will accompany lorries carrying tents.

6. REAR PARTIES.

Rear parties of 1 Platoon per Battalion will be left to clean camp and load tents. They will rejoin Units by civilian trains as soon as possible after the camp is cleaned.

O.C. Platoon will report at Brigade Headquarters before marching off.

7. ACKNOWLEDGE.

Capt.

Captain,
Staff Captain,
1st Highland Brigade.

9th August, 1919.

Copies to :-
G.O.C.
Brigade Major.
Staff Captain.
Brigade Headquarters.
Brigade Signal Officer.
1st Highland T.M.Battery.
52nd Gordon Highlanders.
5th Cameron Highlanders.
10th Argyll and Sutherland Highlanders.
460th Field Coy. R.E.
2/1st (W.R.) Field Ambulance.
No. 2 Coy. Divisional Train.
Brigade Supply Officer.
R.T.O. DUREN.
Highland Division.

(CONTINUED)

Train No.	Sorted Nos.	UNITS	Strength Offrs.	Strength O.R.	Entraining Station.	Dep.	Date	Destination.
11. (12)	A.O.141	10th Btn Arg. & Suth'd. Hdrs.	53	066	Duren	1830	12/8/19	Calais
	A.O.142	1st Brigade Headquarters }	–	–	"			
	A.O.143	1st Brigade Signal Section }	6	100	"			
	A.O.144	No. 2 Coy. Divl. Train	2	40	"			
13. (12)	A.O.150	310th Brigade R.F.A.	30	712	Duren	1355		
	A.O.151	M.V. Section	2	20	"			
14. (13)	A.O.152	312th Brigade R.F.A.	20	722	Duren	1830		
	A.O.153	H.Q., R.A.	5	50	"			
	A.O.154	H.Q., Div. Train	5	25	"			
	A.O.155	No. 1 Coy., Divl. Train	6	00	"			
15. (14)	A.O.156	D.A.C.	16	379 214	Duren	1355		
	A.O.157	2/3rd (W.R.) Field Amb.	4	136	"			

Captain.
Staff Captain.
1st Highland Brigade.

8th August, 1919.

HIGHLAND (62) DIVISION

1st HIGHLAND BDE

5th CAMERON HDRS

1919 MAR – 1919 AUG

(From 9 DIV 26 BDE)

Original

Confidential

War Diary M I

of

5th Cameron Highlanders

1st March 1919 to 31st March 1919

(Volume)

[illegible] [illegible] 21: 3 ·19

46F
I. D.

(6414) Wt. W3906/P1607 2,500,000 7/18 McA & W Ltd (E 3591) Forms W3091/4. Army Form W.3091.

Cover for Documents.

Nature of Enclosures.

Notes, or Letters written.

Page I

Instructions regarding War Diaries and Intelligence Summaries are contained in F. S. Regs., Part II. and the Staff Manual respectively. Title pages will be prepared in manuscript.

WAR DIARY

or

~~INTELLIGENCE SUMMARY.~~

(Erase heading not required.)

5th Cameron Highlanders.

Army Form C. 2118.

March 1919

Place	Date	Hour	Summary of Events and Information	Remarks and references to Appendices
	March			
SOLINGEN	1st		Coys worked. Medical Inspection. Working Party (Range) supplied	ahl
Germany	2nd		Batt: attended Services	ahl
	3rd		P.T. Lewis Gun Classes Drill	ahl
	4th		Ditto. Batt: attended a lecture on 'America & World Politics'	ahl
	5th		Ditto	ahl
	6th		Coys worked	ahl
	7th		P.T. Medical Inspection. Capt: A Macaulay M.C. joined the Bn. Batt: attended	ahl
	~~8th~~		a lecture on 'Industrial Peace after the War'	ahl
	8th		Batt. Billet Inspection. The Batt: Association Team were beaten	ahl
			by the 9th Seaforth Hrs in the semi-final of the Div: Cup	ahl
	9th		Church Parades	ahl
	10th		P.T. Lewis Gun Classes Drill 1st night of finals of Div: Boxing Competition.	ahl
	11th		Ditto. Semi-finals " " "	ahl
	12th		Ditto. Finals " " "	ahl
	13th		Coys worked. Wiring of Outpost Line commenced	ahl
				ahl

(A9475) Wt W2352/P360 600,000 12/17 D. D. & L. Sch. 52a. Forms/C2118/15.

Page II

Instructions regarding War Diaries and Intelligence Summaries are contained in F. S. Regs., Part II. and the Staff Manual respectively. Title pages will be prepared in manuscript.

WAR DIARY
or
~~INTELLIGENCE SUMMARY.~~
(Erase heading not required.)

5th Cameron Hrs

Army Form C. 2118.

Place	Date	Hour	Summary of Events and Information	Remarks and references to Appendices
SOLINGEN Germany	March 14		Wiring. Bathing.	ABL
	15		Wiring Med: Inspection Lt A McRae MC joined the Batt	ABL
	16		Church Parades.	ABL
	17		Wiring Medical Inspection	ABL
	18		Batt: was inspected by Brigadier-Gen: Hore-Ruthven who is vacating	ABL
			the command of the Bde	ABL
	19		Wiring Capt. H Mackenzie MC 2/Lt W. K Fairlie & 2/Lt J.H Scott joined from 1st Batt.	ABL
	20th		Coys carried out training under Coy Cmmdrs	ABL
GEICH	21st		Today the Battalion was transferred to the Highland Division & moved	ABL
			by train to GEICH near DUREN. The Batt: was met by Brig	ABL
			-Gen J. Campbell & was played from the Station at ZULPICH	ABL
			by the Pipes & Drums of the 10th A & S Hrs. The battalion	ABL
			is billetted in GEICH, FUSSENICH, & JUNTERSDORF.	ABL
	22nd		Coys at disposal of Coy Cmmdrs.	ABL
	23rd		Church Parades. Lt A. Miller, 2/Lts J.R.G. Bantock, T. Polson, R St C Shieber, & G.S. Young joined from 11th Bn	ABL
	24th		Bathing. Lieuts. S.S. Cameron, HS Deans, P.D. Rankie, A.B.Smith & 2/Lt J. Mackie	ABL

(A9475) Wt W2358/P360 600,000 12/17 D. D. & L. Sch. 52a. Forms/C2118/15.

Page III

Instructions regarding War Diaries and Intelligence Summaries are contained in F. S. Regs., Part II. and the Staff Manual respectively. Title pages will be prepared in manuscript.

WAR DIARY
or
~~INTELLIGENCE SUMMARY.~~
(Erase heading not required.)

5th Cameron Hrs

Army Form C. 2118.

Place	Date	Hour	Summary of Events and Information	Remarks and references to Appendices
	March			
GEICH	24 (cont)		T. Wallace & F.A. Sowter joined from 6th Bn.	AHL
	25		Baths. Coys at disposal of Coy Cmmdrs. 2nd Lt E G Thomas joined from 6th Bn.	AHL
	26		Inspection of Draft by CO. Batt: Parade. Med: Inspection.	AHL
	27		Coys at disposal of Coy Cmmdrs. No: 200335 Sgt. P. McBean has been	AHL
			awarded the Belgian Decoration Militaire (2nd Class) & Croix de Guerre.	AHL
	28		Most of the Batt: went to Cologne today to see the final of 2nd	AHL
			Army Football Cup in which 1st Cameron Hrs beat 8th Black	AHL
			Watch 2-1.	AHL
	29.		Inspection of billets.	AHL
	30.		Church Parades.	AHL
	31		Baths.	AHL

[signature]
Major
Cmmdg 5th Cameron Hrs

CONFIDENTIAL.

H

47 F

WAR DIARY OF

5th Battalion CAMERON HIGHLANDERS.

FROM 1st May, 1919.

TO 31st May, 1919.

and

FROM 1st April, 1919.

TO 30th April, 1919.

BRITISH ARMY OF THE RHINE,

GERMANY.

Page I

Instructions regarding War Diaries and Intelligence Summaries are contained in F. S. Regs., Part II. and the Staff Manual respectively. Title pages will be prepared in manuscript.

WAR DIARY
or
~~INTELLIGENCE SUMMARY.~~
(Erase heading not required.)

Army Form C. 2118.

FILE

5th Cameron Highlanders
April 1919

Place	Date April	Hour	Summary of Events and Information	Remarks and references to Appendices
FUSSENICH GEICH TUNTERSDORF	1		Coys at disposal of Coy Cmdrs. Baths	RG
Germany	2		Batt: Route march. Capt R. H. Cameron M.C & 2/Lt W. Munro joined	RG
	3		Coys carried out training. Capt H. Grindall M.C & Lt P. Austin joined.	RG
	4		Batt paraded for Ceremonial Drill. Capt A. Harvey MC. Lt D. Gellie	RG
			2/Lt T. McAllister MM & 2/Lt J. S. Orr joined	RG
	5		Inspection of Drafts.	RG
	6		Church Parades.	RG
	7		Baths.	RG
	8		Baths. Education. Drill	RG
	9		P.T. Musketry & Drill. Lt H M D WATSON awarded Chevalier de l'Ordre	RG
			de Leopold with Croix de Guerre. 40745 Sgt. J. Young awarded Belgian	RG
			Decoration Militaire. 2/Lt S. T. Woodsford joined.	RG
	10		Batt: route march.	RG
	11		P.T. L.G. classes. Musketry & Drill.	RG
	12		Billet & Kit Inspections.	RG
	13		Church Parades. Capt. T. Ross joined.	RG

79/4697

Page II

Instructions regarding War Diaries and Intelligence Summaries are contained in F. S. Regs., Part II. and the Staff Manual respectively. Title pages will be prepared in manuscript.

WAR DIARY
or
~~INTELLIGENCE SUMMARY.~~
(Erase heading not required.)

Army Form C. 2118.

Place	Date	Hour	Summary of Events and Information	Remarks and references to Appendices
	April			
	14		Baths.	RG
	15		Baths. Steady Drill	RG
	16		Inspection of Coy by CO. Medical Inspection	RG
	17		Do. Education. Capt D Macdonald MC & 2/Lt R. Aird joined.	RG
	18		Today was observed as a holiday. 2/Lt T. I. Cran joined.	RG
	19		L. G. classes. Inspection of billets	RG
	20		Church Parades.	RG
	21		P.T. Gas Training & Drill.	RG
	22		Adjutant's Parade.	RG
	23		Baths.	RG
	24		Holiday	RG
	25		Ceremonial Drill. Lt A. Miller. Lt O A Walthews & 2/Lt S.J. Cox MM joined the Coy	RG
	26		Route March. 2/Lt W. J. Hanson joined on 25th. Capt W. T. Mackie MC joined	RG
	27		Church Parades	RG
	28		Coy at disposal of Coy Cmdrs.	RG
	29		Batt. Parade under RSM	RG

Page VIII.

Instructions regarding War Diaries and Intelligence Summaries are contained in F. S. Regs., Part II. and the Staff Manual respectively. Title pages will be prepared in manuscript.

WAR DIARY

or

~~INTELLIGENCE SUMMARY.~~

(Erase heading not required.)

Army Form C. 2118.

Place	Date	Hour	Summary of Events and Information	Remarks and references to Appendices
	April 30.		Baths. Education every day	

R Campbell
Lt Colonel
Commanding 5th Cameron Hrs.
Highland Division
Army of the Rhine

(A9175) Wt W2358/P360 600,000 12/17 D. D. & L. Sch. 52a. Forms/C2118/15.

Page 1

Instructions regarding War Diaries and Intelligence Summaries are contained in F. S. Regs., Part II. and the Staff Manual respectively. Title pages will be prepared in manuscript.

WAR DIARY
or
~~INTELLIGENCE SUMMARY.~~
(Erase heading not required.)

5th Cameron Hrs.

Army Form C. 2118.

Place	Date	Hour	Summary of Events and Information	Remarks and references to Appendices
	May			
FUSSENICH GEICH JUNTERSDORF	1		B & D Coys moved to BLENS & HAUSEN into camp.	RS
Germany	2		B & D Coys building ranges. A & C Coys Drill. Education.	RS
	3		Do do do L. G. classes	RS
	4		Church Parades.	RS
	5		B & D Coy on ranges. Coys at disposal of Coy Cmdrs do do	RS
	6		Do A Coy Drill C Coy working on range at JUNTERSDORF. Classes	RS
	7		Do Do Do Do & Baths	RS
	8		Holiday	RS
	9		Do A Coy Route March Do Do	RS
	10		Do A Coy Drill Do Do	RS
	11		Church Parades	RS
	12		B & D Coys on ranges A Coy Drill Do Do	RS
	13		Do Do Do Do	RS
	14		Do A & C Coys Baths Do	RS
	15		Holiday	RS
	16		B & D Coys on range A Coy at disposal of Coy Cmdr Do	RS

(A9175) Wt W2358/P360 600,000 12/17 D. D. & L. Sch. 52a. Forms/C2118/15.

Page. II

Instructions regarding War Diaries and Intelligence Summaries are contained in F. S. Regs., Part II. and the Staff Manual respectively. Title pages will be prepared in manuscript.

WAR DIARY

or

~~INTELLIGENCE SUMMARY.~~ 5th Cameron Hrs

(Erase heading not required.)

Army Form C. 2118.

Place	Date May	Hour	Summary of Events and Information	Remarks and references to Appendices
	17		B & D Coys on ranges. Inspection of A Coy by C.O. C Coy on range at JUNTERSDORF	RS
	18		Church Parades. C Coy moved to HAUSEN.	RS
	19		B C & D Coys on ranges. A Coy firing on range at JUNTERSDORF	RS
	20		Do Do	RS
	21		Do Do Baths	RS
HAUSEN	22		Holiday HQ moved to HAUSEN	RS
	23		Do Do	RS
	24		~~Church Parades~~ Do Do	RS
	25		Church Parades	RS
	26		B & D Coys working on ranges. A & C Coys Section & Platoon Training	RS
	27		C Coy do B & D Coys Do Education. A Coy moved to HAUSEN	RS
	28		B & D Coys do A & C Coys Do	RS
	29		A Coy do B C & D Coys Do Education	RS
	30		B Coy do A C & D Coys Do Do	RS
	31st		C & D Coys do A & C Coys Do Do	RS

R Campbell
Lt Colonel
Comdg 5th Cameron Hrs

(A9175) Wt W2358/P360 600,000 12/17 D. D. & L. Sch. 52a. Forms/C2118/15.

Original.
48 F
g.D.

5TH CAMERON HIGHLANDERS.

War Diary & Appendix
for July 1919
Vol. LI.

[signature] Capt.

1/8/19

R. Campbell.
Lieut.-Col.
Cdg. 5TH CAMERON HIGHLANDERS

Instructions regarding War Diaries and Intelligence Summaries are contained in F. S. Regs., Part II. and the Staff Manual respectively. Title pages will be prepared in manuscript.

5TH. CAMERON HRS. **WAR DIARY** or ~~INTELLIGENCE SUMMARY.~~ JULY 1919

(Erase heading not required.)

Army Form C. 2118.

Place	Date	Hour	Summary of Events and Information	Remarks and references to Appendices
REF. MAP SHEETS			GERMANY 1L & 2K. 1/100.000	
(DROVE–THUM BOICH) H.Q. DROVE	1.		Battn. continues return to encampment at HAUSEN by march route, arriving in camp 12.45 L.	APPT. McGM.
HAUSEN	2.		Settling into camp: 2 Coys. musketry.	McGM
do.	3.		Brigade Ceremonial Parade 09.30 hrs.	McGM.
do.	4.		Coy. training, musketry & education classes 08.00–12.00: 2/Lieut W. MUNROE to U.K. for demobilization	McGM.
do.	5.		Musketry & Coy. training 08.00–12.00	McGM.
do.	6.		Brigade Open Air Church Parade 10.00 hrs.	McGM.
do.	7.		Musketry & Coy. training 08.00–12.00; the following proceed to PARIS to take part in VICTORY MARCH on 14th Capt. A.H. McBEAN; 9966 Sgt. P. DOUGAN D.C.M., M.M. 27749 Sergt. T. GUINEA D.C.M.; 43700 Cpl. J. HUNTER MM; 29662 Pte. J. SORLEY M.M.	McGM

Army Form C. 2118.

Instructions regarding War Diaries and Intelligence Summaries are contained in F. S. Regs., Part II. and the Staff Manual respectively. Title pages will be prepared in manuscript.

5th CAMERON HRS. WAR DIARY ~~or INTELLIGENCE SUMMARY.~~ JULY 1919

(Erase heading not required.)

Place	Date	Hour	Summary of Events and Information	Remarks and references to Appendices
Ref. Map Sheets			GERMANY 1L 92K 1/100.000	
HAUSEN	8.		Coy. training & musketry 08.00–12.00	WGM
do.	9.		Coy. training, musketry & education 08.00–12.30	WGM
do.	10.		Brigade Ceremonial Parade 09.30 hrs.	WGM
do.	11.		Peace Holiday: 5 a side inter-platoon football competition; special cinema performances etc.	WGM
do.	12.		Coy. training & musketry 08.00–12.00	WGM
do.	13.		Church Parade 09.00 hrs.	WGM
do.	14.		Brigade Ceremonial Parade 09.30 hrs	WGM
do.	15.		Musketry, Coy. training & education 08.00–12.30; Lecture on War Savings Certificates 14.00 hrs.	WGM
do.	16.		Coy. training, Musketry & education 08.00–12.30 Lieuts. A A CAMPBELL, D.C.W. MURRAY & W. KEANS join for duty.	WGM
do.	17.		Musketry & Coy. training 08.00–12.00; Medical inspection; first sunny day for a fortnight 2Lt. J. M. STIRLING to hospital	WGM
do.	18.		Musketry & Coy. training 08.00–12.00	WGM
do	~~18~~ 19		Empire Peace Holiday	WGM
do.	~~19~~ 20		Church Parade 09.00 hrs.	WGM
do.	~~20~~ 21		Musketry; Coy. training & education 08.00–12.30 hrs. Disinfection of blankets	WGM

(A9175) Wt W2358/P360 600,000 12/17 D. D. & L. Sch. 52a. Forms/C2118/15.

Instructions regarding War Diaries and Intelligence Summaries are contained in F. S. Regs., Part II. and the Staff Manual respectively. Title pages will be prepared in manuscript.

Army Form C. 2118.

WAR DIARY ~~or INTELLIGENCE SUMMARY.~~ JULY 1919

(Erase heading not required.)

Place	Date	Hour	Summary of Events and Information	Remarks and references to Appendices
REF: MAP	SHEETS		GERMANY 1L & 2K 1/100.000	
HAUSEN	22.		Cross-country run & disinfection of blankets. Education 10.30 – 12.30 Batt. ties 1st with 53rd GORDONS in open Relay Race at 10th A & S H. Games.	McGm
do.	23.		No parades; pouring wet day.	McGm
do.	24.		Regimental Games: dry still day: 'A' Coy. wins inter-coy championship Cup. Battn. wins open Relay Race: 2/Lt. J.M. STIRLING rejoins from hospital	McGm
do.	25.		Clearing up Sports ground. Lecture on Venereal Disease 11.00 hrs.	McGm
do.	26.		Musketry, coy. training & education classes 08.00 – 12.30 hrs; 2/Lt. A. HARVEY to hospital.	McGm
do.	27		Church Parade 09.00 hrs	McGm
do.	28.		Adjutant's Parade 09.00 hrs; C.Os. parade 10.00 hrs	McGm
do.	29.		Inspection by Brigadier at 10.30 hrs. Divisional Horse Show: Battn. wins 1st places with Limbered G.S. wagon, Field Kitchen & Pack Mule; & 2nd places with water-cart & stripped pair mules.	McGm
do.	30.		Battn. picked to be drawn up at G.H.Q in front of COLOGNE Cathedral on occasion of visit of French General FAYOLLE to British G.H.Q; Battn. leaves by Train 08.19 hrs arrives COLOGNE 10.55; Gen. FAYOLLE arrives 12.00, inspects battn. & battn. marches past. 28 offrs & 372 O.Rs. on parade. 2/Lt. J.P. CRAN M.M. carries the Colour. Battn. presents excellent appearance	McGm
do.	31.		Lecture on "Making a modern newspaper" 11.00 hrs. 2/Lt. R. AIRD proceeds to FRANCE to join Chinese Labour Corps. Splendid weather all day; first time this month	McGm

(A9175) Wt W2358/P360 600,000 12/17 D. D. & L. Sch. 52a. Forms/C2118/15.

War Diary
APP I.

OPERATION ORDER NO. 1.
by
Lieut Colonel H. Campbell D.S.O.
Commanding
5th Bn Cameron Highlanders. 29th June 1919.

Reference maps, GERMANY 2 K. and 1 L. 1/100.000.

INFORMATION.
The 1st Highland Brigade is returning to the HAUSEN-BLENS AREA on the 30th June and 1st July 1919.

INTENTION.
The 5th Bn Cameron Highlanders will move to the DROVE - BOICH - THUM AREA by train and march route on the 30th inst and to encampment at HAUSEN on the 1st prox.

INSTRUCTIONS - MOVE.
(1) Entrainment and march to DROVE AREA will be carried out in accordance with appendix A. attached.
March from DROVE AREA to HAUSEN will be carried out in accordance with appendix B. attached. (To be issued later)

(2) Transport.
The following vehicles will move independently of the Battalion under the transport officer by road to HAUSEN in accordance with instructions issued separately to the Transport officer, leaving OPLADEN at 09.30 hours on 30th inst and staying the night of 30th June - 1st July at HUNGERSDORF.
Five limbered wagons, "D" Company cooker, 1 water cart, 3 G.S. wagons and 1 Medical cart, 21 draft animals, and 1 Rider.
Remaining animals and transport will proceed by train to DUREN on 30th June and by road to HAUSEN in Brigade column on 1st July.

(3) Supplies. (a) Supply railhead will remain at OHLIGS up to and including 1st July and will move to DUREN on 2nd July.
(b) All troops will carry unexpired portion of the days rations.
(c) Two days rations for 1st and 2nd July will be carried in bulk as follows:- ~~[illegible]~~
(d) A representative of the Q.M. will report to the supply officer at OPLADEN STATION at 10.00 hours and will take over two days rations for the whole Battalion.
Rations for all ranks proceeding by rail will be kept at station and loaded on to 1st omnibus train on the Q.M. arrangements.
Rations for transport proceeding by road will be reloaded on to supply wagons which will be at the entraining station from 09.00 hours and will be delivered to transport by 526th Company A.S.C. at the end of each days march.
(e) On second July rations will be delivered to the battalion direct by lorry.
(f) On third July refilling will be by supply wagons at FLOITZHEIM at 09.00 hours.
(g) D.A.D.O.S. advance stores at OHLIGS will close on 30th inst

(4) Area Stores. All Area stores taken over in OPLADEN will be left in situ.

(5) Guards. The following guards will remain on duty till relieved
Town Guard OPLADEN, Bridge Guard OPLADEN, Hospital Guard WEISDORF, Eifel Tor Guard.

(6) Billet Certificates. Certificates that all billets occupied in OPLADEN and on night 30th June - 1st July have been left in a clean and sanitary condition will be forwarded to the Orderly Room by Officers commanding companies, H.Q. Transport Officer, and Quartermaster immediately on arrival in HAUSEN on 1st July.

5. ACKNOWLEDGE.

W G M Moffatt
Captain & A/Adjt.
5th Bn Cameron Highlanders.

29th June 1919.

To:- Coys.; H.Q.; C.O.; Q.M.; T.O.; R.S.M.; Adj.; War Diary (2)

APPENDIX A. TO O.O. NO.1.
DATED 29/6/19.

MOVE TO DROVE - BOICH - THUM AREA.

1. PARADE.

Battalion will be formed up in close column of Companies on "A" Company's Square ready to move of at ~~XXXXX~~ 14.00 hours, Markers 13.40 ~~XXXXXXXX~~ hours.

Companies and H.Qrs., will hand to the Adjutant on parade, entraining states showing number of officers and other ranks separately.

A colour Party of 1 sergt and 2 other ranks selected by "C" Company under 2nd Lieut J. Mackie will report at the Mess at 13.40 hours.

2. ENTRAINING.

Battalion will entrain at OPLADEN STATION at 14.30 hours Train departs at 15.00 hours. Battalion will detrain at DUREN at 18.00 hours and proceed thence by march route to billets as follows:-

B	"A" Company.	THUM.
A	"B" "	BOICH.
	H.Qrs.,"C" and "D"	DROVE.

3. ROUTE.

NIDERAU- KREUZAU - DROVE.

4. ORDER OF MARCH.

~~HQ~~ H.Qrs., - "B" - "C" - "D" - "A" Companies.

5. ADVANCE PARTY.

An advance party of 1 N.C.O. per Company and H.Qrs., under 2nd Lieut J.P. Cran will parade at the Orderly Room at 10.30 hours and proceed to DROVE Area by train via DUREN. Train leaves OPLADEN at 10.57 hours, to arrange billets.

6. BAGGAGE.

Blankets rolled in bundles of ten and marked, Officers kits and Company stores will be stacked at H.Qrs and Company billets by 10.00 hours. Three lorries will report to the Quartermaster Stores about 07.00 hours. One N.C.O. and one man per Company and H.Qrs will report to Quartermaster at 09.45 hours. The Quartermaster will send ~~them~~ these men round to collect baggage which they will bring to the Quartermaster Stores on the lorries, There, all other stores will be collected and taken to OPLADEN STATION by the lorries.

The mess cart will collect officers mess kits at 13.00 hours and will convoy them to the station and dump them there with the stores to go with the first omnibus train (see below)

All stores and baggage will be at the station by 14.30 hours.
Conveyance of stores of the battalion, is alloted on the 1st omnibus train leaving OPLADEN at 13.00 hours and arriving at DUREN at 21.00 hours.
Rations, mess kit, camp kettles and as many other stores and baggage as possible will be put on this train.
The Quartermaster will travel by the first omnibus train.
All other baggage and the Transport (see below) will travel by the second omnibus train leaving OPLADEN at 21.00 hours and arriving DUREN at 00,01 hours 1st July. Two covered wagons are allotted the Battalion for baggage on this train. The R.Q.M.S. will accompany the 2nd Omnibus train which loads at 18.00 hours,

6. BAGGAGE CONTINUED.

The Q.M. will hand the Brigade entraining Officer Lieut Millar 10th A.& S.H. an entraining state showing number of Officers and men to proceed by each train immediately on arrival at station.

The two men detailed by Companies to collect baggage will accompany the baggage all through.

Three lorries have been detailed to report to the Quartermaster at DUREN.

The Quartermaster will send off by lorry to DROVE all stores conveyed by first omnibus train immediately they arrive at DUREN. Other stores will be sent off on arrival. Q.M. will remain at DUREN till all stores arriving by second omnibus train have been despatched.

The Q.M. will be responsible that a sufficent number of camp kettles to cook for the whole battalion is put on the first omnibus train. Loading parties at opladen and unloading parties at DUREN are being found by the 52nd Gordon Highlanders and 10th A. & S.H. respectively.

TRANSPORT.

All transport and animals not proceeding by road will proceed by the 2nd omnibus train under the transport sergt. The vehicles will be L.G. limbers, "A" "B" and "D" Company cookers, Mess cart, 1 S.A.A. limber, and 1 Water cart.

The following places are allotted to the Battalion on the 2nd omnibus train:-

Men 45. Axles 22. Animals 33.

Transport will be at the station at 17.30 hours. Train loads at 19.00 hours departs from OPLADEN at 21 hours and arrives at DUREN at 00.01 hours 1st July.

Immediately on arrival at the station the transport sergt will hand the Brigade entraining officer an entraining state showing separately number of men , number of horses, H.D. number of horses L.D. Number of mules, number of axles.

This transport will remain in DUREN during the night of 30th June - 1st July and will proceed to HAUSEN in Brigade column on 1st July under instructions to be issued separately.

8. COMPLETION OF MOVE.

On arrival in billets in DROVE AREA, companies and H.Qrs., will forward certificates of completion of move.

Captain & A/Adjt.
5th Bn Cameron Highlanders.

29th June 1919.

ISSUED TO ALL RECIPIENTS OF O.O. NO.1. OF 29/6/19.

APPENDIX "B" TO OPERATION ORDER NO.1,
DATED 29/6/19.

****

1. STARTING POINT.

Battalion will march to encampment at HAUSEN tomorrow 1st July 1919 passing the starting point at the Junction of the NIDEGGEN - BOICH ROAD and NIDEGGEN - THUM ROAD in the following order and at following times:-

H.Qrs.,	10.30 hours.
"C" Coy.	10.31 "
"D" "	10.32 "
"A" "	10.33 "
"B" "	10.34 "

2. ROUTE.

NIDEGGEN - ABENDEN - HAUSEN.

3. STORES AND BAGGAGE.

All blankets, mess kit, officers kits, stores and baggage of Companies and H.Qrs will be stacked at Company and Bn H.Qrs by 09.00 hours.

Each Company and H.Qrs will detail three other ranks to guard, load, and accompany baggage to HAUSEN.

This baggage will ~~then~~ be collected by lorry under arrangements which will be notified to the Quartermaster.

4. REPORT.

Companies and H.Qrs will report completion of move immediately on arrival in HAUSEN.

W. G. S. Moffatt.

Captain & A/Adjt.
5th Bn Cameron Highlanders.

Issued to all recipients of ~~XXX~~ O.O. No.1. dated 29/6/19.

9 1 Copy to H.Q. 1st Highland Bde

30th June 1919.

49 F

5TH. BATTALION THE QUEENS OWN CAMERON HIGHLANDERS

WAR DIARY VOL. LIV.

and

APPENDICES

AUGUST 1919.

Capt. & A/Adjutant.
5th. Cameron highlanders.

CATTERICK. 1/9/19.

Instructions regarding War Diaries and Intelligence Summaries are contained in F. S. Regs., Part II. and the Staff Manual respectively. Title pages will be prepared in manuscript.

Army Form C. 2118.

WAR DIARY AUGUST 1919

or

~~INTELLIGENCE SUMMARY.~~

(Erase heading not required.)

Place	Date	Hour	Summary of Events and Information	Remarks and references to Appendices
Ref. MAP SHEETS			GERMANY 1L & 2K 1/100.000 & ENGLAND & WALES Sheet 6 2 miles to 1 inch.	
HAUSEN	1.		Range practice & preparing for Bde. games	MHM
			2/Lt. R. AIRD proceeds to join Chinese Labour Corps.	
do.	2.		Brigade Games. Battn. wins the Bde. HIGHLAND GAMES Championship Cup presented by Brig-Gen. T. CAMPBELL D.S.O. with 78 pts to nearest 41. Capt. H. GRINDALL M.C.: Lieuts D. MACDONALD M.C. & A. FRASER M.C. chief winning competitors. Battn. is told that it is shortly proceeding home.	MHM
do.	3.		Church Parade 09.00 hrs.	MHM
do.	4		150 men go for trip on the RHINE; Lt. G. CAMERON rejoins & is taken on strength	MHM
do.	5.		Cross Country Run 08.45.	MHM
do.	6.		Musketry & Baths; message received from the C in C. Gen. Sir W. ROBERTSON G.C.B.	APP I. MHM
do.	7.		Medical Inspection; Checking Mobilization Equipt.	MHM
do.	8		All wagons & mob. stores proceed to ANTWERP. Battn. preparing for move.	MHM
do.	9.		Collection of stores etc. for move. 2/Lt. E. M. ESSON joins from 4th Seaforth Hrs.	MHM
do.	10.		Packing baggage & cleaning camp areas. Move to DUREN Barracks by train commencing 10.30 hrs. Move complete 16 hrs.	APP II MHM
~~do.~~	~~11.~~			
DUREN BARRACKS	11		Cleaning up & preparing for entraining to CALAIS 2/Lt. E.M. ESSON sick to hospital	MHM

Army Form C. 2118.

Instructions regarding War Diaries and Intelligence Summaries are contained in F. S. Regs., Part II. and the Staff Manual respectively. Title pages will be prepared in manuscript.

WAR DIARY ~~or~~ ~~INTELLIGENCE SUMMARY.~~

AUGUST 1919

(*Erase heading not required.*)

Place	Date	Hour	Summary of Events and Information	Remarks and references to Appendices
DUREN BARRACKS	12		Battn entrains, leaving DUREN Station 13·55 hrs. Fairly good journey	APP2
	13		via LIEGE, CHALEROI, ARMENTIERES arriving CALAIS 21·00 h 13th	MGM
			Lieut. D.N. JOHNSTON M.C. proceeds to join Chinese Labour Corps.	
CALAIS	14		Battn embarks with 10th A.T.S.M.; Bde. H.Q. & 460th F. Coy. R.E. 11 hrs. arriving DOVER 15 hrs. Battn entrained 15 hrs.	MGM
CATTERICK	15		Battn arrives CATTERICK CAMP 11·00 hrs.	MGM
do.	16		Baths & settling into barracks.	MGM
do.	17		Church Parade 11·30 hrs.	MGM
do.	18		Coy. training.	MGM
do.	19		Coy. training: Check of rifles, medical inspection	MGM
do.	20		A.T.C. Coys. range practice.	MGM
do.	21		Disinfection & check of blankets.	MGM
do.	22		Coy training 'A' Coy (17 1 O. Rs) proceed on 15 days leave.	MGM
do.	23		Coy. training	MGM
do.	24		Church parade 11·30 hrs.	MGM
do.	25		Coy. training & specialist classes	MGM

(A9475) Wt W2358/P360 600,000 12/17 D. D. & L. Sch. 52a. Forms/C2118/15.

Instructions regarding War Diaries and Intelligence Summaries are contained in F. S. Regs., Part II. and the Staff Manual respectively. Title pages will be prepared in manuscript.

Army Form C. 2118.

WAR DIARY AUGUST 1919

~~INTELLIGENCE SUMMARY.~~

(*Erase heading not required.*)

Place	Date	Hour	Summary of Events and Information	Remarks and references to Appendices
CATTERICK YORKS.	26		Range Practice; Coy. training & education.	[initials]
do	27.		Cleaning camp.	[initials]
do.	28		Coy training 'C' Coy. (170 O.Rs.) proceeds on 15 days leave.	[initials]
do.	29		Coy. training	[initials]
do	30		Coy. training	[initials]
do.	31		Church Parade 11.30.	[initials]
			121 O.Rs. sent for demobilization during August.	
			Change from Germany to home station is not greatly appreciated. Too many rules, regulations & obstructions in obtaining requirements which are easily procured on active service	

[signature]
Captain and Adjutant
5th Cameron Highlanders.

(A9175) Wt W2353/P360 600,000 12/17 D. D. & L. Sch. 52a. Forms/C2118/15.

APP1

GENERAL FAYOLLE'S REVIEW.

****

The following message has been received from the Commander-in-Chief, General Sir William R. Robertson, G.C.B., G.C.M.G., K.C.V.O., D.S.O., A.D.C.

"Begins. Please convey to the Officer Commanding, 5th. Battalion Cameron Highlanders my great appreciation of the way his Battalion turned out, handled their arms and marched past when forming a Guard of Honour to GENERAL FAYOLLE. The way in which the Parade was conducted reflects the greatest credit on Colonel Campbell and the Officers and men of his Battalion. Ends".

The Divisional Commander, having witnessed the Parade, is able to endorse all the Commander-in-Chief has said and sincerely congratulates all ranks.

-----------ooo-----------

APP2

5TH BN CAMERON HIGHLANDERS.

****

Operation Order No.2.
by
Lieut Colonel R. Campbell D.S.O.
Commanding
5th Bn Cameron Highlanders.

****

9th August 1919.

1. The battalion will move to the U.K. via rail and ship leaving HAUSEN, Germany on 10/8/19.

2. Destination in the U.K. :- CATTERICK, YORKSHIRE.

3. Move is divided into the following sub-headings:-

(i) Move to concentration area in DUREN.
(ii) Move to port of embarkation.
(iii) Crossing to U.K. and entrainment to station in U.K.

Each of these are dealt with in separate appendices in detail, to be issued from time to time.

All other arrangements concerning baggage, closing accounts, and details with regard to change of station will also be issued as separate appendices.

4. Transport vehicles and mobilization stores are moving to U.K. via ANTWERP.

Details of this move and of collection of requisitioned and R.E. Stores &c. have been dealt with in Warning Orders and Appendices thereto already issued.

5. ACKNOWLEDGE.

W G H Moffatt

Captain and A/Adjt.
5th Bn Cameron Highlanders.

Issued to	Cop. No.
C.O.	1.
Adjt.	2.
Coys.	3 - 6
Q.M.	7
T.O.	8.
R.S.M.	9
H.Q.	10
File	11
War Diary	12 and 13.

Issued through signals
at

War Diary

Appendix No 1. to O.O. No 2. dated 9/8/19.
****

MOVE TO CONCENTRATION AREA IN DUREN.

1. Battalion will move to DUREN Barracks tomorrow 10th inst by two trains leaving HAUSEN Station at 11.20 hours and 14.50 hours respectively.

2. TRAINS.
(1) "C" Company, "D" Company, all H.Q. personnel and R.Q.M.S. will parade on the Square ready to march off at 10,50 hours. They will proceed by first train(SERIAL LETTER A.)leaving HAUSEN Station at 11.20 hours and arriving DUREN 12.25 hours.
(2) "A" Company (less 1 officer and 20 other ranks as rear party - see below) "B" Company transport and grooms personnel, and the Quartermaster will parade on the Square under the battalion second in Command ready to march off at 14.20 hours. They will proceed by second train (SERIAL LETTER B.) leaving HAUSEN Station at 14.50 hours, and arriving DUREN 15.55 hours. T.M.B. are also travelling by this train.
The battalion will march from DUREN Station to DUREN Barracks to occupy billets taken over by advance party from 8th Black Watch. A guide will be sent for second party.

3. (3) RATIONS AND SUPPLY
All men will entrain with unexpired portion of day's ration, one iron ration, and water bottles filled.
Rations for consumption on the 11th will be delivered at DUREN Barracks by lorry at 10.00 hours.
Q.M. will send representative into DUREN by train at 06.00 hours to take over these rations.
Rations for consumption on 12th will be delivered at DUREN Barracks at 09.30 hours on 11th.
Two days rations for journey to the Base will be drawn at the R.S.O.s Office DUREN Station two hours before entrainment on 12th.

4. TRANSPORT OF BAGGAGE.
Men will carry blankets and Lewis Guns.
No baggage with the exception of utensils used for cooking dinners for second train personnel (i.e. A and B Companies, rear party and transport) will be taken on personnel train.
All baggage will be removed by 3 lorries at 08.15 hours.
If necessary these lorries will do a second journey. Loading Party of one N.C.O. and 12 other ranks will be detailed ~~by~~ from H.Q. They will travel with lorries and unload them at DUREN Barracks. Lorries have been asked for to transport tents. Loading of tents will commence at 08.00 hours and two journeys will probably be necessary. O.C. "B" Company. will detail a loading party of 2 N.C.O. and 20 men for loading tents, to report to Q.M. at 08.00 hours. A sufficient number of these men for unloading will travel with tent lorries on each journey. This party whether all tents have been loaded or not, will accompany their company on second personnel train. After that rear party will see all tents loaded. On no account may lorries for tents be used for luggage and stores.

(Continued)

5. REAR PARTY.

2nd Lieut C.A.C. Hann and 20other ranks of "A" Company will remain behind after 2nd train and all personnel and ~~X~~ baggage have left.

2nd Lieut Hann's duties are:- See that all furniture has been returned to civilians, all R.E. stores have been handed over and signed for, no battalion property left behind, and lines and camping ground left clean and ~~XXX~~ to load onto lorries all tents not loaded before departure of second train.

The above in no way absolves H.Q. and Company Officers from ensuring that the whole area occupied by the battalion is ~~kept~~ LEFT clean.

6. COMPLETION OF MOVE.WILL BE REPORTED.

7. ACKNOWLEDGE.

W G A Moffatt

Captain & A/Adjt.
5th Bn Cameron Highlanders.

COPIES 1 - 13 all recipients of O.O. No 2.
COPY 14. To battalion second in Command.

APPENDIX NO.2 TO O.O. NO.2 DATED 9/8/19.

****

1. INTENTION. The battalion will move to the Port of embarkation, CALAIS, by train leaving DUREN Station at 13.55 hours tomorrow 12/8/19.

2. PARADE. The battalion will parade on the Square in close column ready to move off at 12.15 hours. Markers 12.00 hours. 2nd Lieut R.H. Munro M.C. and 1 Sergt and 2 other ranks of "C" Company will parade at the Orderly Room as a COLOUR PARTY at 12.10 hours.

3. ENTRAINING. Lieutenant Prentice and Lieut Inglis M.C. will carry out entraining duties for the battalion. Special instructions have been issued to all concerned.
No men will entrain till the "ADVANCE" is sounded.

4. RATIONS AND SUPPLIES. The unconsumed portion of the day's rations will be carried. The Q.M. will draw two days rations for the journey at the R.S.O. Office at DUREN Station at 10.00 hours. Hot meals will be issued at 4 HALTES REPAS on the journey. Only FRENCH and BELGIAN money will be accepted at Canteens and hotels at these HALTES REPAS.

5. LOADING AND UNLOADING PARTIES. O.C. "C" Company will detail the following loading parties.
(1) A party of one N.C.O. and 15 other ranks for loading at the Q.M. Stores to report there at 07.30 hours.
None of this party-only Q.M.Stores personnel-will travel by the lorries.
(2) A party of one Officer and 25 other ranks to report to Lieutenant Inglis at the Station at 08.15 hours.
This party will take full kit and rejoin their Companies on its arrival at the Station.
O.C. "D" will detail a party of 1 Officer and 25 other ranks to parade at the baggage wagons on detrainment at CALAIS for unloading the wagons.

6. TRANSPORT AND BAGGAGE. 3 lorries will report at the barracks at 07.30 hours. All baggage less, officers, and mess kit in use and Company cooking utensils will be stacked at the Q.M. Stores by 07.30 hours. Baggage will be loaded on and taken to the station. All mess kit and officers kit will be stacked at B.H.Q. and Company H.Q. Messes by 09.30 hours.
Each company (one for A.B.and C. Coys who are together.) and B.H.Q. will send a mess waiter to report to Lieut Inglis at the station at 09.00 hours. Lieut Inglis will detail the first lorry, to be unloaded, to go round with these men as guides to pick up the baggage at Company and B.H.Q.
Lorry after leaving B.H.Q. will then proceed to the barracks to pick up the cooks gear, which must leave by 11.00 hours, as baggage trucks will be moved from the loading ramp at 12.00 hours. Lieut Inglis will not dismiss any lorries till Q.M. reports all baggage at the station. As far as possible in loading, rations, cooking utensils and mess kit will be kept together on the train.

7. Battalion will probably stay one night in CALAIS.

8. ACKNOWLEDGE.

11/8/19.

W.H.A. Moffatt
Captain & A/Adjt.
5th Bn Cameron Highlanders.

Issued to all recipients of O.O. No 2. Plus Copy No 14 to Lieut P.F. Prentice and COPY No 15 to Lieut J. Inglis M.C.

APP 2

5TH BN CAMERON HIGHLANDERS.

Operation Order No.2.
by
Lieut Colonel R. Campbell D.S.O.
Commanding
5th Bn Cameron Highlanders.

9th August 1919.

1. The battalion will move to the U.K. via rail and ship leaving HAUSEN, Germany on 10/8/19.

2. Destination in the U.K. :- CATTERICK, YORKSHIRE.

3. Move is divided into the following sub-headings:-

(i) Move to concentration area in DUREN.
(ii) Move to port of embarkation.
(iii) Crossing to U.K. and entrainment to station in U.K.

Each of these are dealt with in separate appendices in detail, to be issued from time to time.

All other arrangements concerning baggage, closing accounts, and details with regard to change of station will also be issued as separate appendices.

4. Transport vehicles and mobilization stores are moving to U.K. via ANTWERP.

Details of this movement of collection of requisitioned and R.E. Stores etc. have been dealt with in Warning Orders and Appendices thereto already issued.

5. ACKNOWLEDGE.

M G Moffatt
Captain and A/Adjt.
5th Bn Cameron Highlanders.

Issued to	Cop. No.
C.O.	1.
Adjt.	2.
Coys.	3 - 6
Q.M.	7
T.O.	8.
R.S.M.	9
H.Q.	10
File	11
War Diary	12 and 13.

Issued through signals
at

War Diary

Appendix No 1. to O.O. No 2. dated 9/8/19.
****

MOVE TO CONCENTRATION AREA IN DUREN.

1. Battalion will move to DUREN Barracks tomorrow 10th inst by two trains leaving HAUSEN Station at 11.20 hours and 14.50 hours respectively.

2. TRAINS.
(1) "C" Company, "D" Company, all H.Q. personnel and R.Q.M.S. will parade on the Square ready to march off at 10,50 hours. They will proceed by first train(SERIAL LETTER A.)leaving HAUSEN Station at 11.20 hours and arriving DUREN 12.25 hours.
(2) "A" Company (less 1 officer and 20 other ranks as rear party - see below) "B" Company transport and grooms personnel, and the Quartermaster will parade on the Square under the battalion second in Command ready to march off at 14.20 hours. They will proceed by second train (SERIAL LETTER B.) leaving HAUSEN Station at 14.50 hours, and arriving DUREN 15.55 hours. T.M.B. are also travelling by this train.
The battalion will march from DUREN Station to DUREN Barracks to occupy billets taken over by advance party from 8th Black Watch. A guide will be sent for second party.

3. (3) RATIONS AND SUPPLY
All men will entrain with unexpired portion of day's ration, one iron ration, and water bottles filled.
Rations for consumption on the 11th will be delivered at DUREN Barracks by lorry at 10.00 hours.
Q.M. will send representative into DUREN by train at 06.00 hours to take over these rations.
Rations for consumption on 12th will be delivered at DUREN Barracks at 09.30 hours on 11th.
Two days rations for journey to the Base will be drawn at the R.S.O.s Office DUREN Station two hours before entrainment on 12th.

4. TRANSPORT OF BAGGAGE.
Men will carry blankets and Lewis Guns.
No baggage with the exception of utensils used for cooking dinners for second train personnel (i.e. A and B Companies, rear party and transport) will be taken on personnel train. All baggage will be removed by 3 lorries at 08.15 hours. If necessary these lorries will do a second journey. Loading Party of one N.C.O. and 12 other ranks will be detailed from H.Q. They will travel with lorries and unload them at DUREN Barracks. Lorries have been asked for to transport tents. Loading of tents will commence at 08.00 hours and two journeys will probably be necessary. O.C. "B" Company. will detail a loading party of 2 N.C.O. and 20 men for loading tents, to report to Q.M. at 08.00 hours. A sufficient number of these men for unloading will travel with tent lorries on each journey. This party whether all tents have been loaded or not, will accompany their company on second personnel train. After that rear party will see all tents loaded. On no account may lorries for tents be used for luggage and stores.

(Continued)

5. REAR PARTY.

2nd Lieut C.A.C. Hann and 20other ranks of "A" Company will remain behind after 2nd train and all personnel and ~~X~~ baggage have left.

2nd Lieut Hann's duties are:- See that all furniture has been returned to civilians, all R.E. stores have been handed over and signed for, no battalion property left behind, and lines and camping ground left cleah and ~~XXX~~ to load onto lorries all tents not loaded before departure of second train.

The above in no way absolves H.Q. and Company Officers from ensuring that the whole area occupied by the battalion is ~~kept~~ LEFT clean.

6. COMPLETION OF MOVE.WILL BE REPORTED.

7. ACKNOWLEDGE.

W G A Moffatt

Captain & A/Adjt.
5th Bn Cameron Highlanders.

COPIES 1 - 13 all recipients of O.O. No 2.
COPY 14. To battalion second in Command.

BEF

HIGHLAND DIV formerly
62 DIV

2. HIGHLAND Bde

1/5 GORDONS

1919 MAR to 1919 AUG

~~NO BOX~~

FROM 15 DIV 44 BDE

62 DIV

Aof O

(6392) Wt. W6192/P875 1,500,000 4/18 McA & W Ltd (E 2815) Forms W3091/4.

Army Form W.3091.

ORIGINAL

Cover for Documents.

C O N F I D E N T I A L.

****

Nature of Enclosures.

2 Bde

W A R D I A R Y.

of

5th Battalion, The Gordon Highlanders.

From 1st March, 1919. To. 31st March, 1919.

(Volume. No. 47)

****

Notes, or Letters written.

Army Form C. 2118.

Instructions regarding War Diaries and Intelligence Summaries are contained in F. S. Regs., Part II, and the Staff Manual respectively. Title pages will be prepared in manuscript.

WAR DIARY
or
~~INTELLIGENCE~~ SUMMARY.
(Erase heading not required.)

5th Batt^n GORDON HIGHLANDERS

Place	Date	Hour	Summary of Events and Information	Remarks and references to Appendices
	MARCH			
ROGGANDORF	1st		The usual Divine Services were held	WHL
	2nd		The battalion attended a lecture in MECHERNICH by the REV. W.A. ELLIOT on the subject "CAPE to CAIRO	WHL
	3rd		The battalion was allotted the Divisional Baths for the day. A football match was played against the 2/5th DUKE of WELLINGTONS REGT in the afternoon at OBERGARTZEN	WHL
	4th		The battalion carried out a route march in the morning. A lecture was given in the Brigade hall at 1430 hours in the afternoon on "Social and Economic Problems"	WHL
	5th		The battalion paraded under the R.S.M. for ~~two~~ arm drill on the football field. Cross country paper chases under Company arrangements with a view to selecting "hares" for a battalion paper chase.	WHL
	6th		Training was carried out between the hours of 0930 and 1145. A battalion paper chase was held in the afternoon, one "hare" being selected from each Coy.	WHL
	7th		Training under Coy arrangements. Billeting party left for KERPEN.	WHL

A6945 Wt. W1422/M1160 350,000 12/16 D. D. & L. Forms/C./2118/14.

Army Form C. 2118.

Instructions regarding War Diaries and Intelligence Summaries are contained in F. S. Regs., Par. II. and the Staff Manual respectively. Title pages will be prepared in manuscript.

WAR DIARY
or
INTELLIGENCE SUMMARY.
(Erase heading not required.)

5th Battn. GORDON HIGHLANDERS

Place	Date	Hour	Summary of Events and Information	Remarks and references to Appendices
ROGGANDORF	8th		Divine Service was held in the Protestant church Roggendorf. Orders were issued for entraining at MECHERNICH en route for KERPEN.	WHL
	9th		Battn moved by road to MECHERNICH where they entrained and proceeded by rail to HORREM. Marched to KERPEN, distance about 4 Kms	WHL
KERPEN.	10th		The day was spent in settling down and adjustment of billets. All the men were in single billets and company billeting areas were very large	WHL
	11th.		Training was carried out. Lewis Gun classes and NCOs classes under the RSM were commenced.	WHL
	12th		Usual training and recreation	WHL
	13th		Battalion paraded for route march	WHL
	14th		Usual parades were carried out. A meeting of Officers and NCOs was held in order to start a Sports Club in the Battn	WHL
	15th		The usual Divine services were held.	WHL
	16th		Usual training and recreation.	WHL
	17th		The Battalion ~~mounted~~ supplied the guard for Divisional Headquarters at	

A6945 Wt. W11422/M1160 350,000 12/16 D. D. & L. Forms/C./2118/14.

Instructions regarding War Diaries and Intelligence Summaries are contained in F. S. Regs., Part II. and the Staff Manual respectively. Title pages will be prepared in manuscript.

Army Form C. 2118.

WAR DIARY
or
INTELLIGENCE SUMMARY.
(Erase heading not required.)

5th Battn GORDON HIGHLANDERS.

Place	Date	Hour	Summary of Events and Information	Remarks and references to Appendices
KERPEN	17th (contd)		DÜREN. A party also left the battalion to take over the Divisional Concentration camp from the personnel of English regiments	WHL
	18th		The Battalion supplied two guards to replace those at MONTJOIE and LANGWERE, Strength 3 officers and 50 o.rs, and 18 o.r's. These parties entrained at HORREM at 0700 hours.	WHL
	19th		Adjutants parade.	WHL
	20th		Battalion paraded for route march at 0945 hours.	WHL
	21st		Commanding Officers parade. All employed men in the Battn attended this parade	
	22nd		The morning was given to interior economy. The Commanding Officer inspected the billets of C and D Companies.	WHL
	23rd		The usual Divine Service was held in the Concert Hall at 11.30 hours. A mounted paper chase was held in the afternoon starting from Battalion H.Q.	WHL
	24th		Company training including Platoon and Arm Drill, Physical Training and Bayonet Fighting, was carried out	WHL
	25th		Company training as usual.	WHL
	26th		Battalion paraded for route march.	WHL
				WHL

D. D. & L., London, E.C.
(A8004) Wt. W1771/M2 31 750,000 5/17 Sch. 52 Forms/C2118/14

Instructions regarding War Diaries and Intelligence Summaries are contained in F. S. Regs., Part II. and the Staff Manual respectively. Title pages will be prepared in manuscript.

WAR DIARY
or
~~INTELLIGENCE SUMMARY.~~
(*Erase heading not required.*)

Army Form C. 2118.

5th GORDON HIGHLANDERS

Place	Date	Hour	Summary of Events and Information	Remarks and references to Appendices
KERPEN	27th		Commanding Officers parade was held at 10.00 hours. The usual instructional classes under the R.S.M. and education were carried out. Medical inspection of the Battalion in the afternoon	WHL
	28th		The morning was devoted to interior economy. The Commanding Officer inspected the billets of A and C Companies. During this week the weather has been so bad, that games had to be postponed.	WHL
	29th		Usual Divine Services were held	WHL
	30th		Company training was carried out.	
	31st		Usual company parades and education. The commanding Officer held a conference in the afternoon. The Sports Club also had a meeting, when the Commanding Officer constituted the events for the Shield	WHL
			Strength for month App. I attached	WHL

A. Lyndsay[?]
Lt Colonel
Comdg 5 Gordon Highrs

D. D. & L., London, E.C.
(A8004) Wt. W1771/M2-31 750,000 5/17 Sch. 52 Forms/C2118/14

Army Form C. 2118.

Appendix I

Instructions regarding War Diaries and Intelligence Summaries are contained in F. S. Regs., Part II. and the Staff Manual respectively. Title pages will be prepared in manuscript.

WAR DIARY
or
INTELLIGENCE SUMMARY.
(*Erase heading not required.*)

Place / Date / Hour / Summary of Events and Information	O	OR	O	OR
22.2.19 Effective Strength			36	743
Increase				
Taken on Strength from 9th Gordon Hrs		6		
Decrease				
Men left at Nivelles for Demobilisation		135		
Men officially notified as having been demob on leave		22		
Demobilised 27.2.19		3		
		160		
Difference between Increase & Decrease				154
1.3.19 Effective Strength			36	589
Increase				
Joined from 1st Gordon Highrs	8	60		
Rejoined from Hospital		1		
	8	61		
Decrease				
Taken on Strength of 9th Gordons		16		
Evacuated sick		5		
Over 7 days in FA		2		
Demobilised		9		
		32		
Difference between Increase & Decrease			8	29
8.3.19 Effective Strength			44	618

Summary of Events and Information	O	OR	O	OR
8.3.19 Effective Strength				
Increase Joined from 1st Gordon Hrs	4	18		
" " 6/7 "		2		
	4	20		
Decrease Taken on Str of 9th Gordon Hrs		5		
Re enlisted in Post Bellum Army		1		
Demobilised		8		
Evacuated sick		14		
Struck off Strength (Over 7 days in F.A.		3		
		31		
Difference between Increase and Decrease			4	11
15-3.19 Effective Strength			48	604
Increase Joined from 1st Gordon Hrs	1			
" " 9th "		50		
	1	50		
Decrease Taken on Str of 9th Gordon Hrs	3	8		
Demobilised		2		
To UK Re-enlistment leave		1		
Evacuated sick	1	2		
Taken on Str of 1st Gordon Hrs		1		
Over 7 days in F.A.		1		
Struck off Str on being posted to 1/4 Gordon Hrs	6			
	10	15		
Difference between Increase Decrease			9	35
22/3/19 Effective Str			39	639
Increase Joined from 9th Gordons		22		
rejoined from 1st Hospital	3	14		
	3	36		
Decrease Posted to 1/4 Gordon Hrs	1			
To UK Demobilised on re-enlistment leave		1		
	1	6		
Difference between Inc & Dec.			2	30
29/3/19 Effective Str			41	669

D. D. & L., London, E.C. (A8004) Wt. W1771/M2 31 750,000 5/17 Sch. 52 Forms/C2118/14

SECRET. ORIGINAL.

W A R   D I A R Y.

of

5th Battn. The Gordon Highlanders.

May 1st 1919 to May 31st 1919.

Lieut-Colonel,
Commanding 5th Battn. The Gordon Highlanders.

ORIGINAL

Army Form C. 2118.

Instructions regarding War Diaries and Intelligence Summaries are contained in F. S. Regs., Part II. and the Staff Manual respectively. Title pages will be prepared in manuscript.

WAR DIARY
or
~~INTELLIGENCE SUMMARY.~~
(Erase heading not required.)

MAY 1919

5th GORDON HIGHLANDERS.

Place	Date	Hour	Summary of Events and Information	Remarks and references to Appendices
BIRKESDORF	1.		The usual training programme was carried out. The Battalion was confined to the village of BIRKESDORF owing to the Germans holding processions etc in DUREN.	WHL
	2.		Major R A Wolfe Murray DSO. MC took over the command of the battalion from Major J. B. Wood DSO MC. who proceeded to UK for demobilization. Training as usual. The C.O inspected Coys in their billets during the morning. Kits were laid down	WHL
	3.		Training and Education during the morning	WHL
	4.		The usual Divine Services were held	WHL
	5		Training and Education were carried out.	WHL
	6.		Baths were allotted to the Battalion as usual	WHL
	7.		Battn paraded for route march at 0900 hours. Route HOVEN and return.	WHL
	8		~~The usual training was carried out. One company on the range and the remainder doing musketry and arm drill~~	
	8		All officers and effective ranks paraded at 0715 hours on Battn. parade ground in drill order. Training under Coy arrangements. A lecture on "The NAVY" was given in DUREN by VISCOUNT BROOME. A and D Coys attended this lecture.	WHL
	9.		The usual training was carried out. One company on the range and the remainder doing musketry and arm drill	WHL
	10		Training as usual. A lecture was given by Major HAYWOOD in the Theatre BIRKESDORF at 1100 hours. The G.O.C. 2nd Highland	

D. D. & L., London, E.C. (A8004) Wt. W1771/M2 31 750,000 5/17 Sch. 52 Forms/C2118/14

ORIGINAL

Instructions regarding War Diaries and Intelligence Summaries are contained in F. S. Regs., Part II. and the Staff Manual respectively. Title pages will be prepared in manuscript.

MAY. 1919.

WAR DIARY
or
~~INTELLIGENCE SUMMARY.~~
(Erase heading not required.)

Sheet II

Army Form C. 2118.

5th Gordon Highlanders

Place	Date	Hour	Summary of Events and Information	Remarks and references to Appendices
BIRKESDORF	10		Brigade visited the Battalion and inspected billets cookhouses etc.	WHL
	11		The usual Divine Services were held. The Battn was warned to provide the Divisional Commanders Guard on the 12th	WHL
	12		The C.O. inspected all Coys at 14 30 hours today on the Battn parade Ground. The 2nd Highland Brigade was warned to parade for inspection by the C. in C. Sir William Robertson on the 15th May	WHL
	13		The battalion, less A Coy who proceeded to GROSSHAU to prepare a camp, paraded at 0700 hours outside FACTORY for practice parade under Brigade arrangements in connection with the C in C's inspection. Order of March B Signallers & Pioneers, B, C, and D Coys. Battn returned about 12.30 hours	WHL
	14		Training under Coy arrangements. Battn Cleaned up for C in C's inspection	WHL
	15		Battn was inspected by Sir William Robertson. Paraded at 0730 hours and returned to billets at 12.30 hours. The dress was fighting order. 1st Line Transport was on parade	WHL
	16		Training and education as usual	WHL
	17		Commanding Officer inspected the kits of the battalion today.	WHL
	18		Usual Divine Services were held today.	WHL
	19		Training and Education as usual	WHL
	20		The Baths were allotted to the Battn today. Parades were under Company arrangements	WHL
				WHL

D. D. & L., London, E.C. (A8004) Wt. W1771/M2 31 750,000 5/17 Sch. 52 Forms/C2118/14

ORIGINAL

SHEET VII

Instructions regarding War Diaries and Intelligence Summaries are contained in F. S. Regs., Part II. and the Staff Manual respectively. Title pages will be prepared in manuscript.

WAR DIARY
or
~~INTELLIGENCE SUMMARY~~.

(*Erase heading not required.*)

Army Form C. 2118.

5th GORDON HIGHLANDERS

Place	Date	Hour	Summary of Events and Information	Remarks and references to Appendices
BIRKESDORF	21		Battn paraded for route march at 0900 hours.	WAL
	22		Usual training and education. A lecture was given in Düren by Lt Col Tyson on "Bolshevism" 100 all ranks attended from the battalion	WAL
	23.		Usual training and education	WAL
	24.		Usual training and education. CO inspected billets of all companies	WAL
	25.		Usual Divine Services were held	WAL
	26.		In the morning training and education. In the afternoon the battalion paraded for fatigue to clean out new portion of the factory for a dining hall	WAL
	27.		The Battn was allotted the baths	WAL
	28.		Battn paraded for route march	WAL
	29		Training as per programme. A general interchange of equipment took place as ~~some~~ all WAL companies had both leather & web in their possession. The Battn took over the guard duties from the 51st Battn Gordon Highlanders	WAL
	30.		Usual training and education	WAL

D. D. & L., London, E.C.
(A8004) Wt. W1771/M2 31 750,000 5/17 Sch. 52 Forms/C2118/14

ORIGINAL

Army Form C. 2118.

WAR DIARY
or
~~INTELLIGENCE SUMMARY.~~
(Erase heading not required.)

Instructions regarding War Diaries and Intelligence Summaries are contained in F. S. Regs., Part II. and the Staff Manual respectively. Title pages will be prepared in manuscript.

Sheet 4.

5th GORDON. HIGHLANDERS

Place	Date	Hour	Summary of Events and Information	Remarks and references to Appendices
BIRKESDORF	31.		The Commanding Officer inspected billets	WAH
			Attached Appendix I Effective Strength	
			~~Appendix II Operation Order No F/126~~ WAH	
			[signature] Lt Colonel Commanding 1/5th Bn Gordon Highrs	

D. D. & L., London, E.C. (A8004) Wt. W1771/M2 31 750,000 5/17 Sch. 52 Forms/C2118/14

ORIGINAL

Army Form C. 2118.

Instructions regarding War Diaries and Intelligence Summaries are contained in F. S. Regs., Part II, and the Staff Manual respectively. Title pages will be prepared in manuscript.

WAR DIARY
or
INTELLIGENCE SUMMARY.
(*Erase heading not required.*)

Place	Date	Hour	Summary of Events and Information	O	OR	O	OR
26/4/19			Effective Strength			29	683
Increase							
			Joined from 1st Gordon Highrs		3		
			" " 3rd Corps Conc Camp		1		
			Taken on Str from Royal Scots		18		
			Rejoined from Hospital		2		
			Taken on Str from 9th Gordon Hrs	1			
			" " " " 11th Gordons		100		
				1	124		
Decrease			Struck off Str on proceeding to Gordon Hrs details		1		
			To U.K. for re-enlistment leave		5		
					6		
			Diff between Increase & Decrease			1	118
3/5/19			Effective Strength			30	801
Increase			Rejoined from Hospital		2		
			Taken on Str from 15th Div Area		1		
			" " " III Corps Conc Camp		4		
			" " " 4th Gordon Hrs	5			
			" " " 9th " "		1		
				5	8		
Decrease			To Gordon Highrs details		2		
			To U.K. for demobilisation	1	7		
			Difference between increase & Decrease			4	1
10/5/19			Effective Strength			34	800
Increase			Rejoined from Hospital		1		
			Joined " 9th Gordon Highrs		1		
			" " 15th "		1		
					3		

Place	Date	Hour	Summary of Events and Information	O	OR	O	OR
Decrease			To U.K. for release		10		
			Gordon Hrs details		2		
					12		
			Difference between Increase & Decrease				9
17.5.19			Effective Strength			34	791
Increase			From details 8th Gordon Hrs	2	5		
			Taken on Str from U.K.	1			
				3	5		
Decrease			To 3rd Highland Brigade T.M.B.		16		
			Difference between Increase			3	11
24.5.19			Effective Strength			37	780
Increase			Taken on Strength from Hospital		1		
Decrease			To U.K. for demobilisation	2	6		
			" " re enlistment leave		11		
			Struck off Str on decease		1		
				2	18		
			Difference between Inc and Decrease			2	17
31/5/19			Effective Strength			35	763

(A5475) Wt W2358/P360 600,000 12/17 D. D. & L. Sch. 52a. Forms/C2118/15.

SECRET.

ORIGINAL.

WAR DIARY

of

5th, Battalion GORDON HIGHLANDERS.

From, 1st. JUNE 1919 To. 30th. JUNE. 1919

(Volume LV)

[signature] Lieut-Colonel.

Commanding. 5th, Bn, Gordon Highlanders,

~~Ist~~ June 1919
Sheet I

Instructions regarding War Diaries and Intelligence Summaries are contained in F. S. Regs., Part II. and the Staff Manual respectively. Title pages will be prepared in manuscript.

WAR DIARY
or
~~INTELLIGENCE SUMMARY.~~
(Erase heading not required.)

In Germany

Army Form C. 2118.

5th Gordon Highlanders

Place	Date	Hour	Summary of Events and Information	Remarks and references to Appendices
BIRKESDORF	1		Being Sunday the usual Divine Services were held	WH
	2		Usual training and education	WH
	3		The Birthday of His Majesty the King was observed. The Battalion paraded at 0930 on the Batt. parade ground with the Colours. The remainder of the day was observed as a holiday.	WH
	4		Battalion Route March at 0900 hours	WH
	5		Usual training and education. The Battalion Kitchen Garden [?] was commenced today	WH
	6		A Company moved out to GROSSHAU [?] ... [illegible] the Battalion [illegible] ... "Helping Parent" [?] in the [illegible] DUREN	WH
	7		[illegible] Company [illegible] work on the Kitchen [?] ... [illegible]	WH
	8		The usual Divine Services were held	WH
	9		The Battalion [illegible]	WH

(A9173) Wt W2355/P360 600,000 12/17 D. D. & L. Sch. 52a. Forms/C2118/15.

Army Form C. 2118.

June 1919 — Sheet II — In Germany

WAR DIARY
or
~~INTELLIGENCE SUMMARY.~~

(Erase heading not required.)

5th Gordon Highlanders

Instructions regarding War Diaries and Intelligence Summaries are contained in F. S. Regs., Part II, and the Staff Manual respectively. Title pages will be prepared in manuscript.

Place	Date	Hour	Summary of Events and Information	Remarks and references to Appendices
BIRKESDORF	10.		Training and education.	[illegible]
	11		Batt. on Route march. The Battalion found the 2	
			Bridge Guard DUREN consisting of 1 off. 2 NCOs and 15 OR	[illegible]
	12		The Battalion paraded in clean fatigue to make	
			ready the sports ground for the Batt. Sports.	[illegible]
	13		The Battalion Sports were held in DURENER STRASSE	
			Field & there were no parades.	[illegible]
	14		Battalion was engaged on clearing up the sports ground	[illegible]
	15.		Usual Divine Services were held. Dr SLATER of Edinburgh	
			preached to the Battn.	[illegible]
	16		Usual training and education	[illegible]
	17		In accordance with Operation Order No [illegible] attached, the order to	—
SOLINGEN			entrain came through at 4 am. The Battalion moved to	
			~~to~~ SOLINGEN by trains leaving DUREN at ~~1400~~ and 1730	
			hours respectively, ~~but~~ in accordance with O.O. No 6 and	
			attached amendment. Bn ~~at~~ arrived Solingen 2200 hours.	[illegible]

(A9475) Wt W2358/P360 600,000 12/17 D. D. & L. Sch. 52a. Forms/C2118/15.

June 1919 — Sheet III — in Germany

Army Form C. 2118.

WAR DIARY
or
INTELLIGENCE SUMMARY.
(Erase heading not required.)

Instructions regarding War Diaries and Intelligence Summaries are contained in F. S. Regs., Part II. and the Staff Manual respectively. Title pages will be prepared in manuscript.

5th Gordon Highlanders

Place	Date	Hour	Summary of Events and Information	Remarks and references to Appendices
WALD	17		The Battalion then marched to WALD where they were billeted in the 2nd LOWLAND BDE area	[illegible]
	18		The Battalion rested and cleaned up. Later orders came through that the Battalion would ~~take over~~ relieve the 1st Kings Own Scottish Borderers in the outpost line next day	[illegible]
	19		B & D Companies proceeded to take over from the 2 Companies 6th KOSB in the Bridgehead Perimeter Outpost Line. Operations: See OO No. 7.	[illegible]
	20		The Battn spent the day in cleaning up and preparing to move forward	[illegible]
	21		Training under Company arrangements	[illegible]
	22		Usual Divine Services. The Presbyterian service was held along with 1st KOSB in the church WALD.	[illegible]
	23		Battn cleaned up billets under Coy arrangements.	[illegible]
	24		Training under company arrangements.	[illegible]

(A9475) Wt W2358/P360 600,000 12/17 D. D. & L. Sch. 52a. Forms/C2118/15.

June 1919 — Sheet IV

Instructions regarding War Diaries and Intelligence Summaries are contained in F. S. Regs., Part II. and the Staff Manual respectively. Title pages will be prepared in manuscript.

WAR DIARY
or
INTELLIGENCE SUMMARY.
(*Erase heading not required.*)

In Germany

5th Gordon Highlanders

Army Form C. 2118.

Place	Date	Hour	Summary of Events and Information	Remarks and references to Appendices
WALD	25th		Training under Company arrangements	WHL
	26th		Usual Training	WHL
	27th		Training under Company arrangements.	WHL
	28th		At 1900 hours a wire came through from Brigade	
			Headquarters stating that Peace had been signed (official)	WHL
	29th		Usual Divine Services in WALD.	WHL
	30th		A Coy who was guarding the railway line [illegible] OHLIGS and	
			OPLADEN was relieved today.	WHL
			Attached Appendices I Strength Returns	
			II Operation / Admin Orders No 6?7	
			III Orders for J day	

(A9475) Wt W2358/P360 600,000 12/17 D. D. & L. Sch. 52a. Forms/C2118/15.

Appendix I

Instructions regarding War Diaries and Intelligence Summaries are contained in F. S. Regs., Part II. and the Staff Manual respectively. Title pages will be prepared in manuscript.

WAR DIARY
or
INTELLIGENCE SUMMARY.
(Erase heading not required.)

Army Form C. 2118.

Place / Date / Hour	O.	O.R.	O.	O.R.
Effective Strength 31/5/19			35	763
Increase				
Joined from Base		1		
Taken on Str from 53rd South Wales Borderers		2		
" " " " 51st Gordon Highrs		1		
		4		
Decrease				
Lieut T. I. Ewing taken on Strength 2nd Highland Brigade Light T.M.B	1			
To Concentration Camp for Demobilisation		7		
	1	7		
Difference between Increase & Decrease			1	3
Effective Strength 9/6/19			34	760
Increase Taken on Strength from 4th Gordons		1		
" " " " 9th "		1		
		2		
Decrease				
Taken on strength of 4th Gordons		1		
To Concentration Camp for demobilisation		4		
U.K. re-enlistment leave		2		
Taken on strength of IX Corps Cyclists		2		
		9		
Difference between Increase & Decrease				7
Effective Strength 12/6/19			34	753

Summary of Events and Information	O.	O.R.	O.	O.R.
Effective Strength 12/6/19				
Increase				
Crossposted from 9th Seaforth Highlanders		21		
		21		21
Effective Strength 19/6/19			34	774
Decrease				
To Concentration Camp for Demobilisation		3		
Crossposted to 4th Gordon Highlanders		1		
		4		4
Effective Strength			34	770

(6414) Wt. W3906/P1607 2,500,000 7/18 McA & W Ltd (E 3591) Forms W3091/4. Army Form W.3091.

Cover for Documents.

SECRET.

CONFIDENTIAL.

Nature of Enclosures.

ORIGINAL.
~~TRIPLICATE~~.

WAR DIARY.

of

5th BATTN. THE GORDON HIGHLANDERS.

From.1st July 1919. To.31st July 1919.

VOLUME NO.51.

Notes, or Letters written.

JULY 1919

Instructions regarding War Diaries and Intelligence Summaries are contained in F. S. Regs., Part II. and the Staff Manual respectively. Title pages will be prepared in manuscript.

WAR DIARY
or
~~INTELLIGENCE SUMMARY.~~
(*Erase heading not required.*)

GERMANY

5th GORDON HIGHLANDERS

Army Form C. 2118.

Place	Date	Hour	Summary of Events and Information	Remarks and references to Appendices
	July			
WALD	1		Orders were received for the battalion to proceed back to DUREN and take up the old billeting area. An advance party was sent off to take over the billets in BIRKESDORF	WHL
	2.		The battalion proceeded to SOLINGEN where they entrained for DUREN at 1500 hours. See Oper. Order No 8 (attached)	WHL.
BIRKESDORF	3		The battalion rested and cleaned up equipment + clothing etc	WHL
	4.		The Commanding Officer inspected the battalion by companies on the battalion parade ground during the morning. The remainder of the day was given over to organizing billets etc after the move.	WHL.
	5.		Training and education were carried out as per programme	WHL
	6.		A+B companies moved to GROSS.HAU ~~today~~ and KLEINHAU at 0900 hours. The Second in Command took charge of the party	WHL
	7.		Being Sunday the usual Church services were held.	WHL
	8.		Training and Education as per programme	WHL
	9.		Training and Education as per programme	WHL.

(A9475) Wt W2358/P360 600,000 12/17 D. D. & L. Sch. 52a. Forms/C2118/15.

JULY 1919 — GERMANY — 5th Gordon Highlanders

Army Form C. 2118.

WAR DIARY
or
~~INTELLIGENCE SUMMARY.~~
(Erase heading not required.)

Instructions regarding War Diaries and Intelligence Summaries are contained in F. S. Regs., Part II. and the Staff Manual respectively. Title pages will be prepared in manuscript.

Place	Date	Hour	Summary of Events and Information	Remarks and references to Appendices
BIRKESDORF	10		C, D, and HQ Companies paraded at 0830 hours and marched to the lecture hall in Düren for a lecture by the Divisional Commander Sir David Campbell KCB.	WAH
	11		Today was observed as a holiday. The 2nd Highland Brigade sports were held in the GERMANIA Sports Ground at DUREN today. Teas were served on the ground. The battalion gained 1st prize for best turned out limber and two 3rd prizes for the field kitchen and water cart. After the sports there was an open air concert by the Divisional Troupe and a torchlight procession by C company. All guards in DUREN were relieved by the R.F.A.	WAH
	12		Usual training and education	WAH
	13		Usual training as per programme.	WAH
	14		~~Training as per programme~~ Usual Divine Services	WAH
	15		Training as per programme.	WAH
	16		Training as per programme.	WAH
	17		Training as per programme.	WAH

(A9175) Wt W2358/P360 600,000 12/17 D. D. & L. Sch. 52a. Forms/C2118/15.

JULY 1919

WAR DIARY
or
INTELLIGENCE SUMMARY.
(Erase heading not required.)

GERMANY

5th Gordon Highlanders

Army Form C. 2118.

Instructions regarding War Diaries and Intelligence Summaries are contained in F. S. Regs., Part II, and the Staff Manual respectively. Title pages will be prepared in manuscript.

Place	Date	Hour	Summary of Events and Information	Remarks and references to Appendices
BIRKESDORF	18		As per programme.	WHL
	19.		~~C&D Companies paraded in fatigue dress at 0900 hours to~~	
			~~start work on the new battalion kitchen.~~ Today was observed	WHL
	~~20~~		as a holiday for rejoicing throughout the British Empire at	
			the coming of Peace.	WHL
	20		Being Sunday the usual Divine Services were held	WHL
	21		C&D Companies paraded in fatigue dress for work on the new	
			battalion cook house. A lecture was given at 1100 hours by	
			the Rev. H.G. ROSENDALE on "Turkey in the time of Queen Elizabeth"	WHL
	22		C&D Companies working on the cook house.	WHL
	23		D Company and 10 men of C Company employed on cookhouse	
			and new dining hall. Remainder proceeded on a route march as	
			per programme. British War Medal was authorized today	WHL
	24.		Usual training and education	WHL
	25		C&D Companies on PT. bombing and platoon drill, musketry	
			and extended order drill	WHL

(A9175) Wt W2358/P360 600,000 12/17 D. D. & L. Sch. 52a. Forms/C2118/15.

July 1919.

Instructions regarding War Diaries and Intelligence Summaries are contained in F. S. Regs., Part II. and the Staff Manual respectively. Title pages will be prepared in manuscript.

WAR DIARY
or
INTELLIGENCE SUMMARY.
(Erase heading not required.)

GERMANY

5th Gordon Highlanders

Army Form C. 2118.

Place	Date	Hour	Summary of Events and Information	Remarks and references to Appendices
BIRKESDORF	26		Usual training and education	WHL
	27.		Being Sunday, the usual Divine Services were held	WHL
	28.		Usual Training and education	
	29.		Divisional Horse Show was held today. The battalion had one	
			pack mule & L.G. limber entered for competition	
			The battalion was 2nd with the limber + 2nd with the pack mule	WHL
	30.		Usual training and education. The battalion found the	WHL
	31		outlying picquet in Duren.	
	31		Usual training and education	WHL
			Attached Appendix I Effective Strength, Increase + Decrease	
			Appendix II Operation Order No 8	WHL

R.B. Hosking

(A9475) Wt W2358/P360 600,000 12/17 D. D. & L. Sch. 52a. Forms/C2118/15.

Army Form C. 2118.

Instructions regarding War Diaries and Intelligence Summaries are contained in F. S. Regs., Part II. and the Staff Manual respectively. Title pages will be prepared in manuscript.

WAR DIARY
or
INTELLIGENCE SUMMARY.

(*Erase heading not required.*)

Place / Date / Hour / Summary of Events and Information	O	OR	O	OR
Effective Strength 28.6.19			34	770
Decrease				
To Concentration Camp for Demobilisation	1	1		
To UK for Reenlistment Furlough		3		
Effective Strength 5.7.19			33	766
Decrease				
Posted to Details Battalion The Gordon Highlanders		6		
To Concentration Camp for Demobilisation		3		
		9		
Increase				
Joined from Base		1		
Difference		8		
Effective Strength 12.7.19			33	758

Summary of Events and Information	Remarks and references to Appendices	
Effective Strength 12.7.19		
Decrease		
To Concentration Camp for Demobilisation	6	
Effective Strength 19.7.19	33	752
Decrease		
To Concentration Camp for Demobilisation	1	
To UK re enlistment furlough	1	
	2	
Effective Strength 26.7.19	33	750

(A9475) Wt W2358/P360 600,000 12/17 D. D. & L. Sch. 52a. Forms/C2118/15.

(6414) Wt. W3906/P1607 2,500,000 7/18 McA & W Ltd (E 3591) Forms W3091/4.

Army Form W.3091.

Cover for Documents.

CONFIDENTIAL.

Original.

Nature of Enclosures.

WAR DAIRY

of

5th BATTN. THE GORDON HIGHLANDERS .

From 1st August,1919. To. 31st August,1919.

Volume No. 52.

Notes, or Letters written.

R R Forbes Lt-Col. Commdg.
5th Batt the Gordon Hdrs.

AUGUST, 1919.

Instructions regarding War Diaries and Intelligence Summaries are contained in F. S. Regs., Part II, and the Staff Manual respectively. Title pages will be prepared in manuscript.

WAR DIARY
or
~~INTELLIGENCE SUMMARY.~~
(Erase heading not required.)

5TH GORDON HIGHLANDERS

Army Form C. 2118.

Place	Date	Hour	Summary of Events and Information	Remarks and references to Appendices
	AUGUST			
BIRKESDORF	1st		Battn HQ Details carried out Musketry on 30 yards range – D Coy work on Bn Kitchen	[initials]
	2nd		Educational Training & Inspection of billets	[initials]
	3rd		The Bn moved to MERZENICH (see O.O. No 9 attached) Billets good.	[initials]
MERZENICH	4th		Observed as a holiday.	[initials]
	5th		Training & Education as per programme.	[initials]
	6th		'A' & 'B' Coys rejoined Battn from GROSSHAU and KLEINHAU. 'A' Coy took over duties of Inlying Picquet from 'C' Coy. 'D' Coy usual training	[initials]
	7		Devoted to inspection of kits, cleaning up &c.	[initials]
	8		Battn marched and entrained at Duren for move to United Kingdom. (see O.O. No 11 attached)	[initials]
	9		Continuing the journey in train.	[initials]
CALAIS	10		Arrived in CALAIS about 0400 hours. Battn detrained at 0530 hours and marched to Camp where breakfast was served. Battalion formed up and marched to the boat SS LEOPALD II. Embarked at midday, the pipe band playing "Happy wE've been a' thegither", and arrived	[initials]

AUGUST, 1919

Instructions regarding War Diaries and Intelligence Summaries are contained in F. S. Regs., Part II. and the Staff Manual respectively. Title pages will be prepared in manuscript.

WAR DIARY
or
~~INTELLIGENCE SUMMARY.~~
(Erase heading not required.) 5TH GORDON HIGHLANDERS.

Army Form C. 2118.

Place	Date	Hour	Summary of Events and Information	Remarks and references to Appendices
	AUGUST			
FOLKESTONE	10th		in FOLKESTONE about 1400 hours. Tea was served in the camp at Folkestone. Battn marched to SHORNCLIFFE station and entrained at 1800 hours for CLIPSTONE CAMP.	[initials]
CLIPSTONE CAMP	11th		Battalion arrived at its destination at 0400 hours and a meal which was prepared by the 2nd Battn Lincoln Regt was served. Billeted in Hutments. The day was devoted to organizing of billets	[initials] [initials]
	12th		Cleaning kits & billets &c.	[initials]
	13th		Training & Education	[initials]
	14th		do. do.	[initials]
	15th		G.O.C. 2nd Highland Brigade inspected Battalion Lines.	[initials]
	16th		Cleaning of Huts and C.O.s inspection.	[initials]
	17th		Usual Divine Services.	[initials]
	18th		"C" & "D" Coys musketry on range. "A" & "B" Coys finding Garrison & other duties.	[initials]
	19th		Musketry under Coy arrangements. C.O. lectured to Bn at 1100 hrs on the question of leave.	[initials]
	20th		Training & Education.	[initials]

(A9475) Wt W2358/P360 600,000 12/17 D. D. & L. Sch. 52a. Forms/C2118/15.

AUGUST - 1919

Instructions regarding War Diaries and Intelligence Summaries are contained in F. S. Regs., Part II. and the Staff Manual respectively. Title pages will be prepared in manuscript.

WAR DIARY

~~or~~

~~INTELLIGENCE~~ SUMMARY.

(*Erase heading not required.*) 5TH GORDON HIGHLANDERS.

Army Form C. 2118.

Place	Date	Hour	Summary of Events and Information	Remarks and references to Appendices
CLIPSTONE CAMP	AUGUST 21st		'C' & 'D' Coys musketry on ranges. 'A' & 'B' Coys finding duties	[illegible]
	22		'B' Coy proceeded on 15 days leave. 'D' Coy on ranges. 'A' & 'C' Coys finding duties. Lt Col R.R. Forbes DSO proceeded on leave. Command of Bn taken over by Capt R. Colvin.	[illegible]
	23rd		Kit Inspection under Coy arrangements.	[illegible]
	24th		Usual Divine Services.	[illegible]
	25th		'D' Coy musketry on miniature range. Remainder of Bn Coy Training	[illegible]
	26th		'A' Coy proceeded on leave for 15 days. Usual training	[illegible]
	27th		Training under Coy arrangements. Four O.Rs. proceeded for dispersal.	[illegible]
	28th		'D' Coy musketry on ranges. 76 Other Ranks proceeded for dispersal	[illegible]
	29th		Battn changing beds &c. 6 other ranks proceeded for dispersal	[illegible]
	30th		Inspection of huts &c.	[illegible]
	31st		Usual Divine Services.	[illegible]
			Attached - Appendix I Effective strength, Increase & Decrease	
			do II Operation Order No 9	
			do III do do No 11	

R.R. Forbes Lieut Colonel
Commanding 5th Bn the Gordon Highlanders.

Army Form C. 2118.

Instructions regarding War Diaries and Intelligence Summaries are contained in F. S. Regs., Part II, and the Staff Manual respectively. Title pages will be prepared in manuscript.

WAR DIARY
or
INTELLIGENCE SUMMARY.

(Erase heading not required.)

Place	Date	Hour	Summary of Events and Information	O	OR	O	OR
			Effective Strength 26.7.19			33	450
	Decrease		To Concentration Camp for release		3		
	Increase		Joined from Northern Division		1		
			Difference		2		
			Effective Strength 2.8.19			33	448
	Decrease		Taken on Strength of Rhine Army Reception Camp		3		
			To Concentration Camp for release		1		
			Transferred to R.A.S.C.		2		
			Major R.A. Wolfe Murray DSO proceeded to War Office 23/7/19 Struck off Strength	1			
				1	6		
	Increase		Taken on Strength from Details Bn		2		
			Taken on Strength from A&SH		1		
			Difference Decrease	1	3		
			Effective Strength 9/8/19			32	445

Summary of Events and Information	O	OR	O	OR
Increase Taken on Strength from 2nd A&SH		3		
" " London Scottish		3		
Proceeded to Concentration Camp for release & retaken on Strength on being [illegible]		1		
		7		
Decrease Taken on Strength of Military Governor Rhine	1	1		
" Establishment of Rhine Army Reception Camp		3		
	1	4		
Difference	1	3		
Effective Strength 16.8.19			31	448
Decrease Struck off Strength on being declared a deserter		1		
Increase Taken on Strength from Hospital		6		
Difference		5		
Effective Strength 23.8.19			31	453
Decrease Proceeded to Concentration Camp for release		88		
Effective Strength 30.8.19			31	665

(A9475) Wt W2358/P360 600,000 12/17 D. D. & L. Sch. 52a. Forms/C2118/15.

SECRET.
****

OPERATION ORDER No.11.

7th August 1919.

1. Orderly Officer for tomorrow..................2/Lt.A.R.Stronach.

2. Routine.

Reveille.	0600 hours.	Dinners.	1200 hours.
Breakfast.	0630 "	Teas.	1500 "

The Battalion will move to England to-morrow.

Hour or Parade.
A,B,D and H.Q.Coys will parade ready to march off at 1615 hours. Head of column at Tramway Station, Merzernich, facing South East.
C. Coy will join the Battalion at the junction of the Mezernich-Cologne-Duren roads at 1630 hours.
Order or march H.Q., A,B,D and C.Coys.

Colour Party.
Colour Party consisting of the following will report at H.Q.Mess at 1600 hours.
2nd Lieut.H.Burns,2nd Lieut.W.Mearns? and one N.C.O. from A, B and C.Coys.

Haltes Repas.
The train will halt at the following places for meals.
HUY. CHALEROI. CHISLENCHEN, and MERRIC.

Parade States.
O's C. Coys will render Daily Parade States to Orderly Room to-morrow as usual.

Billets.
O's C.Coys will render a certificate to Adjutant by 1500 hours that Billets are in a clean condition and will ensure that they are left as such.

Requisitioned Stores.
O's C. Coys will render a certificate to the Adjutant by 1200 hours that no requisitioned stores or material are being taken out of Germany by any Officer or man of their Coys.

(Sgd) I.M.FRAME, Capt & Adjt.
5th Battn. The Gordon Highlanders.

AMENDMENTS TO ADMINISTRATIVE ORDERS ISSUED UNDER H/198.

Reference para.1, C. Coy's Mess kit and Officers' valises and stationery box will be dumped outside Coy.H.Q. by 0815 hours.

Reference para.4, C.Coy'sn dixies will be dumped outside Coy.H.Q. at 1545 hours

(Sgd) I.M.FRAME, Capt & Adjt.
5th Battn. The Gordon Highrs.

ACKNOWLEDGE.

5th Battn. The Gordon Highlanders.

Operation Order No.9.
2nd August 1919.

SECRET.
****

The Battalion will move to MERZENICH tomorrow, Sunday 3rd August 1919.
Parade outside Factory Gates, ready to march off at 1000 hours.
Dress - Full Marching Order.
Order of march. 'D' Coy, Headquarters Coy, and Transport.
The parade will be under Capt.R.Cowie.

ADMINISTRATIVE INSTRUCTIONS.

Colours ~~Party~~. Lieut.W.G.Henderson.M.C., will be i/c of Colours ~~Party~~ which will proceed in first lorry leaving BIRKESDORF.

Blankets. Blankets rolled in bundles of ten will be dumped outside Q.M. Stores by 0800 hours. Palliasses will be dumped at the same hour. A & B. Coys blankets will be kept separate from the remainder and will be picked up by a lorry and taken to GROSSHAU. Officers' valises and Officers' and Sergts Mess kit will be dumped at Q.M.Stores at 0900 hours.

Fatigue Parties. O.C.'D' Coy. will detail the following fatigue parties.
One N.C.O. and 10 men to report to R.Q.M.S. at Q.M.Stores at 0800 hours to travel on lorries and act as unloading party under Lieut. W.H.Lyell.A.M., on arrival at MERZENICH.
1 N.C.O. and 10 men to report to R.Q.M.S. at Q.M. Stores at 0800 hours to act as loading party for the day.
6 men of B.Coy. who were to attend torchlight tattoo, to bring all education material to Q.M.Stores. Report to 2/Lt A.R. [illegible] at 0800 hrs
The remainder of A & B.Coys (Torchlight Tattoo) to report to Cpl.Walker, Sanitary Cpl., at 0745 hours at the Factory Gates to remove all latrines, ablution benches and tubs from Coy. areas to Q.M.Stores.
1 N.C.O. and 12 men to assemble all ovens and soyer stoves in the Factory Square by 0900 hours. These will be picked up by a lorry in the Square.

Tables & Forms. The R.Q.M.S. will be responsible that 100 tables and 200 forms are collected from the Factory and conveyed to the new area. Battn. Headquarters men plus loading party will be utilized for this.

Beds. O's C. Coys will utilize the remainder of their Coys. in bringing all beds to the Pioneers' Shop. A return showing the amount of beds stored will be handed to the Adjutant by 1000 hours tomorrow.

Transport. Transport Officer will detail one limber to report to Orderly Room at 0900 hours to collect Orderly Room stores and convey same to new area.

Billets. O's C. Coys will render a certificate to the Adjutant before leaving that billets have been left clean.

(Sgd) I.M.FRAME, Capt & Adjt.
5th Battn. The Gordon Highlanders.

BEF

HIGHLAND DIV formerly
62 DIV

2 HIGHLAND BDE

51 GORDONS

1919 MAR to 1919 AUG

NO BOX

Highland [illegible] 62 DIV

SECRET. **ORIGINAL.**

2 Bde Vol I

WAR DIARY

-of-

51st Bn. Gordon Highlanders

1st March 1919 to 31st March 1919.

VOLUME 1

[signature]
Lieut. Colonel,
Commanding, 51st Bn. Gordon Highlanders.

To- Headquarters,
186 Infantry Brigade.

Herewith original copy War Diary, for your information.

Capt & Adjt
J. Boswell Lt-Colonel.
3rd. April, 1919. Commanding 51st. Bn. Gordon Highrs.

Original

57th Bn. Gordon Highlanders

Army Form C. 2118.

WAR DIARY
or
INTELLIGENCE SUMMARY

(Erase heading not required.)

Instructions regarding War Diaries and Intelligence Summaries are contained in F. S. Regs., Part II. and the Staff Manual respectively. Title Pages will be prepared in manuscript.

Place	Date	Hour	Summary of Events and Information	Remarks and references to Appendices
DUNKERQUE	21/3/19	12.00	Battn disembark sailing from Dover. left Dover 09.45. Night of 21st 22nd in No 4 Rest Camp DUNKERQUE.	J.G.B.
DUNKERQUE.	22/3/19.	10.00.	Battn entrain for destination in Germany. 38 offrs 905. O.R.	J.G.B.
HORREM.	24/3/19	09.30	Battn. detrain. and march from HORREM to TURNICH. area Battn billeted A Coy & B Coy BALKHAUSEN. 'C' Coy. KERPEN. 'D' Coy. BRUGGEN. Hqrs. TURNICH SCHLOSS.	J.G.B.
TURNICH	25/3/19.		'C' Coy move from KERPEN to BRUGGEN. A.B.D. Coys Training	J.G.B.
TURNICH	26/3/19 to 31.3.19		Training	

J.G. Birch.
Lt. Col.
Cmdg
57 Bn The Gordon Highlanders

2449 Wt. W14957/M90 750,000 1/16 J.B.C. & A. Forms/C.2118/12.

Secret.

Original

H

WAR DIARY

of

51st Bn. Gordon Highlanders.

From 1st May. 1919. to 31st May, 1919.

ORIGINAL

Army Form C. 2118.

Instructions regarding War Diaries and Intelligence Summaries are contained in F. S. Regs., Part II. and the Staff Manual respectively. Title Pages will be prepared in manuscript.

WAR DIARY
or
INTELLIGENCE SUMMARY

(Erase heading not required.)

Place	Date	Hour	Summary of Events and Information	Remarks and references to Appendices
DUREN to	1st MAY 31st MAY		Training	
	2nd MAY		Major R.A. CHRYSTAL 4th A.S. Highrs. proceeded home demobilised	
	4th MAY		Capt. Rev. A.T. LAWRENCE. granted leave 4th – 11th May '19.	
	1st MAY		Lieut. J.S. AIKMAN. asst. Adjt. to 2nd Hd. Bde. Hqrs. for duty.	
	7th MAY		Lieut. J.J. SUTHERLAND. proceeded to England for demobilisation	
	8th MAY		2/Lt. P.W. BARNETT. appointed Assistant Adjt.	
	10th MAY		RAILWAY GUARDS taken over from 53rd Bn Gordon Highrs. 2 Officers 10 NCOs & 66 men	
	10th MAY		Lt. T. McGREGOR. to Highland Div. Hqrs. for duty as Signalling Instructor	
	12th MAY		Lt. J.B. MATHER. R.S.F. to Div. Education School duty as Adjutant & Q.M.	
	13th MAY		'A' & 'C' Coy. Pipers & Drummers Pioneers & Signallers parade at aerodrome for rehearsal C in C. inspection	
	15th MAY		A & C Coys. Pipers & Drummers. Pioneers & Signallers inspected by Commander in Chief (Garrison Parade).	
	14th MAY		Battalion march as strong as possible to DUREN STATION to welcome MARSHALL FOCH	
	20th MAY		Transport inspected by MAJ. GENERAL SIR DAVID CAMPBELL K.C.B. Commdg. Highland Division	
	16th MAY		Lt. A.D. SUTHERLAND & 2nd Lt. J.A. DONALDSON proceeded to UK. demobilised	
	15th MAY		'C' Coy. take over 'INLYING PICQUET' from Coy of 5th Bn Gordon Highrs.	Operation Order No 3.
	21st MAY		A Coy. COMMENCE MUSKETRY COURSE ADDENDUM 4.	
	24th MAY		BARRACKS. inspected by Major. GENERAL SIR DAVID CAMPBELL K.C.B. Commdg. Highland Division	
	30th & 31st MAY		REGTL Sports. MEETING. 4th Corps SPORTS GROUND. DUREN. Coy. Championship – 'C' Coy. Individual Championship Cup – Pte Hutcheson 'C' Coy.	

R. M. Dudgeon, Lieut. Colonel Commanding 51st Bn Gordon Highlrs.

2449 Wt. W14957/M90 750,000 1/16 J.B.C. & A. Forms/C.2118/12.

Secret.

Original.

War Diary

of

51st Battn. Gordon Highlanders

From 1st June 1919 to 30th June 1919.

(Volume IV.)

[illegible] Lieut.-Colonel
Comdg. 51st Bn. Gordon Highrs.

51st Bn. Gordon Hrs

WAR DIARY
or
~~INTELLIGENCE SUMMARY.~~

Original

Army Form C. 2118.

Instructions regarding War Diaries and Intelligence Summaries are contained in F. S. Regs., Par. II. and the Staff Manual respectively. Title pages will be prepared in manuscript.

(Erase heading not required.)

Place	Date	Hour	Summary of Events and Information	Remarks and references to Appendices
DUREN.	2/6/19	–	2nd LIEUT. H.J. THOMPSON GORDON HIGH^RS taken on strength (Instructor Div. Education School)	131/19 (10)
	3/6/19	–	BIRTHDAY of HIS MAJESTY THE KING. CEREMONIAL PARADE General Holiday.	
	5/6/19	–	A. Coy. Complete Musketry Course Addendum IV. at DUREN-STOCKHEIM range	
	6/6/19	–	B. Coy. Commence Musketry Course Addendum IV at DUREN-STOCKHEIM range	
	10/6/19	–	B. Coy. move from BARRACKS to houses at RANGE	138/19 (5)
	9/6/19	–	Lieut. R.C. MATHEWS 4th BORDER REGT. taken on strength (Divisional Concert Party)	138/19 (6)
	9/6/19	–	D. Coy. take over inlying picquet from 5th Bn GORDON HIGH^RS	O.O. No 3.
	11/6/19	–	LECTURE by Command Paymaster at DUREN on PAY & MESS BOOKS.	
	15/6/19	–	Officers Shooting Competition DUREN STOCKHEIM range. 1. Capt. R.B.D. McLEOD M.C. (2) 2nd Lt. D.W. BARNETT (3) MAJOR LAWRENCE DSO, M.C. DCM	
	16/6/19	–	D. Coy relieved at INLYING PICQUET by 4th Bn GORDON HIGH^RS.	
	17/6/19	–	BATTALION move to SOLINGEN	
	18/6/19	–	BATTALION takes over OUTPOST LINE from 51st HLI A. Coy. (RIGHT) C (Centre) D (Left)	M.O. No 3
		–	B. Coy in support at SOLINGEN KAISERSAAL.	
	28/6/19	–	B Coy Concert & dance in KAISERSAAL SOLINGEN. Peace signed (Bde wire G.83)	
18 –	30/6/19	–	Battn holding OUTPOST LINE.	

R. M. Anderson. Lt-Col
Commdg. 51st Bn Gordon Hghrs

A6945 Wt. W11422/M1160 350,000 12/16 D. D. & L. Forms/C./2118/14.

SECRET.

Schedule; No 5.

1st July, 1919 to 31st July 19

Original

WAR DIARY

OF

51st Battn. "Gordon Highlanders."

PERIOD. From 1st July 1919. — 31st July 1919.

Original

Instructions regarding War Diaries and Intelligence Summaries are contained in F. S. Regs., Part II. and the Staff Manual respectively. Title pages will be prepared in manuscript.

WAR DIARY
or
~~INTELLIGENCE SUMMARY.~~
51st Bn. Gordon Hrs
(Erase heading not required.)

Army Form C. 2118.

Hour, Date, Place	Summary of Events and Information	Remarks and references to Appendices
1/4/19. SOLINGEN.	Battn. holding outpost line	
2/4/19. SOLINGEN	Battn. relieved by 51st H.L.I and move to DUREN. & resume quarters in BARRACKS.	Movement ~~[illegible]~~ Order No. 4
5/4/19. DUREN.	'A' Coy move to GEY. for training	B.R.O. 158/19. 3
5/4/19 DUREN.	'C' Coy. move to RANGE DUREN STOCKHEIM road for Musketry Course	BRO 158/19 4
9, 11/4/19. DUREN.	2nd HIGHLAND BDE. SPORTS. Peace Celebrations GERMANIA SPORTS GROUND.	
21.4.19 DUREN.	D. Coy. move to ~~[illegible]~~ RANGE. DUREN STOCKHEIM Road for Musketry Course	BRO 170/19 5
	C Coy move from RANGE to BARRACKS.	
22.4.19	B Coy move to GEY for Coy. Training	B.RO 171/19. 10
	A Coy move from GEY to BARRACKS	
15/4/19 to 29/4/19.	LIEUT COL RM. DUDGEON DSO MC on leave to U.K. MAJOR T.B. LAWRENCE. DS.O. MC. in command.	
29/4/19.	HIGHLAND DIVISION HORSE SHOW.	

R. M. Dudgeon. Lt Col
Commdg. 51st Bn Gordon Hghrs

(73989) W4141—463. 400,000. 9/14. H.&J.Ltd. Forms/C. 2118/10.

Secret.

Schedule No. 6
Original

WAR DIARY

of

51st Gordon Highlanders.

Period from 1st August, 1919 to 31st August 1919

51st Bn. Gordon H.

Original.

Army Form C. 2118.

Instructions regarding War Diaries and Intelligence Summaries are contained in F. S. Regs., Part II. and the Staff Manual respectively. Title pages will be prepared in manuscript.

WAR DIARY
or
INTELLIGENCE SUMMARY.
(*Erase heading not required.*)

Place	Date	Hour	Summary of Events and Information	Remarks and references to Appendices
DUREN.	1/8/19.		D. Coy on RANGE (ADDENDUM IV) B. Coy. Coy. (Coy. Training) A & C Coy. Barracks. Training. duties.	
"	8/8/19.		Baggage train depart to ANTWERP from DUREN. 2/Lieut ROSE proceeds with baggage	Special Order
"	8/8/19.		Advance Party under CAPT. R.B.D MACLEOD. MC. proceed to CALAIS.	B.R.O. 183/93
"	9/8/19.		Battn proceed from DUREN STATION. to CLIPSTONE CAMP. NOTTS. ENGLAND night of 10/11th 8-19 at rest camp CALAIS.	2nd (H) Bde SC. 7/8/19 172/1 (Our M1410)
CLIPSTONE	19/8/19.		Musketry recommenced on CLIPSTONE RANGE. (annual musketry Course) Coys. on Musketry and Training	B.R.O. 184/19 para 2
	23/8/19		Battn takes over Garrison duties for week	
	22/8/19		'B' Coy. proceed on leave until 6/9/19.	
	26/8/19		'C' Coy. proceed on leave until 10/9/19.	
	30/8/19.		2/Lt. R.M. Brown proceeded to GULLANE to attend Course of Instruction in Gas.	

R.M. Dudgeon. Lt Col
Commdg 51st Bn Gordon Highrs

(A9475) Wt W2358/P360 600,000 12/17 D. D. & L. Sch. 52a. Forms/C2118/15.

www.ingramcontent.com/pod-product-compliance
Lightning Source LLC
Chambersburg PA
CBHW081430300426
44108CB00016BA/2339
9781474533737